Sea Islands Heritage

Sea Islands

Heritage

Resonances of Africa
in Diasporic Communities

Mary A. Twining

Alpharetta, GA

Some names and identifying details have been changed to protect the privacy of individuals.

The author has tried to recreate events, locations, and conversations from his/her memories of them. In some instances, in order to maintain their anonymity, the author has changed the names of individuals and places. He/she may also have changed some identifying characteristics and details such as physical attributes, occupations, and places of residence.

ISBN: 978-1-61005-685-4

10 9 8 7 6 5 4 3 2   0 8 1 8 1 6

Printed in the United States of America

∞ This paper meets the requirements of ANSI/NISO Z39.48-1992 (Permanence of Paper)

To Congressman James E. Clyburn for his long, distinguished service to the Sea Islands region and support in the creation of the Gullah Geechee Cultural Heritage Corridor Commission for the understanding, management, and development of the endangered history and traditions of the Sea Islands Region.

Also to my family and the memory of my elder son, Thomas Sherman Twining, who passed away on April 1, 2016, and who always encouraged me by saying, "Ma, you should write about all this."

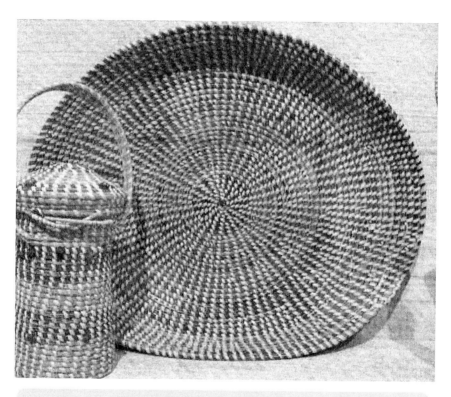

Two baskets from Mt. Pleasant, South Carolina. The basket on the right is a fanner for grain by Ms. Mary Manigault of Hamlin Sound, South Carolina.

Table of Contents

PART II

"Tryin' to Make It": African Spiritual Endurance, Artistic Strength, and Technology

Foreword

Althea Natalga Sumpter, DAH

I am a native of St. Helena Island, South Carolina, and I am relevant. I grew up learning how to walk the land and smell the tidal changes in the marsh and the seasons in the newly turned soil. Spirits were real, as they still are, and preserving the stories of the elders has become more important today than I realized while my grandmother was still alive and telling stories of my ancestors. Those stories I still try to capture, as I gather with siblings and talk about the way we were taught, about the medicinal herbs growing wild in the swamps, and about running barefoot on hot sand that never burned.

Owning the name "Gullah Geechee" to identify myself took years of overcoming cultural shame as a desegregation kid of the 1960s. It took years before I would understand the relevance of a culture now celebrated for its longevity and uniqueness, as a creolization of ethnic groups from West Africa who survived kidnapping and enslavement to grow the wealth of crops that would build a Southern economy.

I learned about my culture not as a child, but as an adult. I had already endured a childhood of cultural shame after years of desegregation, crossing the bridge to integrate the public schools in the Lowcountry town of Beaufort, South Carolina. However, my formal education really began as a doctoral student working on a degree that I first thought would include Anglo-Saxon creolization. I wanted to know why I spoke English. With that question in mind, I sought to combine my first career as a documentary producer/editor with anthropology and history. My own interest in the combination of media, anthropology, and history would, I hoped, answer the question of why, throughout my life, I saw much of life through a different lens. That lens included the awareness that there is a tangible link between the seen and the unseen, where haints and ancestors live in the same realm and wrestle for the care of those on the other side—the living.

After years in the production industry encountering those more interested in the lilt in my speech than in the perspective of my world view, I decided to work on a doctorate exploring why I spoke English. In 1992, I met Mary A. Twining and Keith Baird, both professors at Clark Atlanta University. Twining understood immediately the significance of my background before I did, before I acknowledged that I am Gullah Geechee and my culture has relevance. While pursuing an independent studies project with Twining as my advisor, I started reading, which would last the summer.

I read the books of others—*Drums and Shadows* (1940), Clyde Kiser's *Sea Island to City* (1932), and Edith M. Dabbs's *Sea Island Diary: A History of St. Helena Island* (1983), to mention a few—writing about the Gullah Geechee culture in order to know what exists and how the culture has been represented by others. While I read the familiar, I also realized what was missing: the life I have lived on the Islands. Starting with a few selected books, I ended up absorbing and notating my own culture in nearly twenty publications. I surprised myself. Mary A. Twining was thrilled and she became my mentor, helping me integrate the perspective of a participant/observer who can document a way of life using the technology from my life as a producer with the academic traditions of a scholar.

In this work, Mary A. Twining tells the stories of her experience living on Johns Island and St. Simons Island, becoming part of each community and learning how to walk the land. She shares her knowledge as an accepted member of each island and as a scholar documenting a culture and adding to the scholarship of others.

Beginning as an outsider, Mary became a participant in the community, learning folkways and how to walk the roads, which in turn informed her scholarship, returning to an academic life in order to understand the experience in such a way that those outside of the Gullah Geechee culture can understand how we want to live. The unintentional observer experience, because her introduction to the Islands was in support of civil rights activities, captures in *Sea Islands Heritage* voices of the elders from the 1960s and reminds the contemporary reader that the culture still exists.

Keith Baird adds the language that we both know and understand from birth. As I claim him my professor forever, his link to the Sea Islands as a Bajan provides the linguistic knowledge of language origins and transmutation from Africa and Europe. The creolization of language into the sounds spoken from his home on Barbados and those from my home on St. Helena Island bears similarities that help conjoin familiarity and understanding.

I read in *Sea Islands Heritage* about the words of my father as he ebbed and flowed in and out of Gullah and English, depending on the need to code-switch for those on the island or for mainlanders as he shopped for the few things we needed from in town.

I read in *Sea Islands Heritage* about the quilts from my grandmother, hand stitched, passed along, and used to tuck each grandchild into bed during cold winters. My brothers and I would tell stories from the quilts because we remembered the clothes that we wore before the warmth of strip patterns were made heavy from the old blankets creating its insides. I still have the strip pattern quilt made for me when I went away to college.

I read in *Sea Islands Heritage* about the healing herbs used by my midwife grandmother who sent us children into the swamps and the woods to collect her medicine. We survived and thrived during a time when segregation meant limits to medical care or waiting while the one white doctor available in the county would see whites first, then anyone in the colored waiting room of his office.

The last twenty years have been about my writing my own stories collected from elders of my culture. With Mary A. Twining still as my mentor forever and Keith Baird my professor forever, I have moved beyond taking a special life experience for granted. With an appreciation for the life lived on the Gullah Geechee Corridor, and contributing to the formation of the Gullah Geechee Cultural Heritage Corridor as a federal commissioner, weaving life experience along with my own developing scholarship is where

I find myself. Mary A. Twining still provides a road map for me as she tells her own stories weaving her experience on the Islands along with the scholarship she unfolds in *Sea Islands Heritage*.

In 2006, the National Heritage Areas Act (Public Law 109-338, Title II, Subtitle I) established the Gullah Geechee Cultural Heritage Corridor. The Gullah Geechee Corridor, which stretches from southern North Carolina, continues along the coast of South Carolina and Georgia, and ends in southern Florida, incorporates the coast-to-thirty-mile-west designation posed in Special Field Order, No. 15 by Major General William T. Sherman in 1865. The significance of the similarities did not go unnoticed in the Gullah Geechee community. The selection of the first group of commissioners in 2007 was charged by the Department of the Interior to develop a management plan to create an organization that would recognize and celebrate the culture by listening to the voices of the Gullah Geechee community. I was selected as one of those initial twenty-six commissioners. On July 18, 2012, the management plan became available to the public, and the following year a float representing the Gullah Geechee culture became a part of the Presidential Inaugural Parade.

The Thirty-Seventh Presidential Inaugural Parade on January 21 celebrated the second inauguration of President Barack Obama. As I watched the float of the Gullah Geechee Commission glide across the television set with commissioners hailing the crowd, I became "full up," feeling a sense of joy and on the edge of tears. I am relevant. We are relevant! The culture has survived and is now recognized as a member of the floats representing the heritage of the First Family. The Gullah Geechee heritage of First Lady Michelle Obama establishes the culture on the international stage.

In 2014, I was privileged to be elected the chair of the Gullah Geechee Cultural Heritage Corridor Commission.

Acknowledgments

First and foremost, I extend my eternal gratitude to the people of the Sea Islands for their acceptance and graciousness. I have carried away some life lessons never to be forgotten. Their fortitude and courage will stay with me always. Residents of Johns Island, South Carolina, and St. Simons Island, Georgia, chiefly were among my teachers, but there were visits to other islands that opened up vistas too.

I would like to thank Dr. Paula Ebron of Stanford University for her faith in me as a "foundational scholar" of the Sea Islands region. I recognize and appreciate the work she is doing about the Sea Islands and her role in teaching the next generation of scholars. This is only part of what I had hoped to do, but illness in my family has curtailed my ability to devote myself to my scholarship. I offer my essays, which were often used as textual material at Clark Atlanta University in the courses I taught during my tenure there. My collection of quilts and basketry is housed at the Clark Atlanta University Art Galleries in gratitude for having had them in my possession for as long as I did. I am grateful to Tina Dunkley, director of the galleries, for her acceptance of the collection and her working with me to teach the students over the years.

I am obliged to Judith Palache Gregory for her turning over the Gregory Papers to use as I saw fit in future endeavors. They have been placed in the Gregory Archives among my files in Decatur, Georgia.

I am beholden to the librarians at the Charleston County Library, Charleston, South Carolina; Indiana University Library; the Bobst Library at New York University; the Woodruff Library at the Atlanta University Center; and all librarians, as they do invaluable work in guarding the written sources and guiding us to their valuable contents.

The publishing staff at BookLogix has been a mainstay in helping me to complete this book, as I had almost given up hope of completion as the years rolled by. Their work has greatly enhanced what I aspired to do.

My family has always encouraged me to continue on and I appreciate their support. I am especially grateful to my husband, Keith E. Baird, who has not only supported me in exploring my scholarship, but also joined in editing our first book, *Sea Island Roots*. Furthermore, he has written the chapter on the connections between the languages of the Sea Islands and his home in the Caribbean for this volume.

Last but not least, I am beholden to Jerry Immel for all his unflagging assistance and advice in overcoming technical challenges.

Introduction

To *Sea Islands Heritage*

This book addresses a number of aspects of Sea Islands culture and society. It will provide information for readers who are not acquainted with this distinct area as well as those who have some knowledge of the area but would like to understand more. The Sea Islands and mainland area stretch four hundred miles along the southeastern coast of the United States. Many captive Africans were brought to these isolated areas to work the plantations with their special agricultural skills.

Escapees from plantations came to these remote areas, which the Euro-Americans were not anxious to penetrate because of the diseases that swamp-land could generate. Marginalized to these secluded regions, the Africans made the best of their situation and thrived as well as they could until the late twentieth century when coastal land was made safe by drainage and insect control by the real estate developers, thereby rendering it unaffordable for the Islanders.

The story of the Sea Islands is a long and fascinating one that is rarely completely understood. This gap in understanding exists partly because the history of the region and its people has been told from the point of view of the English and other European colonists and plantation owners who brought the Africans to these "barrier islands," as they are sometimes called, in the first instance. Two factors have an important bearing on the history of the Sea Islands: the first is the relative isolation of the Islands from the mainland and from one another, and the second is the ever-present annoyance and health hazard presented by hosts of mosquitoes. Until recently, transportation, both island-to-island and island-to-mainland, had to be done by boat so that in pre-emancipation as well as post-emancipation times the Africans remained marginalized and separated geographically from the European population. The mosquitoes, multitudinous and malaria-bearing, served to maintain a distance between the two populations, since the Europeans—unprotected by the sickle-cell gene borne by the Africans and in mortal danger from the unrelenting onslaught of the insects—avoided contact with the Islands and their transplanted African inhabitants.

For the most part, the Euro-Americans left the Islanders to their own devices. The Sea Islands culture that resulted was made up of African customs, languages, music, dance, methods of community governance, sympathetic movement, economic behavior, healing practices, religious sensibilities, and many more subtle manifestations of their ability to create or recreate various agricultural implements as well as household tools and other artifacts necessary for their day-to-day survival. They made clothing and household articles, which rendered their modus vivendi, if not elegant, at least relatively comfortable. As their congeners in the Caribbean Islands would put it, they knew how to "tek trik an mek luck." Some of these behaviors are peculiar to the Islands but they are also part and parcel of most of the African World, which has many unique characteristics, many of which are universal both within the continent and the lands of the diaspora.

There are a number of motivations and inspirations that brought me to write scholarly essays and ultimately this book. The civil or human rights movement brought me to the Sea Islands and Charleston area to participate in this significant human-rights struggle, which was part of a self-determinative movement sweeping the unjustly colonized African World. At the same time the population of the territory that came to be called Ghana was freeing itself from colonialism in the 1950s, the Afro-American bus riders were beginning their heroic sit-ins against what was for them an oppressive, colonial regime. Since then, I have learned a great deal more about humans' inhumanity to other humans, but I owe the beginnings of my education in such matters to my friends on the Sea Islands and in Charleston, South Carolina.

My involvement in the Sea Islands endeavor began when I saw on television the police attacking young people with hoses and dogs. I was outraged and politicized by what I regarded as un-American behavior, since I believed our nation had fought the Second World War to put an end to such actions on the part of the Nazis toward their minority populations. I resolved to do whatever I could to assist in the struggle for human and civil rights in which these heroic Sea Islanders were engaged. I inquired among people who I knew to be of a progressive bent as to how I might make the necessary connections. It was Guy and Candie Carawan who met me in New York and directed me to Esau Jenkins, Bill Saunders, and others on Johns Island; here was a place where I found a life's work and an enrichment of my life I could not have dreamed possible.

On Johns Island, a man who had only a fourth-grade formal education, Esau Jenkins, founded a school on his home island. In spite of his having to leave school as a young boy to help his family, Mr. Jenkins, possessed of a quick intelligence and a compelling urgency to learn, educated himself to take a leadership role, which he played in the Charleston and surrounding communities until his untimely death. His struggle for self-determination was in line with that waged by others in the African World at the time, as African people strove to shed the yoke of colonial rule. Although the Sea Islanders were embedded in the body politic of the United States, they and other African American communities needed to establish much more control over their own affairs. Mr. Esau, as we called him, felt that issues—such as education, commerce, community governance—were far too important to leave in the hands of people whose attitudes were hostile and ungenerous toward the Island populations.

I had the rich experience of working with Mr. Esau and his close associate, William Saunders, in community organization. We began with voter registration and moved on to aspects of rural community life, which had tremendous importance to the residents but which they were not empowered to deal with on their own behalf because of the Euro-supremacist sociopolitical climate still pervading the South at that time.

Mr. Jenkins dispatched me to go around Johns Island to make sure all the older residents were signed up for Social Security. I tramped impassible roads in boots and went into remote neighborhoods where people had a very indistinct idea about Social Security or who I was. The Islanders taught me about their lives, how they fished and farmed, worshipped and sang, raised their families, and survived. I read everything available at the time on the language, folklore, and history, and I learned how to ask questions and what questions to ask. Lorenzo Dow Turner's foundational work, *Africanisms in the Gullah Dialect*, was the work I consulted most often because of the wealth of information manifesting all around me.[1] It was only later, when I realized how vicious the captive labor system had been and how deeply ingrained injustice and violence were in the South, that I began to understand more fully and to appreciate the strength and endurance of the Sea Islanders and other African American people.

What became apparent as I circulated around the Island communities was the fact that I was within a different language community, within a different cultural milieu, and among people of a deep, historic-social heritage that merited further respectful study. The Islanders anthropologized me, and I them, as we endeavored to understand each other as we discussed issues of voting rights, community control, and the importance of the struggle in which we were engaged.

Clearly, the most pressing issues were access to enfranchisement and provision of education. Strategizing was all-important as we battled with administrators of the Head Start Program, who sent us salaries for personnel but no stove for the cook and no transportation to school for the children on the second largest island of the United States. I learned from the children, some of whom were the first in their families to go to school or be literate. The Islanders were very welcoming and gracious, making real their philosophy expressed in a favorite song of theirs, "Ain't You Got a Right to the Tree of Life?"

I moved successively from the Social Security project to voter registration to an agricultural project to assisting government teams in implementing programs such as Catch Up and Speed Up by serving as a liaison between them and the Islanders. These teams were designed to help young people in remote rural communities be able to compete in the schools as deseg-regation went forward. The strategy of the African American planners was to move from desegregation to integration to a separatist stance. The earlier efforts to send young African American students into the mainly Euro-American schools had resulted in dropouts, nervous breakdowns, and downright physical injuries.

While I was in and out of the island homes, I began to be aware of the distinctiveness of the culture of the people, which plunged me into study that would increase my knowledge and understanding of it. I found corroboration of the cultural phenomena I was seeing and hearing every day and became convinced I could add to the store of information about this region and its people. It was a period of intensive research both in the field and in the library.

As I began to understand the depth and strength of the African World, I saw that the Sea Islands fit into a cultural continuum that began in Africa, moved through the Caribbean, and continued on to the Southeast coast of the United States. The sweep of autochthonous Africans spread in a number of directions, including the Sea Islands area, where the Charleston and other slave markets functioned as entry ports for thousands of Africans who brought their cultural belongings with them in their minds. Some sociologists and historians use the terminology of the economic condition which brought the Africans to these shores by calling them "slaves." However, when considering the cultural matrix and manifestations of the people of an ethnic and geographic identification, it is more appropriate and humanistically valid to refer to them in terms of the society or ethnic group from which they came if at all possible. Robert Farris Thompson coined the terms Afro-Georgian or Afro-Carolinian in referring to the Islanders of African descent. It is that kind of reference to the ethnic and cultural origin that needs to be employed when speaking of cultural retentions in both scholarly and social interactions.

The library research I have done over the years has grown as more information has been added to the amount of knowledge we have about the Islands. Melville Herskovits has influenced at least two generations of scholars with his groundbreaking work in African World studies. Teachers such as Daniel Crowley and Alan Merriam influenced my thinking in a Herskovitsian frame of reference. Some of Herskovits's work was established through actual fieldwork, but some of his ideas were speculative about what might be found in the future. So few scholars from the African World were researching in his time with a culture contact perspective that he could only look forward to the time when others, besides his students, would be doing the kind of field research he knew would yield rich results. He acknowledged the expanse of the African World when others did not. William Pollitzer has indicated he follows the scholarship of Melville

Herskovits in his *The Gullah People and Their African Heritage*.[2] While the Herskovitsian model is a worthwhile one, the work in the field has moved to broader and more African-based sensibilities. For instance, Pollitzer reprints Herskovits's "scale of intensity of New World Africanisms," which by now is at least sixty years old and seriously underestimates the artistic output of the Sea Islands along with non-kinship institutions, although it was statistically worthwhile and possibly predictive at the time. My fieldwork exposed me to the aesthetic cultural imperatives in the quilting, basketmaking, storytelling, secular and religious musical expression, dance, and movement. The institutions within the community such as the Praying Band, credit ring banking, death benefit, insurance societies, the church, and social clubs are part of the fabric of the society woven in with the kinship connections.

Many scholars could not have gone forward without the groundwork of people like Herskovits, Bastide, A. C. Jordan, Leo Hansberry, Lorenzo Dow Turner, and researchers like William Pollitzer, whose article from 1958 inspired me to know that there was scientific proof of the genetic Africanity of the Charleston and Sea Islands population. Many scholars and professors doubted the cultural connections with Africa of any part of the diaspora, so it seemed important to me to begin with the physical basis of the Sea Islanders' connection with Africa. Pollitzer's 1999 book has built further upon that research, which combines technical scientific information with an appreciation of how that information impacts contemporary studies on the culture and people of the Lowcountry.

Since there is a greater wealth of information, a truer picture of the Sea Islands is coming into focus. Patricia Jones-Jackson took Lorenzo Dow Turner's work in *Africanisms in the Gullah Dialect* for her model in *When Roots Die*.[3] Other new scholars are working without being beholden to any school of thought or doctrinaire approach; they search for the objective data and information, which will yield a more extensive body of knowledge.

Sea Islanders themselves are weighing in in increasing numbers to write about their own culture. Marquetta Goodwine has edited a volume of essays and poetry, *The Legacy of Ibo Landing*—generated from her home in St. Helena Island, South Carolina.[4] It is a mixture of poetry, visual art, scholarly essays, and translations into literary Gullah. Dr. Althea Sumpter, also of St. Helena Island, completed her dissertation, *Navigating the Gullah Culture Using*

Multimedia Technology, about her home island and may have been the first islander to write her doctoral dissertation about the Islands.[5] The ideal is to have persons in the culture teaching the reader about their own society from the inside. To this array of scholars—European, African (continental and diasporic), and felicitously, Sea Islanders—I bring essays on different aspects of Sea Islands culture. Much of this material is taken from my fieldwork with scholarly support where it is reflective of the culture or needed for corroboration. The scholarly books and articles are illustrative of the historical depth of the culture and the interest in it.

While much of the information is descriptive ethnography, it all makes several points when taken together. The African World connection, self-determinative activity, and the durability of the people and their culture all speak to a society which has a great deal to contribute to a world mad with acquisitive materialism. It furthermore shows a picture of people who did not take capture and enslavement lightly. The rebellions such as the Stono Rebellion of 1739 and Denmark Vesey's of the 1820s indicate that African men were acting in a manner appropriate to their cultural upbringing and commensurate with their understanding of their roles as males in their ethnic group.

Michael Gomez's *Exchanging Our Country Marks* makes the point that the defeated Muslim troops in the wars surrounding the Futa Jallon region of West Africa were taken off to Sierra Leone for transshipment to the Americas.[6] Clearly some elements remained of a trained, experienced, frustrated military force, comprising Muslim as well as traditional African warriors, launched into servitude on the plantations where their military skills were not forgotten. For the good of their families and community, they knew they had to strive for the survival and freedom of their bodies and minds as they had in West Africa. Their dramatic actions demonstrated their sense of control of themselves and their destinies. Those efforts were crushed unmercifully for those who were caught. Some escaped, however, and arrived down in Florida to eventually fight in the so-called Seminole Wars. These liberation struggles are in line with those of the Caribbean Maroon fighters.

In recent years, two books have been published, distinguished by their having been written by Islanders themselves: Cornelia Bailey of Sapelo Island, Georgia, wrote *God, Mr. Buzzard, and the Bolito Man* and Marquetta

Goodwine wrote *The Legacy of Ibo Landing*.[7] They provide unique perspectives from inside the culture. This vantage point has been the missing angle, and these works begin to fill in the lacking material that we need for a full view of the history and culture. The African World connection is one made manifest in the traditional culture—such as the modes of verbal expression in song and story as well as the more tangible products like quilts and baskets. Self-determinative activity certainly began with resistance to captivity and forced labor, from the people who jumped overboard during the Middle Passage to later, more organized escape plans. Such expression presently resists negative, reductionist stereotyping of Sea Islands people, the legacy of which still bedevils presentations on the Sea Islands experience.

In less sensational daily life, actions were underway to empower people to escape in less spectacular fashion through the use of domestic arts. The secular and religious dance exercised their sense of control over their own bodies. The aesthetic reaffirmations of quilts, brooms, and baskets recalled their African traditions and reinforced their feelings of control over elements of design and a technology that was theirs alone.

The sexual life of the Islanders also demonstrated their commitment to retaining control of their own bodies and reproductive selves. Although some scholars have opined that polygyny—a normal practice of many traditional African communities—did not survive, my own fieldwork and knowledge of the community in which I lived indicated that it did indeed survive, but people just did not talk about it much. Needless to say, serial monogamy was noted but polygyny was also practiced. Sea Islanders retained their autonomous attitude toward themselves and their personhood by way of exercising their individual rights to their own bodies through a well-developed realization of their cultural identity in sensual, sexual, artistic, and movement behavior. This immanent awareness of power they retained informed their personhood and culture until better days would come in social, political, and economic future times.

In this book, the culture is seen through the lens of the African background and experience. The Sea Islands culture is also apprehended through sound transmission, dance, and movement communication. It is through these important cultural imperatives that I learned what was, and still is, of consequence to Sea Islands people as they communicated through modalities of word, song, and texture.

The first section of the book introduces the culture and its concerns. "Talkin' Up a Giffie" concentrates on the uses of language in oral lore, drama, folk stories, poetry, and religious expression. Verbal communication is the vehicle for much of the cultural transmission and is, therefore, of primary importance. A "giffie" is a stormy sky, and the ability to bring it on through one's verbal power is both feared and respected with a certain amount of humor. Oral expression is highly valued in African World societies for its flexibility, teaching capabilities, messaging, entertainment, and documentation. Whether or not it is written down, its deepest roots and most vital expression lie in its orality. Oral transmission also finds expression in song: religious, secular, or downright scatological. All forms are grist to the mill since song can be spontaneous in its utterance to reflect the mood of the moment or ritually expressed in recognition of sacred feeling.

The second section, "Tryin' to Make It," deals with cultural survival as exhibited in concepts, actions, and products. Movement is not only nonmaterial and evanescent, but also productive of early inculcated and well-remembered motor patterns that remain for a lifetime. These repetitive and meaningful movements may be recalled in an instant as a rhythmic pulse begins. The teaching of it is by imitation and early patterning beginning in the womb of the baby's mother. When the verbal instruction is added, the picture becomes more complete.

Giving texture to life comes by means of the manipulation of the natural products of the earth, such as seagrass and palmetto sewn into baskets, brooms fashioned from broom sedge, material scraps reconfigured into artistic quilts, and fishnets knitted from cord with palmetto or plastic needles. This texturization is found in the lives of women on the Islands and the decisions and skills they must exercise every day. The economic fabric is comprised of the productivity of fishing, agriculture, and the managing of their money through "Savings Society."

With their heads, hearts, and hands, the Islanders have reaffirmed their connections with Africa by utilizing the cultural modalities that were functional there, modifying them to suit the new surroundings in which they found themselves. Such a fabric of their lives might well be suggestive of the "patchy" quilts they make because they bring together in artistic harmony the elements of their pasts and presents. The Afterword sketches in the economic elements, which constitute the basis of survival in any culture but especially in these communities that have been marginalized for many years. Light and attention have been focused through a recent infusion of welcome interest due to the good offices of the Honorable James Clyburn in establishing the Gullah Geechee Cultural Heritage Commission.

---

[1] Lorenzo Dow Turner, *Africanisms in the Gullah Dialect* (Chicago: University of Chicago Press, 1949).

[2] William Pollitzer, *The Gullah People and Their African Heritage* (Athens: University of Georgia Press, 1999).

[3] Patricia Jones-Jackson, *When Roots Die: Endangered Traditions on the Sea Islands* (Athens: University of Georgia Press, 1987).

[4] Marquetta Goodwine, *The Legacy of Ibo Landing: Gullah Roots of African American Culture* (Atlanta: Clarity Press, 1998).

[5] Althea Sumpter, *Navigating the Gullah Culture Using Multimedia Technology* (DAH diss., Clark Atlanta University, 1999).

[6] Michael Gomez, *Exchanging Our Country Marks* (Chapel Hill: University of North Carolina Press, 1998); Dr. B. G. Martin mentions these circumstances as giving rise to some of the Muslim presence in the United States in "Sapelo Island's Arabic Document: The 'Bilali Diary' in Context," *The Georgia Historical Quarterly* LXXVII, no. 3 (Fall, 1994), 589–601.

[7] Cornelia Bailey, *God, Dr. Buzzard, and the Bolito Man: A Saltwater Geechee Talks About Life on Sapelo Island, Georgia* (New York: Doubleday, 2000); See note 4.

Prologue

Voices in the Wilderness

These white People here are sincere but they've never had an opportunity to hear another opinion or another voice. . . . The time is going to come when these people, despite the local paper, are going to face a situation . . .

The Gregory Papers, Charleston, SC
February 17, 1959

A group of community leaders in Charleston, South Carolina, in 1959, knew they were risking their lives, their livelihoods, and their sacred honor to meet to talk about a society that had stressed them and their families for far too long. Their lives were barely tolerated, their means of making a living were limited to their own communities, and thus, constrained by the larger society. They were not credited as human beings possessing a sense of self, with emotions, desires, and aspirations, nor individually or collectively entitled to life, liberty, and the pursuit of happiness.

Thus marginalized, these people of talent, ability, and sensitivity were relegated to living within a restricted, permitted framework that devalued the significance of their lives and work. Even having toed the line and measured up to the standards of the dominant group, they found it was not sufficient to win them full citizenship and the human rights to which they knew they were entitled. The time to run that risk and take that chance was fast arriving, and they needed to discuss issues.

Meeting as an interethnic group brought with it hazards that all were willing to undergo. Septima Clark, the author of *Echo Within My Soul* and a courageous teacher and organizer, was hosting this meeting in her own home.[1] It would have been noticeable but unremarkable at that time for Euro-Americans to visit in the African American community, but quite remarkable and unacceptable the other way around and very likely to raise comments and questions.

The group, including Esau Jenkins of Johns Island, South Carolina, was quietly gathered to exchange information from various perspectives: Northern/Southern, African/European American, male/female, religious/secular, and Charlestonian/non-Charlestonian. It also met to strategize ways to better the repressive situation in which they all lived. Their meetings were organized because of violent incidents in the community, which were symptomatic of the dangerous and toxic climate that prevailed in Charleston County.

Mr. Jenkins had been willing to throw himself into the fight against segregation all along. Once he learned the concept of developing and spreading leadership, he enthusiastically enlisted other community leaders on the model taught by the Highlander Folk School, which Myles Horton patterned on the European folk schools—people of all ethnicities could meet and discuss common problems, decide how to face them with constructive engagement, and work toward positive solutions.[2]

This modality of cooperation accorded well with an African concept of mutual assistance to accomplish heavy and difficult tasks, common in traditional diasporic African communities—such as the Sea Islands where Mr. Jenkins originated. The persons who attended Highlander got a chance to think, away from the scenes of conflict and threat in which they lived daily. They then could go back to their own communities and begin to make life more bearable for all concerned. Taking their lives in their hands, people of European American and African American ethnicities met to deliberate on how to effect significant change. Some of their conversations are revealing of how confined they were in the apartheid of the South. As James Jenkins shows in his poem, "What is de Hour?" the time had come to take action.[3] This group was working in the community in terms of evolution, not revolution, but they knew that something more had to be done.

One troubling problem was the hesitancy of the church or any church establishment to engage with the issue of racism in the community. Mamie Fields, Afro-Carolinian author of *Lemon Swamp and Other Places*, tells of relationships among Methodist women that seemed to be thriving, which she describes as ". . . interracial church meetings across jurisdictional lines."[4] These interactions unaccountably vanished, and efforts to revive them were unavailing after the 1954 Supreme Court decision outlawing segregation in schools.

Another burning issue they discuss in the meeting concerns the lines of communication between the segments of the communities. Septima Clark speaks about the South Carolina Federation of Women's Clubs meeting up to 1955. Ms. McAdoo contributes a hopeful note about relationships in the YWCA. Many of the statements include tentative language—such as ask, try, would like, vote defeated for statements, and positions thought about but not taken. It was a frustrating time—full of hope and promise in some ways and very daunting in others. "We [that is, the colored branch of the YWCA] have nothing to do with the planning."[5] Ironically, this remark came after the statement about the relationships between staff and board being good.

Ms. Cornwell recounts a meeting that almost did not happen since none of the European American women knew anyone in the African American church community to connect with in order to make a plan. The meeting was to find out what was happening in the African American churches and to report to the national committee. Eventually, the very secret meeting took place with the European Americans asking what the African Americans wanted. This revelation provoked laughter among the Charleston group at Ms. Clark's home, and credit was given to the Euro-American women for their sincerity, if not their effectiveness. They labeled the meeting in such a way as not to reveal who did or said what while still being able to utilize the points of discussion in their report. Coming out as leaders of such discussions would ruin their ability to continue to influence the situation. Ms. McAdoo states, "They would never admit it, if it came out in the paper, that there is a reign of terror." Mr. Jenkins: "Can we get anywhere being silent?"

Mr. J. Arthur Brown relates an anecdote about bringing a man with his tax receipt to register and the annoyance of one of the registrars at his appearance with the incontrovertible proof of the man's eligibility to register to vote. The interplay among Mr. Brown, his friend the policeman, the registrar, and the hopeful registrant typified the drama that was being enacted all over the South. The registrar's efforts to get Mr. Brown removed from the registration procedures is a humorous story about a deadly serious struggle. It illustrates the spirit with which African Americans have always met the obdurate attitudes of the prejudiced Euro-Americans in the South in spite of the climate of fear that pervaded the society.[6]

Highlander Folk School in Tennessee was initiating citizenship education projects in meetings in the South to bring together European and African Americans to talk over issues that could influence change in their communities. Founded by Myles Horton on the model of folk schools in Scandinavia and using folklore and life, songs, games, etc., to help teach self-determination and human rights, Highlander was a retreat where all groups could meet, sing, and eat collectively at their leisure. The prospect of traveling that far from home was frightening enough that some of the Sea Islanders brought their own food, sure they would not like whatever was prepared for them.

Guy and Candie Carawan, authors of *Ain't You Got a Right to the Tree of Life?*, and William "Bill" Saunders, Esau Jenkins's right-hand man, have told the story about all the participants being arrested on some trumped-up charge, among them Septima Clark. The participants, who had previously indicated that they had no money, found the cash quickly when Ms. Clark was threatened. Their respect for her was great, and it hurt them to see her treated roughly by the Tennessee constabulary.

Returning from workshops in the hills of Tennessee, Islanders went about participating in the democratic process as well as community organizing, which they had learned to do at Highlander. Esau Jenkins was a prime mover in the Charleston and Island community. He drove a VW bus that proclaimed "Hate is Expensive!" on the side—his declaration of independence from the restrictions of Southern society.

It was into this climate of ferment and renewal that I arrived in Charleston one rainy February in 1966. I had met with Guy and Candie Carawan in New York to receive some instruction from them as to who to contact when I got to Charleston. They sent me right to Esau Jenkins at the J & P Café near the Ashley River Bridge. It was a rendezvous point for Islanders trying to hook up with rides home or to have a meal or a drink of coffee. Moultrie, the chef, wore a high white hat and turned out African American Southern cooking at its best; Katheryn chopped pig tails far into the night; and Ms. Jenkins and Mr. Polite managed the establishment while Esau Jenkins was away on civil rights business.

Guy and Candie Carawan had come down earlier to live on Johns Island, Jenkins's home island, for Highlander's citizenship projects. They had pulled together material for a book and had gone back North to edit and publish *Ain't You Got A Right to the Tree of Life?* Their house on Johns Island had been a focal point for local activities and a way station for rights workers needing a meal or a bed.[7]

My roommate Jan, a theology student from Union Theological Seminary in New York City, my son Tim, aged two, and I moved into the Felder house, as it was locally known. We had many meetings and rehearsals for the Johns Island Silhouettes, as the gutbucket band had named themselves. Jan and I entertained visiting government teams such as Speed Up and Catch Up, which were brought into being to aid with educational needs and help students who wished to challenge the segregated school system.

The young people were the "Talented Tenth" being sent, like Shaka's warriors, into battle to test the enemy's strength. The European American establishment turned out to be powerful and unrelenting toward the young people who were vastly outnumbered in the first efforts to integrate the schools. When it looked as though Esau Jenkins might win a seat on the school board, they changed the position from elected to appointed. Fortunately, they appointed Ms. Septima Clark, who was a stalwart advocate for the people. Many of the young people in the vanguard came away bruised and nervously shattered by the pressure of being, for example, one of six African Americans among the one thousand strong Euro-American student body.

They suffered beatings, rejections, and indignities designed to discourage them from wanting to participate in band practice, school clubs, or dances (many of which were cancelled so as not to run the risk of their dancing together or more). Many dropped out under these assaults and became unable to function, so the plan to disable these smart young people succeeded. The gradual plan toward desegregation had been set up for failure, so a new strategy had to be devised.

Ms. Clark's group had educational issues as a foremost topic, not only that of young children but people who wished to get career or professional training that would stand them in good stead in the marketplace as they strove for decent jobs. Ms. Clark had been a teacher since she was sixteen years of age, and so she knew education was the way up and the way out. She waded in wherever she was needed and people loved her for it. She stopped a young man one day who was escaping from a local store with some stolen goods, racing through the parking lot. Ms. Clark talked with him and persuaded him to return the goods and stay on a righteous path, which would lead him to a better life.[8] She had begun her teaching career in the creosote (black) painted schools to which African American students were relegated. Later in her career, she taught workshops for Highlander Folk School where European and African Americans were learning how to bring about and, subsequently, move into a more equitable society. She went to California to do a workshop with prisoners out there. Herman Blake told me that as he was taking her to this event, he was anxious about her meeting with the men and how they would react to her gentle manner. He asked her what on earth she would say to them. She answered that she would just be there to love them a little. Well, the prisoners loved her and were reluctant to let her go when time came to leave. Her genuine love for them and fearless association with them had won their hearts—just one credit in a long life of proving humanity.

Meanwhile, back on Esau Jenkins's home island, where Ms. Clark had taught in her early career and some twelve miles' distance from the city of Charleston, Jenkins's fellow Islanders had lived for hundreds of years reaffirming their African heritage in the many aspects of their farming and fishing lives. Like the Charleston meeting group, they too were involved in self-determination. Their continuation of their culture and identity had been dictated by the practices of their ancestors who had brought a mind full of information and cultural patterns as their only luggage in the unwilling migration from their homes in West Africa.

---

[1] Septima Poinsett Clark with Legette Blythe, *Echo in My Soul* (New York: E. P. Dutton, 1962).

[2] Myles Horton with Judith and Herbert Kohl, *The Long Haul: An Autobiography* (New York: Teachers College Press, 1999).

[3] James Jenkins in "The Weapon of My Song: Two Sea Island Poets" in this volume.

[4] Mamie Fields, *Lemon Swamp and Other Places* (New York: Free Press, 1983).

[5] Ms. McAdoo in The Gregory Papers.

[6] The Gregory Papers, 1959, section II, 4.

[7] Guy and Candie Carawan, *Ain't You Got a Right to the Tree of Life?* (New York: Simon and Schuster, 1972).

[8] The Gregory Papers, 1959, section II, 4.

Ms. Bessie Jones of St. Simons Island, Georgia.

"By the Waters of Babylon"

The Sea Islands as a Delineated Region

The Sea Islands, a group of coastal areas and islands located from North Carolina to Florida, are an integral part of the United States politically. The inhabitants, however, are in the majority culturally as well as part of a broader framework of the African World and some of its creolized communities in the Caribbean and South America.

African World: American Life

The islands themselves, actually a part of the coastal plain, are surrounded by sea, streams, riverine waterways, and brackish marshes separating them from the mainland. Some of the Islands are located far enough out in the ocean to require boats for transportation while others are now connected (since the 1930s) to the mainland by bridges or causeways, making access possible by car or bus. Although Sapelo and Daufuskie are less accessible, a key factor in their economic and social life, it is the isolation that has so significantly operated to preserve the folklore and culture of the Sea Islands. These factors have been reinforced most recently by the incursions of developers.

Areas of those islands have been rendered even more culturally, socially, and economically remote by their actions. Within the past twenty years or so, the social and interethnic situation began to alter, producing a course of events that affected the economic conditions as well.

Sea Islands as Folk Region

This group of islands is generally regarded as constituting a cultural or folkloric region. It may be useful to discuss theories of regionalism, the better to understand the concept and its terms of reference. To recognize a locality as a folk region is not to isolate it absolutely from its larger geographical and cultural relationships. In the words of Rupert B. Vance, "any practicing member of the social science fraternity who undertakes to use the regional as a tool for research will soon find, in Howard W. Odum's felicitous phrase, that the choice he has made is not that of regionalism *or* but regionalism *and.* The missing term is nation or world, for the region gains its significance only from its relation to a total structure. The relation that regionalism presumes to study is that of parts to wholes."[1] In this case, the Sea Islands area is the part related to the whole African World. In *American Regionalism,* based in part on H. E. Moore's publication of 1937, Howard Odum and H. E. Moore deal with this matter very specifically.[2] Their study has political and economic emphasis, which can be used, but there is also interest in the definitions concerning the cultural unity of regions. This unity may be established by inner cohesion through culture, exterior marginalizing pressures through societal strictures that confine them to certain areas, or historic events such as capture, transshipment, and enslavement. The area has a long history of exploration and appreciation; visitors have recorded the climate and vegetation and general aura of the place since the Spanish explorations. They recognized the differences, subtle and obvious, that made this place a good one in which to settle. Historian William Leuchtenburg quotes Eudora Welty's poetic description of why place matters in an excellent discussion of regionalism as a determining factor in understanding human beings. Leuchtenburg indicates that regionalism may be making a comeback from its heyday when Odum and Moore were first laying out the theory. Interestingly, it is the artists who have the most sensitivity to the taste, color, sound, and feeling of the home place or region. He quotes or refers to Joyce, Stegner, Durrell, Lawrence, and, of course, Welty to shore up his argument.[3] Although so many areas—such as architecture, brand-name clothing, and food articles—have come to be the same nationally and worldwide, there still remain the distinctive regions, changed but yet recognizable in their sense of themselves as belonging to one place and not another. The sense of things and persons unseen also contributes strongly to the feeling of belonging in the African World as well as what is visually obvious.

Although these various authors, Johnson, Forten, et al., clearly show they are defining a certain area in their explorations and descriptions, the terms "Sea Islands" and "Lowcountry" did not come into more general usage until the twentieth century.

Willie Lee Rose, in her fine historical work on the Port Royal area, *Rehearsal for Reconstruction,* treats the era of great change and action just at the end of the Civil War.[4] The "contrabands of war," as the African American population was known, were displaced by the war because their owners abandoned them along with their property, and they were left to shift for themselves in the face of oncoming battles, artillery, and soldiers. The abnegation of these responsibilities by the landed class created a great deal of flux among the Afro-American population. Port Royal and the surrounding islands were under observation by the United States government at this time and were administratively well defined for that reason. Missionary societies were also arranging for groups of teachers to go south to this area and teach basic reading, writing, and arithmetic. The newly emancipated captive workers and their families could now legally learn to read and write because they were entering a money economy for the first time and needed training in the handling of money. This well-intentioned intrusion is the point at which the system of the field-hand gangs on the large plantation islands, preserved through isolation factors and large population statistics, began to disintegrate.

Out-migration to the northern cities, especially New York, that followed this era has had a further weakening effect on the African-based culture and language of this area, influencing it in the directions of the dominant Euro-American cultural dilution. Out-migration resulted in the apparent disappearance of the Gullah language as Guy Johnson experienced it on St. Helena Island thirty years later. [5]

Subsequent research—such as that of Baird, Jones-Jackson, Mufwene, and Hopkins—has established that Sea Islands Creole is still alive, though in modified form.[6] Other groups of Euro-Americans or Afro-Americans may possess one or two of the same cultural traits, folkloristic events, and linguistic usage of the Sea Islanders, but it is the whole complex of the shared mutual experience and its endurance through time that constitutes the folk region.

In their introduction, Odum and Moore identify six major regions for the United States. Their system obviously places the Sea Islands area in the

Southern region. Odum and Moore speak of these divisions as ". . . portraying the new pluralism of the American nation and for interpreting its growth through the orderly processes of the people and their institutions within the living geography of a natural and cultural heritage."[7] This statement pinpoints the ecology of the area as influencing the lives and culture of the people and begins with the ecological foundation, which finds the people farming and fishing. Any group at a given time within this ecological setting will have been making their living on the land and water.

To authenticate the Sea Islands area as a folk region, we must consider two coordinates that help to define a culture, namely, the synchronic day-to-day activities and diachronic timeline of the group. The culture must be shared at any one given time, and it must move through time as well by being passed on from generation to generation. The shared elements are evident in the internal culture, and its dimensions are also defined by the boundaries beyond which the folkways of the Sea Islands are seen as strange and esoteric or exotic by outsiders.

The Sea Islands region actually relates to more than one "total structure." It is connected by culture to the African and European continental origins of many of its residents. It is consociated by cultural, social, and economic ties and political orientation to the United States mainland. So, it is the American "nation" and the African "world" and culture to which the Sea Islands relate as a region. It is problematic to define a region as a comprehensive unit in an ethnographic vacuum. A region is, by this definition, interdependent with its larger unit or units—this being the characteristic of region. The Sea Islands are also interconnected with the Caribbean Island societies with which they share a creolized population group and culture. Thus, the Sea Islands region can be seen as part of the whole in juxtaposition to Africa, the Caribbean, and the United States.

The existence of politically established units has the effect of predetermining the status of a subunit as a region. As a result, the distinctive character of a subunit as a discrete social and cultural entity can be obscured, since political boundaries often cut across or subsume sociocultural dividing lines. "If there were natural subregions which could actually be delimited in terms of realistic boundaries and units susceptible of social implementation as major regions, they could be preferably utilized. But they do not exist. The states do exist and under the American system must continue to exist and are therefore essential units."[8] Furthermore, the geographic divisions, islands and mainland, continue to define essential units. During the era of European control, this subsumptive factor operated in the division of continental Africa into political units irrespective of the ethnic groups which were separated by this action. For the determination of folk regions and culture areas, strict adherence to political divisions can thus often be hampering rather than helpful. In the case of the Sea Islands, however, the stated divisions—North and South Carolina and Georgia—can be used as principal subregions, and one may proceed directly to the establishment of a substate division of upland and lowland areas. For example, in Virginia they are called the Piedmont and Tidewater. The Sea Islands areas of the states of South Carolina and Georgia are referred to as the Lowcountry. Relevant to this geographically based concept of region is that noted thus by Lewis Mumford: "Between the continent and the historic village is an area sometimes larger, sometimes smaller than the political state. It is the human region."[9]

A number of studies or series focused on such human regions in the United States have been undertaken at one time or another. Erskine Caldwell edited a group of publications in what Odum and Moore refer to as "... the older authentic literary regionalism." Its contributors have produced studies which are very uneven in literary worth and content. *Mormon Country* by Wallace Stegner stands out among the others for research skill as well as literary merit.[10]

In seeking to establish the Sea Islands area as a folk region, the inquiry really falls somewhere between literary interests, on the one hand, and more geographical-political-historical on the other. The real danger in working with regionalism as a concept is that the attempts to characterize a large area and its people by inclusive descriptive terms may be marred by generalizations and clichés. Certainly, the Sea Islands are no exception; there are varieties of linguistic, social, musical, and dance behavior, which make for a certain amount of internal variation and differences within the designated culture area. Actually, the Lowcountry, divided already as island and coastal region, could be subdivided again; this is where the political state boundaries could be useful.[11] Robert F. Thompson suggests the terms Afro-Carolinian or Afro-Georgian for use in referring to objects of African American manufacture in those areas. Besides the African heritage, which is more marked in this island and coastal region, it is possible there is a wider separation between the ethnic groups which inhabit this region than in other sections of the country. Linguistically, all the long-term residents, Euro-American and Afro-American alike, speak some form of Sea Islands Creole as is true in other English-language, creole-speaking communities—such as Jamaican, Barbadian, and Providencian.

Throughout the history of African peoples in intensive contact with Europeans in the New World, the process of creolization has been at work; there was a mixing of peoples, languages, and cultures from two or more ethnic groups in each instance. The languages formed in the culture contact between African and European peoples in human traffic markets, seasoning farms, and plantations are presently undergoing a process of decreolization due to increased communication with speakers of English, either through personal intercourse or by way of the spoken/heard or oral/aural culture.

Provincial locality from which loyalties, patriotism, and folkways radiate certainly covers the various aspects—such as the historical unity, the loose economic unity (because of the type of plantations here), the language and culture loyalty, and the richness of the folklore and folklife.[12]

Some specific factors in the lives of the people can help to establish a cultural unity. Further, folklore and folklife evidence illustrate some of the traits that distinguish this area from others and set it apart as a folk region, as well as traits that join it in language and culture with others of the African World. Vance encapsulates the dimensions of regional studies in these terms: "To show its dynamic aspects and to relate it to history and social change, the region must be interpreted both as structure and functions, as process and product."[13] This statement is one which relates to all human societies in which the structure is the framework within which the members of the society function. The product is the result of the process within that function. Thus, they are part of the determinant of societies which contribute to the definition of the human region. At one level, there are the values of the culture which dictate the process and the use to which the local materials will be put to yield the product, which in turn represents the culture and its world view.

The assumption has been made that this area exists. Many researchers writing in terms of the Sea Islands have not defined the area, not thinking such definition important or necessary. For example, researchers could set the limits of the Sea Islands region as that area occupied by the persons who speak the Gullah Creole language (also called Sea Islands Creole). This procedure could be too limiting as there are Sea Islands Creole speakers in Prince Edward Island, Canada, Mexico, Texas, New York, and Los Angeles, to name a few, due to further diasporic spread. The region could also be defined as the Islands together with an area of an indeterminate number of miles inland from the actual coastline, which is often difficult to establish, as the coastline is quite uneven and often interrupted by rivers and streams and marshes.

History

These islands have been written about as a source of interesting cultural phenomena since before the days of the American Revolution.[14] Often the accounts in the nineteenth and early twentieth centuries tended to stress the exotic nature of the customs in some of the literature. This perception is not entirely surprising to the Gullah people, who, although native to the United States, actually manifest in their speech, customs, and general manner of life features which show greater affinities to the Afro-Caribbean populations and to indigenous African peoples than do other Americans of African origin.

The Sea Islands area has a long history of exploration and appreciation; writers have recorded the climate and vegetation and general atmosphere of the place since the coming of the Spanish voyagers—such as Lucas Vasquez, who came to Florida and Saint Helena Island in the 1520s. French Huguenots were not far behind the Spanish adventurers, as they arrived in Port Royal in the 1650s in order to escape the persecutions at home, much as the English did in the following century.[15]

The Sea Islands area or the Lowcountry has inspired authors and travelers to write in different eras about the natural land and seascapes, the beauty of nature, the language, the stories, the people, and the social interactions. Lanier's poem, "The Marshes of Glynn," is a praise song to the natural beauty of the coastal marshes where so much of our evolving life exists.[16] The northerners who came to the Sea Islands area after the Civil War—Allen, Ware, and Garrison—wrote of the language, its expression in song and speech, and the moving quality of the songs (1867).[17] Gonzales wrote *With Aesop along the Black Border* (1924) about the folklore and language, and later, Mason Crum completed a book (1940) about the language and lore.[18] These latter two authors were Southerners and had certain attitudes about African people and their ways. Elsie Clews Parsons, an independent—in spirit and means—New Yorker, researched *Folklore of the Sea Islands* (1924).[19] In the 1930s, Lorenzo Dow Turner, an African American linguistic scholar, was completing groundbreaking research in the Gullah language and its relationship to African languages, thereby bringing the discourse about the Gullah speakers into a more objective framework.[20] In the 1940s, when Turner's book was finally published, Lydia Parrish, the wife of famous artist Maxfield Parrish, turned out *Slave Songs of the Georgia Sea Islands,* which gave the world some of the songs and games of the Island people.[21]

A great deal of research—social, historic, linguistic, and folkloric—was focused on St. Helena Island, South Carolina; Arthur Huff Fauset, brother of novelist Jessie Redmond Fauset, Guy B. Johnson, Guion Griffis Johnson, T. J. Woofter, and Claude Kiser all contributed field-researched material about this area.[22] Some folk stories of Johns Island, South Carolina, can be found in *Ain't You Got a Right to the Tree of Life?* by Guy and Candie Carawan.[23]

Since it has been a center of interest and activity from the 1500s, there are many writings about the Islands that may be consulted. These are just a few examples. This region has been a mine of information and material for creative writers as well. William Gilmore Simms set his novels—such as *The Cassique of Kiawah* (1859) and *The Yemassee* (1835)—in South Carolina, especially the Sea Islands area where there was a coming together in the 1700s of the Native Americans, Euro-Americans, and African Americans in a frontier and colonial situation. He makes attempts at reproducing the speech patterns of these various groups. He represents the characters according to the temper of the times in which he wrote, casting the Native Americans as noble or ignorant savages, African Americans as doughty but ignorant frontiersman or servants, and European Americans as powerful colonists, crafty maneuverers, or brave warriors.[24]

A Sea Islands character appears in Caruthers's *The Kentuckian in New York* (1834), which contains a fictionalized vignette of Bilali, who was an actual historical person who lived on Sapelo Island, as part of the plantation establishment of the Spauldings. The small, leather-covered booklet the author mentions in the description of this man still exists and is archived in Athens, Georgia. The language of the main characters in reference to the displayed person is typical of the times.[25]

In the 1920s, Julia Peterkin wrote several novels illustrative of the Sea Islands people and their lives. She won the Pulitzer Prize for her *Scarlet Sister Mary*. She internalized quite a bit of the folk culture in the stories and built the human interactions around them. One scene in *Black April* (1927) is a quilting gathering of women on an island. The Bible quilt she describes bears a superficial resemblance to the famous Bible Quilt, which was made by Harriett Powers of Athens, Georgia.[26]

The first one . . . was Adam and Eve and the serpent. Adam's shirt was blue, his pants brown, and his head a small patch of yellow. Eve had a red headkerchief, a purple, wide-skirted dress, and a tall black serpent stood straight up on the end of its tail. The next square had two men, one standing up, the other fallen down—Cain and Abel. The red patch under Abel is his blood, spilled on the ground by Cain's sin.[27] Peterkin also had an ear for the spoken Gullah language and wrote it down as she heard it:

> Maum Hannah's deep sigh broke into the stillness. "I ever did love Boy-chillen, but dey cause a lot o'sorrow. My mammy used to say ev'y Boy-child ought to be killed soon as it's born." "How'd de world go on if people done dat?" Bina asked. "I dunno. Gawd kin do a lot o'strange t'ings."[28]

Some of the dialogue she has written in her books is reminiscent of the transcribed Gullah language from field-collected folk stories.[29]

In more modern times, Paule Marshall, an author of Barbadian descent, has written *Praise Song for the Widow* (1983), which is a story of a woman from the Sea Islands undergoing an epiphany on a Caribbean island during which she connects with her past including the African diaspora.[30] Her aunt tried years before to help her make that connection, but Avey had resisted. She finally comes to recognize that her Sea Islands past and the atmosphere and culture of Grenada and Carriacou in the present all belong in the same continuum from the continent of Africa. She then knows she must pass on the knowledge of that cultural heritage to her descendants. The Sea Islands provide the area in which the heroine must work out her destiny.[31]

Tina McElroy Ansa is a transplant to the Islands, but has taken them to her heart. Her *Baby of the Family* (1989) shows us a heroine who we know from birth and who, with the wisdom and clear vision of childhood, sees beyond the ordinary. Lena was born with a caul, which to the Sea Islands belief system endows her with "the sight." Ansa uses the natural beauty of the seashore to set off the dramatic vision Lena has of Rachel.

> As she strolled down the beach, she stopped for a while to watch a school of mullet leap and splash not three feet from where she stood at the water's edge. Lena could see the dragonflies and sand flies and gnats hovering above the water's smooth still surface. Each time a big fat mullet, going after an insect, jumped out of the muddy water, the sun turned it silver-colored as it fell back in on its side, and Lena let out a little cry of appreciation.[32]

This tranquil scene gives way to an unsettling visitation from a woman of the past who reveals the sadness of slavery times and her experiences. Through this encounter, Lena learns of the African background and the pain of African American involvement in the separation from the homeland and harsh treatment under enslavement. The literature clearly shows use of the landscape by entities seen and unseen, which contribute to the character of the place.

The Sea Islands, like the Caribbean, were the site of large plantations worked by gangs of enslaved Africans who were chiefly directed by overseers, by drivers, or by the owners whenever they were in residence. Population statistics on the Islands reflected a majority of enslaved Africans and a minority of Euro-American people. Most enslaved Africans during the plantation era, which ended with the Civil War, worked in field gangs, but a select few, often of mixed parentage, were house servants. African field hands existed in greater numbers than either the house servants or the Euro-Americans, and were, thus, more often left to their own devices than those members of the African population whose duties tended to involve them more directly with the Euro-American population. As a result, they were more able to preserve the remembered and transmitted culture from their lost homes in Africa.

The previous isolative constraints and the slavery-imposed restrictions in the South were only somewhat relieved in the post-World War I era by boat travel to the mainland. It is difficult to judge the relative importance of the various isolating influences. Geographic location is certainly basic, however, and to a certain extent, other considerations such as the uses of the terrain for escape and concealment arise from this physical delimitation.

Only after the 1930s, when the Works Progress Administration (WPA) built some roads and bridges, was some pattern of geographic integration imposed. Although some island people have traveled on the boats, much greater numbers were later to use the roads and bridges.

After World War II had dramatically emphasized the need for change, the war veterans expressed their feelings, saying it was long in coming and is still in process. As a result, some peonage conditions remain among the farming population in spite of the efforts toward ameliorations of social and economic inequalities.

The civil rights movement of the 1960s helped to raise the social awareness of the Islanders and effected some few alterations in their lifestyle designed to better their way of life through increased economic opportunity. More mobility because of developing transportations and communications between the mainland and the Islands together with socioeconomic progress from the civil rights movement tended to mitigate the isolative factors. These factors of change had not yet been strong enough to completely extinguish the manifestation of distinctiveness in such cultural modes as language, oral lore, social and economic organization, and some aspects of material productions, such as the basketry.

The Sea Islands constitute a subregion of the Deep South, but there are factors of isolation which make it distinct from the rest of the South and its people and from the rest of the African American population too. Historical factors can also account for the cultural conservatism which has developed here. During slavery times, the Africans escaped to marginal areas—in Jamaica, they fled to the mountains; in Dahomey (Benin), they hid in the lacustrine marshes; in the Sea Islands area, they ran and secreted themselves in the mosquito-filled swamps. In the Sea Islands, Benin, and Jamaica, they were partially protected from the ravages of mosquitoes by the presence of the sickle-cell gene. It was in these marshy, forested areas that the Sea Islanders lived, organized themselves, and buried their dead.

Locality is a consideration in this definition too, though it is neither mere locality nor isolation alone which determined the distinctive qualities of this area, but a combination of all these aspects—locality (coast and island), language, geographic, social and runaway isolation, and the fact of its being a subregion of the South and of the whole African American population group. Joseph Himes writes in his introduction to *Sea Island to City*, "On St. Helena Island they lived as members of an isolated all-black society. They enjoyed relative freedom, independence, and cultural integrity."[33]

A little more broadly, one could define it as the area inhabited by the people who retain definitely identifiable practices, and can, therefore, be said to possess a cultural integrity.

In the understanding of this area as a folk region, we have to deal with a predetermination or predisposition. Writers refer to the Sea Islands area confident that readers will know what they mean. Christensen uses the term Sea Islands in the title of her book.[34] Jones employs the expression thus— "We refer to the swamp region of Georgia and the Carolinas, where the lingo of the rice field and sea island Negroes is *sui generis*."[35] Jones is, in somewhat circular terms, telling us that the Sea Islands is where they speak Sea Islands Creole, and by so doing, the Islanders fit into the theory which states that the region may be defined by the language loyalty of its speakers. In the title of his book, he utilizes the geographic designation "Georgia Coast," mainly to distinguish between the area where the plantation was located and inland Georgia. Some of the early writers can help to give us an historical perspective on the continuity of Sea Islands identity and culture.

Some regional studies tend to be like photographic vignettes, suffering from the myopia of the ethnographic present. Processual as the nature of human culture may be, fieldworkers are limited by finite vision and can only record what they hear and see at any given moment. They may also limit themselves by means of the conventional academic use of the concept of the ethnographic present. As Vance points out, however, the relationship of the subregions to the larger units must be kept in mind, which in this case are Africa and the United States.[36]

While one can cite the past, particularly when delving into memory culture, and record the present, one can only wonder about the future and its consequences for the area in which one does research. Sometimes the best that can be done is record the culture as well as possible in an effort to preserve as much as is feasible. The anthropologist or folklorist may also function as a cultural barrier by providing linguistic and cultural augmentation which bear the stamps of their own mindsets (possibly to increase the readers' comprehension). Indeed, "Naked texts divorced from living frames . . . "[37] challenge the researchers as purveyors of their cultures and test the cultural researchers' ingenuity in presenting a meaningful experience or situation to members of a different group. These subregions, which have not been homogenized into the "melting pot," may contribute to the cultural plurality mentioned by Odum and Moore in their introduction.

The future of the Islands is already unfolding as the natural resources and the residents, war with the developers driven by profit motives. Both neglect the needs of the African American population who become ghettoized and economically imperialized and are never mentioned as being among the resources worth saving. These areas, so developed, will cease to have their unique characteristics and lose the distinguishing features of the folk region. As the ethnomusicologists have a legitimate complaint about the missionaries and their gross interference with autonomous culture groups, so do the scholars of traditional lifeways have such feelings about the developers whose irresistible money and bulldozers cause irreparable damage to the cultural integrity of some isolated areas whose powerless populations cannot prevent the damage to their lives and culture.[38]

On the good side, however, the developments sometimes bring some economic opportunities to the folk who live there. Furthermore, the so-to-speak submerged folk are flexing their cultural muscles and realizing that their folkways can be exploited—by them. There are various festivals during the year, which draw thousands of people, bringing much needed money and trade to the Islands. They are, furthermore, exploring ways to continue a relexification of their language and a recreolization of their culture by utilizing or creating economic opportunities within the new setting of condominia and resorts. Jeanne Moutoussamy-Ashe's poignant work on Daufuskie Island highlights the serene beauty lost as the island is developed by the condominium/resort builders.[39] People such as these developers have an eye for the commercial exploitation of the beauty of the surroundings, but there is no appreciation for the danger to a way of life, which, deprived of its place of being, will die.

The regions as we have known them are not only vanishing in one sense, but their people are also changing, as any culture group must. Academic field-workers can continue to document the changes as they appear and learn to find the folklore in recent adaptations and in its new setting. The process of decreolization is moving quite quickly on the Islands due to development and cataclysmic events in addition to increased opportunities for exposure to the outside world through education, travel, and television. The process of decreolization also goes on in other segments of the African diaspora. The Caribbean societies, to which the Sea Islands are culturally related—Jamaica, Barbados, and other Afro-English-speaking groups—are also changing under the onslaught of postcolonialism, outside economic power and cultural impact. From the Sea Islands all the way south to the circum-Caribbean coasts of Central and South America is a culture area which shares definite characteristics, many of which have certain African societies as their source. The Caribbean creolized languages and societies are made up of a mixture of European, African, and Native American elements as well as a later admixture from the imported Asian workers. Each group has had its impact on the Creole languages and customs as well as oral/aural society moving and changing in response to culture contact. It is theorized now that increased communications and faster travel have brought about a decreolization process in these societies. In fact, it is likely that the process of creolization has always been a mobile phenomenon because of the oral/aural nature of these groups. Their unwritten language and folkways can yield to cultural pressure more swiftly than a culture bound more rigidly by a strong literary tradition. Creolization and decreolization are different aspects of continuing dynamic culture contact and its resultant change.

It is clear that the people and culture of the Sea Islands constitute a region by any one of the definitions offered, though V. B. Stanbery's may be the most suitable: "A region may be described . . . as an area of which the inhabitants instinctively feel themselves as part."[40] This area might once have been characterized by R. H. Whitbeck's statement, ". . . The region is distinguished by the use to which it is put by its occupants."[41] As the developers move in, the vital issue now is that of survival; it is a problem that African Americans have been confronting since slavery times. The question now is whether their coping skills will stand against the forces now in operation as well as they have done in the past on a personal and community level. Meanwhile, decreolized though the language and culture may be to a certain degree, the region, its people, and their survivability endure for now.

The coping mechanisms of the folk culture, oral and material, have been the mainstay of the culture when they were left to their own devices. The oral transmission has been the strong thread which has kept the Sea Islands society connected. It has been the continuing voice of the culture in the storytellers, the singers, the actors, the game players, and the poets. The spirit of the persisting culture will also be represented by the writers who draw upon the rich customs of the Sea Islands to inform the characters in their stories.[42]

---

[1] Rupert B. Vance, "The Regional Concept as a Tool for Social Research," in *Regionalism in America*, ed. Merrill Jensen (Madison: University of Wisconsin Press, 1951), 119.

[2] Howard W. Odum and Harry E. Moore, *American Regionalism* (New York: H. Holt and Co., 1938).

[3] Willliam E. Leuchtenburg, *The White House Looks South* (Baton Rouge: Louisiana State University Press, 2005), 5.

[4] Willie Lee Rose, *Rehearsal for Reconstruction* (New York: Vintage, 1960).

[5] Claude V. Kiser, *Sea Island to City* (New York: Columbia University Press, 1932).

[6] Keith E. Baird, "Semantics and Afro-American Liberation," *Social Casework* 51 (May 1970), 265–269; Patricia Jones-Jackson, *When Roots Die: Endangered Traditions on the Sea Islands* (Athens: University of Georgia Press, 1987); Salikoko Mufwene, *The Ecology of Language Evolution* (Cambridge: Cambridge University Press, 2001); Tometro Hopkins, ed., *The Carrier Pidgin* (Miami: Florida International University).

[7] Howard W. Odum and Harry E. Moore, *American Regionalism* (New York: H. Holt and Co., 1938), vi.

[8] Ibid.

[9] Lewis Mumford, "Regionalism and Irregionalism," *The Sociological Review* 19 (October 10, 1934), 277–288.

[10] Wallace Stegner, *Mormon Country* (New York: Duell, Sloan, and Pearce, 1942).

[11] Howard W. Odum and Harry E. Moore, *American Regionalism* (New York: H. Holt and Co., 1938), 168.

[12] Ian Hancock, "A Provisional Comparison of the English-Derived Atlantic Creoles," in *Pidginization and Creolization of Languages,* ed. Dell Hymes (Cambridge: Cambridge University Press, 1971), 287–291.

[13] Rupert B. Vance, "The Regional Concept as a Tool for Social Research," in *Regionalism in America*, ed. Merrill Jensen (Madison: University of Wisconsin Press, 1951), 124.

[14] Katharine Jones, *Port Royal Under Six Flags* (Indianapolis: Bobbs-Merrill, 1960), 67–97, 118.

[15] Ibid., 19–45, 47–65; Peter H. Wood, *Black Majority* (New York: Knopf, 1974), 3–6.

[16] Sidney Lanier, "The Marshes of Glynn," in *The Literature of the American South*, eds. William Andrews et. al. (New York: W. W. Norton, 1998).

17 William Francis Allen, Charles Pickard Ware, and Lucy McKim Garrison, *Slave Songs of the United States* (1867; repr., Freeport, NY: Books for Libraries Press, 1971).

18 Ambrose Gonzales, *With Aesop along the Black Border* (Columbia, SC: State Co., 1924); Mason Crum, *Gullah: Negro Life in the Carolina Sea Islands* (1940; repr., New York: Negro Universities Press, 1968).

19 Elsie Clews Parsons, *Folklore of the Sea Islands, South Carolina*, Memoirs of the American Folklore Society, vol. 16 (Cambridge, MA: The American Folklore Society, 1923).

20 Lorenzo Dow Turner, *Africanisms in the Gullah Dialect* (Chicago: University of Chicago Press, 1949).

21 Lydia Parrish, *Slave Songs of the Georgia Sea Islands* (New York: Creative Age Press, 1941).

22 Lydia Parrish, *Slave Songs of the Georgia Sea Islands* (New York: Creative Age Press, 1941); Arthur Huff Fauset, "Folklore from St. Helena Island, South Carolina," *Journal of American Folklore* 38 (1925), 217–238; Guy B. Johnson, *Folk Culture on St. Helena Island, South Carolina* (Chapel Hill: University of North Carolina Press, 1930); Guion Griffis Johnson, *A Social History of the Sea Islands* (Chapel Hill: University of North Carolina Press, 1930); T. J. Woofter, *Black Yeomanry* (New York: H. Holt and Co., 1930); Claude V. Kiser, *Sea Island to City: A Study of St. Helena Islanders in Harlem and Other Urban Centers* (1932; repr., New York: Atheneum, 1969).

23 Guy and Candie Carawan, *Ain't You Got a Right to the Tree of Life?* (New York: Simon and Schuster, 1967).

24 William Gilmore Simms, *The Cassique of Kiawah* (1859; repr., Gainesville, GA: Magnolia Press, 1989); William Gilmore Simms, *The Yemassee: A Romance of South Carolina* (New York: Redfield, 1835).

25 William Caruthers, *The Kentuckian in New York* (New York: Harper and Bros., 1867).

26 Julia Peterkin, *Scarlet Sister Mary* (Indianapolis: Bobbs-Merrill, 1928); Julia Peterkin, *Black April* (New York: Grosset and Dunlap, 1927).

27 Julia Peterkin, *Black April* (New York: Grosset and Dunlap, 1927), 171.

28 Ibid., 170.

29 See "Telling Lies: Adult Stories of the Sea Islands" in this volume.

30 Paule Marshall, *Praise Song for the Widow* (New York: Penguin Group, 1984).

31 Ibid.

32 Tina McElroy Ansa, *Baby of The Family* (New York: Harcourt Brace and Company, 1989), 155.

33 Joseph Himes, preface, to Claude V. Kiser, *Sea Island to City: A Study of St. Helena Islanders in Harlem and Other Urban Centers* (1932; repr., New York: Atheneum, 1969), 1–7.

[34] Abigail M. H. Christensen, *Afro-American Folklore Told round Cabin Fires on the Sea Islands of South Carolina* (Boston: J. G. Cupples Co., 1892).

[35] Charles Colcock Jones, *Negro Myths from the Georgia Coast* (Boston: Houghton, Mifflin, and Co., 1888), v.

[36] Rupert B. Vance, "The Regional Concept as a Tool for Social Research," in *Regionalism in America*, ed. Merrill Jensen (Madison: University of Wisconsin Press, 1951), 125.

[37] Ibid.

[38] Lynne Duke, "A Touch of Africa Makes a Last Stand," *The Washington Post,* March 23, 1991, A1, A8, A9.

[39] Jeanne Moutoussamy-Ashe, *Daufuskie Island* (Columbia: University of South Carolina Press, 1982).

[40] V. B. Stanbery, quoted in Howard W. Odum and Harry E. Moore, *American Regionalism* (New York: H. Holt and Co., 1938), 2.

[41] R. H. Whitbeck, quoted in Howard W. Odum and Harry E. Moore, *American Regionalism* (New York: H. Holt and Co., 1938.

[42] Tina McElroy Ansa, *Baby of The Family* (New York: Harcourt Brace and Company, 1989).

Ms. Bessie Jones of St. Simons Island, Georgia, with her granddaughters.

The Gullah-Caribbean Connection

Keith E. Baird

> *So there is a race against time to preserve these things because of the human elements that are holding the authenticity of who we are. And language is critical to our identification.*
>
> Rosalyn Browne, St. Helena Island, SC, June 2009
> Meeting of the Gullah Geechee Cultural Heritage Commission

The African-descended population of the lowland coastal area of South Carolina and Georgia in the United States has maintained to the present day a profound sense of the historical and cultural continuity, which animates their consciousness of their distinctive peoplehood. Similarly, the people of African origin in the Caribbean and circum-Caribbean, although separated by vast expanses of sea and ocean, possess a deep awareness of their common African origin and share the same sense of optimistic aspiration, political self-confidence, and transatlantic destiny. This commonality of circumstance is neither accidental nor insignificant.

Genetic and cultural lines of descent can be traced geographically in relation to both of these transatlantic African aggregations transplanted from West Africa to the Americas. The nature of this tri-continental interaction involved the displacement of indigenes of one continent (the West Africans) by indigenes of another continent (the Europeans), an encounter both remarkable and historic. These tricontinental events took the form of the infamous human trafficking in African people taken from their homelands by Europeans, transported against their will across the Atlantic Ocean to the Americas, and forced to work on plantations there as unpaid, captive laborers. The impact of this European enterprise on the African captives, as well as on the almost-eradicated Amerindian people, have left their marks on the people of both the United States Sea Islands, as on the people of the Caribbean and circum-Caribbean area. Obvious effects on religion, music, dance, folksay, folk arts and crafts, savings societies, work patterns, games, etc., are to be seen in the various cultures of these African-originated island societies, north and south. An important result of this African-European cultural contact and interaction is linguistic in nature.

The people of African origin living in the lowland coastal area of South Carolina and Georgia in the southeastern United States and, specifically, of the Sea Islands, which lie adjacent to those regions, speak the language known as Gullah in South Carolina and Geechee in Georgia. (The names Gullah and Geechee are geographical in origin: Gullah from the place-name Angola, located in the southern region of the African Guinea Coast, and Geechee from the place-name Kissi, in present day Liberia in the northern reach of that West African stretch of land.) Interestingly, Gullah (also sometimes referred to as Gullah Geechee) is quite similar to the speech of the African-descended population of Barbados, Jamaica, other formerly British-ruled Caribbean islands, and circum-Caribbean locations such as the Bahamas, Bermuda, and Guyana (formerly British Guiana) on the northern coast of the South American continent. These languages have two notable character-istics in common: (1) their vocabulary is drawn mainly (lexified) from English, with an admixture of words from African languages together with a few words drawn from Portuguese and Spanish, and (2) their syntactical patterns exhibit remarkable non-English structural similarities.

This product of an African-English language contact we have designated elsewhere (Twining and Baird 1991) as Afrish (cf. Span*ish*, Dan*ish*, Pol*ish*). In fact, it is today generally accepted by linguists that this speech formed as the result of the language contact between speakers of West African languages and speakers of English is a linguistic continuum that embraces Gullah as well as the comparatively more English-lexified African American speech variety, which has been described by J. L. Dillard (1972) as Black English reflecting, unintentionally perhaps, the color coding of its speakers— connected with imperialism and exploitation associated with the myth of "race" involved with the subsumption of African stupidity.

During plantation times in the United States, especially in the southern states where the plantations were located, as well as in the Caribbean islands where the plantation system first flourished, the fact that the speech of the captive Africans was not readily intelligible to their English-speaking captors and overlords was attributed to the presumed mental incapacity of the laborers. Scholarly reference to the speech of the Africans' attempts to communicate with their Anglophone overlords tended to be negative, demeaning, and generally dismissive both with regard to the language and also, by extension, to its speakers. The failure of the Africans to speak intelligibly to their captors, in the prevailing Euro-supremacist world view then confidently and unapologetically propagated by the European human traffickers, was buttressed by an intentional discourse of domination. In his work, *Africans and Native Americans: The Language of Race and the Evolution of Red-Black Peoples* (1953), Jack D. Forbes deals extensively and authoritatively with the matter of terminological misuse imposed and derogatory abuse inflicted on Native Americans and African Americans during the human trafficking period and persisting into the present.

A most significant event in the scholarly study of Gullah and its Caribbean congeners was the publication in 1949 of the work *Africanisms in the Gullah Dialect* by the African American linguist Lorenzo Dow Turner. Turner provides, *inter alia*, a number of examples of the derogatory terms of discourse created and utilized to justify the European transatlantic atrocity inflicted on the captive Africans held as unpaid laborers in the Americas, of which the following is typical. Turner introduces Ambrose E. Gonzales as a scholar who " . . . has edited several volumes of Gullah folktales and whose interpretation of the dialect has been generally accepted as authoritative," and follows with this quotation from Gonzales's work, *Black Border: Gullah Stories of the Carolina Coast* (1922):

> Slovenly and careless of speech, these Gullahs seized upon the peasant English used by some of the early settlers and by the white servants of the wealthy colonists, wrapped their clumsy tongues about it as well as they could, and, enriched with certain expressive African words, it issued through their flat noses and thick lips as so workable a form of speech that it was gradually adopted by the other slaves and became in time the accepted Negro speech of the lower districts of South Carolina and Georgia (Gonzales, qtd. In Turner 1949: 8).

It should not be surprising in the face of such demeaning commentary from a presumably respectable scholar that Gullah, far from being regarded as a medium of communication, was scorned and ridiculed by large portions of the United States and European public as an ineffective and grotesque jargon, unintelligible to human beings other than their fellow Africans. The use of language is a faculty which distinguishes humans from animals, and an indication of the human's capacity for rational thinking. James Pope-Hennessy, in his *Sins of the Fathers: A Study of the Atlantic Slave Traders 1441–1807*, makes a relevant comment:

> We have noticed that, on the steaming Gulf of Guinea, the comforting myth of the savagery and low mentality of Africans gained welcome sway over the minds of European slavers, and was spread by word of mouth and published books through Europe. Born of a callous and insolent ignorance, this myth crossed the Atlantic in the shark-ridden wake of the slave ships (1967: 114).

Such characterizations were fully supportive of the Euro-supremacist exploitative world view and moral conduct the sequelae of which are still in practice today. Not all assessments of Gullah, however, were derogatory. As early as 1941, Melville J. Herskovits, a colleague of Turner's, had published his *Myth of the Negro Past*. In this work, Herskovits, documenting the persistence of African cultural survivals in the Americas, cites Turner's research findings regarding African linguistic continuities and calls attention specifically to Gullah in this regard. The occurrence of Afrish, both in the Sea Islands area and in the Caribbean, is due, if not to strictly identical circumstances, to similar historical events. It is to be noted that a number of European-language speakers came through both the United States Sea Islands and the Caribbean areas, including Spanish, French, Portuguese, and Dutch. It is English, however, which remained in such vigor in the United States and the Caribbean as to be combined with the African contributions to create the Gullah Geechee language as well as the Caribbean Afrish. Both of these varieties arose out of the Afro-English language-contact phenomenon.

The circumstances in which the African-European language contact occurred originated in the entrepreneurial activities of European adventurers beginning with those from Portugal who, with the encouragement of their Prince Henry, called the Navigator, became engaged in the exploration and commercial exploitation of the West Coast of Africa early in the fifteenth century. Other Europeans followed, as we have mentioned above, but as Gilbert Schneider has remarked significantly, the British are credited with carrying the bulk of African products during the eighteenth century and were the preeminent agents engaged in the human trafficking of captive Africans being transported to the Americas during that period (1967: 11).

For example, the first European adventurers to arrive at Barbados were Portuguese, who had also visited the island in 1536. By that date, the indigenous Arawak people, who had lived there before the Portuguese visit, had abandoned it. The Portuguese did not claim it for their sovereign nor establish a settlement there. As they approached the shore, they were struck, it seems, by the sight of the tall trees there from which long vine-like growths hung; they named the location the "isle of the bearded (Ptg. *barbados*) trees." In 1627, an English ship arrived at Barbados, bringing several dozen individuals; Peter H. Wood remarks that one man out of every four men in this company was African. English interest in the colony was immediate, states Wood, and within two years over a thousand English individuals had been sent out to Barbados as tenants (1974: 6, 7).

Wood provides some useful information in *Black Majority* relating to the interaction between the Caribbean islands, especially Barbados and Jamaica, on the one hand, and the United States mainland, especially South Carolina, on the other. Of particular reference to the linguistic connection between Afro-Caribbean creole language (particularly Barbadian and Jamaican) and the creole language of United States Sea Islands of coastal South Carolina and Georgia is Wood's chapter entitled "Gullah Speech: the Roots of Black English" (1974: 166–191). Wood's narrative usefully brings together speakers of English and speakers of African languages in a situation which required that the Afrophone laborers, having no mutually pan-African language at their disposal to communicate among themselves, were compelled to try to understand the language of their anglophone overlords. Thus English, no doubt with the assistance of some pantomime to communicate action (and thus verbs) and show-and-tell to indicate designated objects (and thus nouns), could serve as a lexifying procedure and a means of obtaining and expanding vocabulary drawn from a common source—English.

Africans were few at first in the settlement, but small numbers of captive African laborers were purchased from Dutch ships or brought from Spanish colonies to supplement the considerable flow of indentured labor from the British Isles (O'Callaghan 2001: 92–3).

Jamaica, captured from the Spanish in 1655, was formally ceded to the English in 1670. It remained a British colony thereafter, gaining independence from Britain in 1962. Two reports published in 1789 on the order of the Jamaican House of Assembly provide information indicating the numbers and ethnic origins of captive Africans brought into Jamaica between the years 1764–1774 and 1779–1788. Geographically, the Africans are listed as drawn from some six regions along the Guinea coast of West Africa and ethnically from at least eight African population groups. These data provide some insight into the number and places of origin of Africans, albeit in captivity, into social relation and linguistic contact with speakers of English.

In 1953, Uriel Weinreich published his work *Languages in Contact: Findings and Problems*. Weinreich was able to demonstrate that, out of the contact between two or more languages, it was possible for a new language to be created; in fact, by such interaction, new languages could and, by such means, had actually been created. Free of the self-serving, Euro-supremacist notions associated with the forced-labor plantation era, scholars now explain the origins of pidgins and creoles—such as Gullah and its Caribbean congeners—not in terms of intellectual deficiency in the Africans but as a natural outcome of language contact between speakers of African languages and speakers of English.

Much of the foregoing has dealt with the phenomena related to the genesis and development of languages. In this connection, the role of pidginization and creolization as stages in the process of "new language" creation has been touched on more by implication than by explication. The illuminating notion of "languages in contact" introduced by Weinreich provided an explanation for the genesis of new languages which could, and did, occur without the sociopolitical domination of one participating language group over another.

Discussion of the origin and development of Gullah and its Caribbean congeners has been vitiated and distorted in the process of explaining and accounting for the circumstances in which the African-European language contact occurred. In the fifteenth-century transatlantic encounter, what was for the Europeans an activity of enlightened self-interest was for the Africans the perpetration of unprovoked and undeserved atrocity. Obviously, the European human trafficking and forced-labor practices were not approved of by all the citizenry of all the nations participating in that transatlantic enterprise. Eventually, economic, no less than moral, considerations operated, after three centuries, if not completely to end, to at least significantly to attenuate the European exploitation and abuse of African humanity. Scholars such as Philip Curtin, W. E. B. Du Bois, Eric Williams, Sterling Stuckey, and Orlando Patterson have documented these events and their outcomes.

The account of the African-European language contact is fraught with terminology which demeans what European scholars have designated as the creole languages. As a matter of fact, the word *creole* itself is reflective of the notion of European domination and African subjugation. Thus, the authoritative *Romanisches Etymologisches Wörterbuch* by W. Meyer-Lübke traces the Spanish word *criollo* from its origin in the Latin *creare* (Eng. create) by derivation from the Portuguese *crioulo* and French *créole*, with the explicit meaning in German "der im Hause geborene Neger," that is, "the negro born in the (master's) house" (1935: 213, #2305). It might be noted here that in the languages of the European traffickers, the color-referent descriptive word in the Portuguese and Spanish, the adjective *negro,* both derived from the Latin *niger* meaning "black," has been taken into the language of other, non-Latin-derived European languages specifically and exclusively to denote a human individual of African origin. A person so indicated may in fact, on the basis of visual recognition, conform to the accepted physical characteristic of having a very dark complexion; the term is also applied to a person having a complexion more usually indicative of European origin, particularly if the individual under scrutiny is known or believed to have African social or cultural associations. Accordingly, the Latin word *niger* has yielded the German and Dutch *Neger,* the French *nègre,* and the Italian *negro* (a noun designating an African person), displacing the normal *nero* (a descriptive adjective referring to a color).

As we have discussed above, the human-trafficking activity of a number of European nations provided the conditions for language contact between African—especially West African—peoples and European peoples. Gullah (or as we prefer, Sea Islands Afrish) as we have indicated, the most distinctive of the forms of African-English contact languages, is greatly outnumbered by those of the Caribbean region. As in the case of English-speaking human traffickers, entrepreneurs from other European nations participated in the resulting language contact, beginning with the enterprising activities of the Portuguese and the Spanish. In academic circles, it is the practice to refer to such languages as Latin, Greek, Hebrew, Sanskrit, and some other ancient languages as the classical languages and to languages such as French, Spanish, Portuguese, German, Italian, and some other languages, especially European ones presently in use, as modern languages, without offense to any national amour-propre. The gratuitous insult to the sensibilities of a number of sovereign nations will be avoided or assuaged when their comparatively newer languages are referred to not as "creole languages," shameful products of opprobrium and exploitation, but as "postmodern" languages, no better, no worse, than our respected "modern languages." A number of major European languages have contributed considerably to the present lexicons of the "postmodern" languages and are likely to continue to be drawn on in the future. Portuguese, Spanish, Dutch, and English are notable in this regard. Gullah falls into the English-lexified, postmodern category of Afrish, as do Jamaican, Barbadian (more often and affectionately referred to as Bajan—pronounced BAY-jun), and others—about a dozen, mutually intelligible.

It has been my (the author's) experience both in the Sea Islands-Charleston region of the United States and in the Caribbean and circum-Caribbean areas that speakers of Gullah Geechee and speakers of Caribbean Afrish (especially in Barbados, Jamaica, and other links in the United States Sea Islands-Caribbean Afrish linguistic continuum) generally are bilingual. To communicate with persons they do not credit with being likely to understand the Afrish language of the locality—e.g., Gullah, Bajan, nation-language (i.e., Jamaican)—the Afrish speaker speaks the standard English taught in school; with persons they have reason to identify as speakers of the Afrish language, they speak the Afrish. Linguists call this procedure code-switching. Some researchers in the Sea Islands-Charleston area as well as in the Caribbean, returning to the Afrish-speaking community after an absence of a decade or two, have reported that the Africa-connected language has practically disappeared from usage. Thus, in December 1967, Guy B. Johnson, who has written extensively on African American folklife and folklore, presented a paper entitled "The Gullah Dialect Revisited: A Note on Linguistic Acculturation," read before the American Anthropological Association, stated:

I will say this: after forty years I would make only a slight modification of the earlier views that African traits were relatively scarce in the Gullah dialect, and I would still insist that in the long run acculturation process the contribution of African language patterns to American English will be almost nil.

A rebuttal to this assertion of Johnson's appeared in the June 1980 issue of the *Journal of Black Studies*, which pointed out that Johnson ". . . did not sufficiently consider factors other than the lexical in his assessments of Gullah."

[Johnson's] judgements of the nature and present status of the Sea Island speech were circumscribed by his Eurocentric predisposition to see Gullah as a dialect of English rather than as a language in its own right. His approach, not surprisingly, led him to overestimate the importance of the indisputable quantitative fact that Gullah has a preponderantly English-based lexicon, and to minimize important qualitative sociolinguistic factors which were involved in the dramatic confrontation and dynamic interaction and linguistic and cultural interface encounter which took place between African peoples and speakers of the English language. His insistence on "white-to-black" cultural transmission caused him to overstress Euro-American sociopolitical dominance and to disregard African adaptive and creative capability (Baird, 1980: 425–435).

Pidgin and Creole Linguistics in the Twenty-First Century, edited by Glenn Gilbert (2002) provides illuminating examples of the progress made by linguists in more recent times regarding the origin, nature, and even the continuing process of Afrish language formation and development. It needs to be remarked that interest in, even concern about, the present status and continuing existence of the Gullah Geechee and Caribbean Creole Language components are matters of social and political interest in these creole-speaking societies. In the Sea Islands-Charleston community there are groups which actively support the preservation and promotion of the Gullah heritage. For instance, St. Helena Island is the location of Penn Center, which houses the Institute for Gullah Studies, a project devoted to the teaching of teachers and other interested groups the history and culture of the Gullah people.

A particularly significant scholarly event is the republication in 2002 of Lorenzo Dow Turner's magnum opus, *Africanisms in the Gullah Dialect*. This publication is singular in that it not only presents the text of the original work as published by the University of Chicago Press in 1949, but contains a new introduction by Katherine Wyly Mille and Michael B. Montgomery.

Professor Mille is a native of the South Carolina Lowcountry; she now resides in Columbia, South Carolina. She is an independent scholar and a 1996 Fulbright Professor of sociolinguistics and women's studies in Finland. She has done linguistic research on Gullah. Michael B. Montgomery is Distinguished Professor Emeritus of English and Linguistics at the University of South Carolina. He is the editor of *The Crucible of Carolina: Essays in the Development of Gullah Language and Culture*.

Professors Mille and Montgomery have in their introduction to *Africanisms* enhanced the value of this work. They have placed Lorenzo Dow Turner's masterpiece clearly within the context of his time, of his scholarly intent, and of his singular achievement. Readers will find particularly helpful the informative notes and the bibliographical information included in their introduction to the Turner work.

A matter of concern for linguists interested in Sea Islands or Caribbean Afrish is that with the passing of time the number of speakers of the language is considerably diminished, as is the likelihood of hearing it. In the Sea Islands, as educational and other opportunities for better living conditions arise for young people, Sea Islanders tend to use English in public and in communication with strangers, but speak Afrish with elders, children, and in the company of close friends. In the Caribbean, a similar usage is practiced, except that with many of the countries becoming independent, sovereign nations, code-switching between English and Afrish occurs as the occasion may require. In the context of nationalist consciousness, Afrish is regarded as an important part of popular cultural expression and is referred to as "nation-language" and utilized in artistic productions.

Fortunately, the tapes of Gullah made by Turner in the United States and the use of the creole in artistic productions and the intentional reproduction and preservation of speech-mediated social, cultural, and even political events are occasions and activities which contribute to the preservation of Gullah creole language. Continuing academic research has also provided opportunities for the study of these Afrish linguistic artifacts in the context of ethnolinguistic, sociological, and related areas of humanistic inquiry.

Following are some texts in Gullah and in Caribbean, mostly Bajan/Jamaican, which might serve to convey some impression of the Gullah-Caribbean Afrish connection.

Gullah Texts

[This text is one of a number of examples of Gullah speech presented by Turner in *Africanisms in the Gullah Dialect*. The topic is illustrative not only of the Gullah language but also of a preoccupation of African people—religion.]

SIKIN

(By Hanna Jenkins, Waccamaw, South Carolina)

And I gone out in the wilderness, and I beg the Lord to forgive me for me sin. And I have pass through many danger; have pass through many danger before I commence to see good. And all the sin what I have done in this world when I was a dancer, I had that load to pass before I could see goodness. And I beg the Lord to forgive me and have mercy upon me for Christ's sake. And he carry me right through a pounding mill—gone through that pounding mill. And it appear like I weigh on a scale. You see? And when I first come through before day that morning, I come a shouting.

[The text that follows is taken from a translation into Gullah of the New Testament of the Bible done by the Sea Islands translation team in cooperation with Wycliffe Bible Translators. The work, entitled *De Nyew Testament*, was published in 2005 by the American Bible Society. In a preface to this Bible translation into Gullah, the translators have given an indication of their intent and attitude with which they approached their task. We think it is appropriate for all the right reasons, before presenting an excerpt,

Philippians 4:8, of the Gullah version, to cite the first paragraph of the translators' preface as an example of historical sensitivity and conscientious scholarship.]

> Gullah, also known as Geechee or as Sea Island Creole, is a language traditionally spoken along the coastal areas of South Carolina and Georgia. While in the past Gullah was mistakenly characterized as poor English, today it is recognized as a distinct language. It is an English creole, born several hundred years ago out of a contact language situation where Africans were taken from various nations and language groups to grow rice in the marshy Lowcountry area along the Southeastern coast of the American colony (Sea Island Translation Team, 2005).

[The Gullah text corresponds to The King James Version of Philippians 4:8, "Finally, brethren, etc. . . ."]

> Me Christian bredren, las ob all, A da tell ya, mus keep on da study bout jes dem ting wa good mo den all an wa people oughta gii praise fa. Study bout dem ting wa true, dem ting wa honorable, dem ting wa right een God eye, dem ting wa ain neba mek people sin, dem ting wa mek ya wahn fa lob um, and dem ting wa people know fa be good fa true (*DE NYEW TESTAMENT*).

Caribbean Texts

In the summer of 2008, we (Mary A. Twining and I) made a visit to my homeland, Barbados. On a previous visit, I had given one of the local newspapers an interview in which I had spoken about the connection between Bajan and Jamaican in the Caribbean and Gullah in the United States. We had hardly unpacked our luggage in our lodgings before our friend, Mrs. Judy Straughn, a retired secondary school principal and senator, stopped by to bid us welcome home and, no less importantly, to regale us with the account of a Gullah-Caribbean Afrish related incident. Some six or eight lads, aged between twelve and fifteen, sons of the professional couples inhabiting the well-kept homes of a sedate neighborhood, were engaged in an informal game of cricket in a nearby pasture. It was dinnertime and the mothers had singly deployed without success their vocal resources to summon their progeny home for the evening meal. Frustrated at their failure, their number had grown to five, and the mothers were about to consider what more drastic means might be employed when a young Chaka, all of seven years old, appeared. As if with one voice, they said to him, "Go and tell those boys on the pasture that their mother wants them at home at once." The youngster trotted off on the assignment and said something, very brief, and the young cricketers, as one, turned and headed homeward. The youthful messenger returned to the assembled mothers at a somewhat quicker pace than the cricketers. The grateful mothers, lost in wonder, love, and praise, to which might be added intellectual curiosity, asked him "What did you say to those boys?" He responded, "All o' unna mudda call wunna," a locution equally effective as to semantic import and structural configuration whether in the United States, Sea Islands, Jamaica, or Barbados. The final word in the Sea Islands communities might emerge as "yunnah" or "hunnah."

Caribbean, Jamaican, and Barbadian Sayings

Caribbean Afrish has not received as much attention from linguists as has Sea Islands Afrish. The comparative isolation from the mainland has favored the cultivation and preservation of a strong sense of distinctive community self-expression. In the United States, Gullah tales, secular and religious songs, and other forms of Gullah expression have been collected by mainland Euro-American writers and scholars to an extent not existent in the Caribbean area. The following are examples of the proverbs and maxims with which Afrish speakers inhabiting the Caribbean Islands arc from Jamaica to the north and reaching Guyana on the north coast of the South American mainland flavor their discourse up to this day.

Words is win, but blows is unkine.

High win know weh ole house.

God don' like ugly.

Start befo' yuh ready, yuh sure get lef.

Wha' don' kill does fatten.

Ef yuh en got a horse, ride a cow.

De higha monkey clime de mo' e show e behine.

Wha fuh yuh, fuh yuh.

Wha sweet goat mout' bu'n e tail.

While de grass growin' de horse starvin'.

Wen yuh got yuh head in de lion mout,' yuh got to ease it out.

References

Baird, Keith E. "Guy B. Johnson Revisited: Another Look at Gullah." *Journal of Black Studies* (June 1980), 425–435.

Dillard, J. L. *Black English: Its History and Usage in the United States.* New York: Random House, 1972.

Forbes, Jack D. *Africans and Native Americans: The Language of Race and the Evolution of Red-Black Peoples.* Urbana: The University of Illinois Press, 1993.

Gilbert, Glenn. *Pidgin and Creole Linguistics in the Twenty-First Century.* Frankfort: Peter Lang, 2002.

Gonzales, Ambrose. *Black Border: Gullah Stories of the Carolina Coast.* Columbia, SC: State Co., 1922.

Herskovits, Melville. *The Myth of the Negro Past.* New York: Harper and Bros., 1941.

Hymes, Dell, ed. *Pidginization and Creolization of Languages.* Cambridge: Cambridge University Press, 1974.

Johnson, Guy B. "The Gullah Dialect Revisited: Thirty Years Later." Paper delivered at the American Anthropological Association. Washington, DC, 1967.

Montgomery, Michael, ed. *The Crucible of Carolina: Essays in the Development of Gullah Language and Culture.* Athens: University of Georgia Press, 1994.

Meyer-Lübke, Wilhelm. *Romanisches Etymologisches Wörterbuch.* Heidelberg: Carl Winters Universitätsbuchhandlung, 1935.

O'Callaghan, Sean. *To Hell or Barbados.* Dingle, Ireland: Mount Eagle Publications, 2001.

Pope-Hennessy, James. *Sins of the Fathers: A Study of the Atlantic Slave Traders 1441–1807*. London: Weidenfeld and Nicolson, 1967.

Schneider, Gilbert D. *West African Pidgin-English*. Athens: Center for International Studies, Ohio University Press, 1967.

Turner, Lorenzo Dow. *Africanisms in the Gullah Dialect*. Eds. K. Wyly Mille and Michael Montgomery. Columbia, SC: University of South Carolina Press, 2002.

Twining, Mary A. and Keith E. Baird, eds. *Sea Island Roots: African Presence in the Carolinas and Georgia*. Trenton, NJ: Africa World Press, 1991.

Weinreich, Uriel. *Languages in Contact: Findings and Problems*. New York: The Linguistic Circle of New York, 1953.

Wood, Peter H. *Black Majority*. New York: Knopf, 1974.

Left to Right: Vanessa Jones, Bessie Jones, and Mary Twining.

"Bringing in the Sheaves"

Collectors of African American
and Sea Islands Folklore

E arly writers and collectors gave an erroneous impression of the state of mind and emotions of the captive Africans as they sang. William Smith opines, ". . . Virginia slaves were the happiest of the human race."[1]

It was this kind of statement that Frederick Douglass calls attention to in his autobiographical narrative of 1845 as he commented on the presence of song in the Maryland plantations he had known in his youth:

> I have sometimes thought that the mere hearing of those songs would do more to impress some minds with the horrible character of slavery, than the reading of whole volumes of philosophy on the subject could do.[2]

He appears to have rejected any interpretation of the songs other than as emblematic of despair and admonished:

> I have often been utterly astonished, since I came to the north, to find persons who could speak of the singing, among slaves, as evidence of their contentment and happiness. It is impossible to conceive of a greater mistake.[3]

Fanny Kemble, an English actress married to Southern planter Pierce Butler, recalled in her reminiscences of 1865 the experience of attending a slave's funeral during her residence on her husband's plantation in the Georgia Sea Islands region in 1838:

> Presently the whole congregation uplifted their voices in a hymn, the first high wailing notes of which—sung all in unison . . . sent a thrill through all my nerves . . . I cannot tell you how profoundly the whole ceremony . . . affected me . . . I began to cry very bitterly . . .[4]

These observations from "within" and outside of the music of antebellum African American folk-rural culture, admittedly from different regions, point up both the complexity and the "problematique" that lie in wait for the student of that culture.

Though there are other early allusions to music—such as the unsigned article which proclaims, ". . . the African nature is full of poetry and song"[5]— and other folklore of antebellum African Americans in the plantation South, widespread collecting of the folklore had begun with the Civil War.

Port Royal

Northern missionary societies in New York, Pennsylvania, and Massachusetts dispatched teachers in 1862, after emancipation was declared, to the Port Royal region of South Carolina, where former slaves were settled by the federal government to whose lines they had escaped. *The Journal of Charlotte Forten* reflects the Port Royal experience from the perspective of an African American.

> Coming over in the boat, the men sang one of the most beautiful hymns I have ever heard.

> "Praise believer, praise God, I praise my God until I die Jordan stream is a good old stream and I aint but one more river cross I want some valiant soldier to help me bear the cross."[6]

James McKim, an organizer of the Port Royal movement, came with his daughter, Lucy McKim Garrison, an accomplished musician herself, who found the musical subtleties of the spirituals and other songs especially intriguing. Along with the Reverend W. F. Allen and his cousin Charles Ware, Lucy Garrison collected and published a book of spirituals, shouts, and work songs of the Sea Islands, *Slave Songs of the United States* (1867), which was the first of its kind, to reveal the range of the hidden heritage these songs communicated.

The songs include Sea Islands interpretations of Biblical texts; Jacob and the Angel is a popular theme as seen in "Wrestle On, Jacob" and another example from Biblical text is "I Saw the Beam In My Sister's Eye." Some of the songs we know now—such as "Rock O' My Soul," "There's a Meetin' Here Tonight," and "Roll Jordan Roll." Work songs such as "Round the Corn Sally," "Shock Along John," "Michael Row," and "Poor Rosy" are also recorded, but are far outnumbered by the religious element. Songs of play, dance, and a lighter character—such as "I'm Gwine to Alabamy" and "Charleston Gals"—are few in the collection. Shout songs like "O Shout Away" and "Shout On Children" have survived until today.[7]

Thomas Wentworth Higginson, writing during and after the Civil War, recounted the feelings of revelation he experienced. He sent accounts back to New England of his sojourn in the Union Army as a colonel at the head of the First South Carolina Volunteers regiment of African American soldiers, many of whom were Sea Islands natives of the Port Royal region. These writings, first published in *The Atlantic Monthly*, later appeared in his *Army Life in a Black Regiment* (1869).[8] The chapter entitled "Negro Spirituals" served to popularize the songs in a setting which helped people come to know the singers as well as the songs. He recorded work songs, such as "The Coming Day," which helped the boat rowers establish the rhythm, and communitarian songs, like "Bound to Go," in which members of the group were named in each succeeding verse. "My Army Cross Over" was used as a marching song. Higginson felt wonder at the sheer poetry of "I Know Moon-rise." He transcribed an account of how "The Driver" came into being as the enslaved Africans vented their disgust and anger at one of their own treating them in such a harsh manner.

Colonel Higginson was an avid abolitionist and well known to Charlotte Forten, who had James McKim as an advocate for her plan, in 1862, to go to South Carolina to teach the so-called "contrabands of war" at the school Laura Towne had set up on St. Helena Island. She was able to go, and in her journal, she recounts some of her adventures. Her first purpose was to help educate the newly freed young people of St. Helena Island at the school, which later became Penn Center. Along the way, however, she recorded some of the songs she heard and the impressions she gathered. She characterizes the shout songs as ". . . very wild and strange," testifying to their Africanity, though she did not express it in those terms.[9] She noted some of the same songs as Higginson and Allen, Ware, and Garrison so, in spite of herself, she was a minor collector.

Hampton

Hampton Institute published *The Southern Workman*, a periodical, which made significant contributions to folklore study. In 1893, Miss A. M. Bacon, a teacher at Hampton, declared in *The Southern Workman*:

> If within the next few years care is not taken to collect and preserve all traditions and customs peculiar to the Negroes, there will be little to reward the search of the future historian who would trace the history of his people from the African continent, through the years of slavery, to the position which they will hold a few generations hence.[10]

She proposed the establishment of the Hampton Folklore Society to accomplish the tasks enumerated. Notice was taken in the "Notes and Queries" section of the *Journal of American Folklore*. In order to foster the project, Bacon presented the idea of a "Folklore and Ethnology" section in *The Southern Workman*, which became a focal point for many short contributions that were coming in on a regular basis.[11] In succeeding notes, queries, articles, and contributions, A. M. Bacon, Susan Showers, Portia Smiley, and others published various collected pieces consisting of "old sayings" such as "A good run is better than a bad stand" and stories like "The Fool Hunter" and "Jack and the King" in which Jack, the hero/trickster, outwits the "king." Religious songs, such as "Don't Leave Me Behind Lord," and prayers were reported from services and camp meetings. Lighter genres like children's games, such as "Peep Squirrel" (1900: 56), later published by Bessie Jones in *Step It Down* in 1972, and riddles were taken in with the weightier forms in the new "Folklore and Ethnology" section of *The Southern Workman*.[12]

Joel Chandler Harris

In 1880, Joel Chandler Harris published the first of his many Uncle Remus books, and the fame of their most frequent protagonist, Brer Rabbit, began to spread.

Harris, a writer for the *Atlanta Constitution*, was one of the instruments in the post-Reconstruction project of creating an attractive picture of the New South advocated by Henry Grady, the editor of the *Atlanta Constitution*. Harris invented the kindly old Uncle Remus, set in a romanticized image of the plantation South, to frame the animal stories he knew from his boyhood in Middle Georgia. The animal stories and the idealized setting charmed his Euro-American audience; the tales were also translated into many languages and delighted readers around the world.[13]

In addition to the Uncle Remus stories, Harris introduced at least two characters from the Sea Islands area, Aaron (*Aaron, Son of Ben Ali* and *Aaron in the Wildwood*) and Daddy Jake. Aaron is considered to have special powers, which might be attributed to his unusual looks and his knowledge of animals and Arabic. He purports to be the son of Bilali, or Bu Allah, a historical resident of Sapelo Island, Georgia. Bilali was the foreman on the Spalding Plantation, where he was much trusted and well known for possessing a small, brown leather book. The book is described in *Aaron, Son of Ben Ali* as he shows the children the Bilali manuscript. (There is more on the Bilali story in the chapter "Hold Your Light" in this volume.) Since the book was written in Arabic, few understood it, and different interpretations ensued as to what the book actually contained. *Aaron in the Wildwood* includes scenes depicting the captive workers' withdrawal into the thick swamp area.

Harris considered himself a writer first and folklorist, if at all, next. In "An Accidental Author," he tells how he backed into a career as a teller of African American tales.[14]

Harris realized in 1895, when he read Heli Chatelain's collection from Southwest Africa, *Folk Tales of Angola* (1894), that the tales he had heard in Middle Georgia—such as the trickster tales where one animal deceives another—contained the same elements as the stories Chatelain had recorded in Africa.[15] The animals in the African stories were somewhat different in kind and name, but they enacted the same rituals. Alan Dundes formulated the structure of such folktales. They begin with friendship, making a pact (to do some cooperative work), deception, breaking the pact and hence the friendship bond, and outright chicanery that Brer Rabbit, Bear, Fox, et al., visit upon one another.[16] The famous Tar Baby is echoed in Chatelain's "Leopard, Monkey and Hare" in which no less than two tar babies (girls) are adorned to lure monkey and hare.[17]

The American Folklore Society

With the creation of the American Folklore Society in 1888, on the model of the Folk Lore Society in England, folklore collecting, including African American folklore, entered a "scientific age." It is notable that Joel Chandler Harris was one of the founding members along with other distinguished figures—such as Henry Wadsworth Longfellow; Mark Twain (Samuel Clemens); Charles Colcock Jones of Sapelo Island, Georgia; William F. Allen, collector of Sea Islands folksongs; Thomas Higginson, colonel of a regiment made up of Sea Islands men; Abigail Christensen, collector of Sea Islands tales; Oliver Wendell Holmes; Francis Parkman; Franz Boas; James Mooney; Andrew Lang; and others. The society established a journal called the *Journal of American Folklore*, which committed itself to publishing the work of collectors among its other articles.

Among the charter members of the American Folklore Society were collectors, such as Charles Colcock Jones, who issued books on the lore of African American Sea Islanders. He indicated that the language and tales of his home in the coastal Sea Islands region of Georgia were different from those of Uncle Remus's location. Jones's collection, *Negro Myths from the Georgia Coast* (1888), is extensive. There are many stories involving animals and humans—i.e., "De Fiddler, Buh Tiger an' Buh Bear" (130). A captive fiddler plays his irresistible fiddle, Tiger and Bear dance until they fall exhausted, and the fiddler makes good his escape. "De Ole King and de Noung King" (131–2) is a very interesting story in light of the political situation in the South after the Civil War. In addition to the stories, Jones also includes sketches on plantation dentistry (137–143), spirits, and Daddy Jupiter's vision (158–166); these writings give us a certain picture of plantation life on the Sea Islands in the latter part of the nineteenth century.[18] Other collections followed—such as the 1894 Sea Islands collection of Abigail Christensen.

Abigail Christensen attempted to fulfill some of the stated aims of the Society in collecting and publishing the stories of African American Sea Islanders in order to preserve them. She notes the African provenience for the stories and the influence of matrifocality in African and Sea Islands culture. The narrator, Prince Baskin, likens himself to Brer Rabbit as the little man trying to survive. (Prince) Baskin in Christensen's book and (Daddy)

Jupiter in Jones's book are presented as actual persons in contrast to the fictional Uncle Remus and Daddy Jake.[19]

Representative of a new generation of anthropologically trained folklorists who came to the fore in the twentieth century was Elsie Clews Parsons, a New Yorker of independent means who studied varied folkloric cultures, including those of the African World. Stories have circulated about the colorful Ms. Parsons, her big hats, cigars, and unconventional dress. Beneath the surface of apparent eccentricities and open rebellion against the mores of her day, she was an intellectual who went about collecting folklore in an orderly, scientific fashion. It is in her collections we begin to see a range of African American folklore, which was not apparent in the selective vision of Harris and others. She travelled among Native Americans and African peoples in the United States and the Caribbean. From 1917, during the First World War, to the 1930s, Parsons investigated and published folklore and anthropological materials. She strove to bring a scientific disciplinary approach to the materials she collected in the field. She numbered her stories and thought out classificatory schemes for her collectanea. She also helped to finance the research of other scholars, and contributed funds to the American Anthropological Association and the American Folklore Society, bodies of which she was president at one time or another.

Parson's chief venues for publication were the organs of the American Folklore Society: The Journal and the Memoirs.[20]

The Harlem Renaissance

Numbered among anthropologically trained folklorists is Arthur Huff Fauset, a beneficiary of Elsie Clews Parsons's guidance and support in his fieldwork. He was also a protégé of the Harlem Renaissance mentor Alain Locke, who had a great interest in folklore. In the 1920s, Fauset collected in Philadelphia and later in Alabama, Mississippi, Louisiana, and Nova Scotia. He was a part of the cultural explosion of the Harlem Renaissance, and his article, "American Negro Folk Literature," appeared in Alain Locke's *The New Negro* (1925). He contributed to the *Journal of American Folklore* and published *Folklore from Nova Scotia* (1931) under the aegis of the American Folklore Society. He is also known for an anthropological study, *Black Gods of the Metropolis* (1944).[21]

Among the artists of the Harlem Renaissance, Zora Neale Hurston forged a special identity for herself as a folklorist. She studied anthropology at Barnard College under the tutelage of Franz Boas, listened to the tenets of the folk-oriented ideology of Alain Locke, and accepted the financial support of Charlotte Osgood Mason, a connoisseur of "primitivism." Hurston, at the end of the 1920s, did research in the South, originally in her childhood home, Eatonville, in Central Florida, and later in other environments, such as New Orleans. The product of this activity emerges both in her folk-conscious fiction and her folklore collection *Mules and Men* (1935). In the introduction to *Mules and Men*, she tells her readers something of her views:

> Folklore is not as easy to collect as it sounds. The best source is where there are the least outside influences and these people, being usually underprivileged, are the shyest. They are most reluctant at times to reveal that which the soul lives by. And the Negro, in spite of his open-faced laughter, his seeming acquiescence, is particularly evasive. You see we are a polite people and we do not say to our questioner, "Get out of here!" We smile and tell him or her something that satisfies the white person because, knowing so little about us, he doesn't know what he is missing.[22]

Hurston returned to her roots on such field-collecting trips. Her fiction and her fieldwork share the same sources, the African American people themselves. She based her fiction on her folkloric collections, which were coupled with her personal knowledge. Her folkloric fiction reads like art writing, and simultaneously, her novels read like realistic pictures of rural life. Her sympathy and affection for her subject were patent, although she did not hesitate to show people as they were.[23]

In 1915, in "Some Types of American Folksongs" (*Journal of American Folklore*, 28: 1–17), John Lomax began to lay foundations for the consideration of folklore in many settings. Through his collections, he expanded the definition of the folk to include such populations as prisoners. With his son, Alan Lomax, he published *American Ballads and Folksongs* (1934). Alan Lomax published prolifically in liner notes and booklets accompanying recordings—such as "Yazoo Delta Blues and Spirituals," "Negro Sinful Songs as Sung by Leadbelly," "Negro Prison Songs from the Mississippi State Penitentiary," and "Georgia Sea Islands Volumes I and II." His books include

The Rainbow Sign (1959), *The Folksongs of North America in the English Language* (1960), and his comparative work, *Folksong Style and Culture* (1968).

He was one of the first to recognize the usefulness of a movie camera in recording folklore as it occurred in work situations and the accompanying paralinguistic gestures of singers and taletellers. He honored individual artists, such as Vera Hall and Huddie Ledbetter, by encouraging careers and performance. He was instrumental in launching the Sea Island Singers onto the concert circuit. They were already singing locally on the Sea Islands. He went beyond mere collecting and anthologizing by looking at overall patterns in different societies and beginning to formulate theoretical conclusions, which could be drawn from a broad comparative approach.[24]

John Lomax's daughter, Bess Lomax Hawes, also participated in folklore collecting and is best known for her collecting work on African American Sea Islands games with Bessie Jones, *Step It Down* (1972).[25]

Chapel Hill

At the University of North Carolina in the late 1920s and '30s, there was a group of scholars who looked at the sociological implications of African American life and experience as depicted in folk culture.

As early as 1909, Howard Odum, then at Clark University in Massachusetts, collected material and assembled a manuscript of African American songs. When he came to North Carolina, he and Guy Johnson drew on that manuscript and on some of Thomas Talley's 1922 collection as a nucleus for their collaborative works, *Negro Workaday Songs* (1926) and *The Negro and His Songs* (1927). In the 1926 work, the editors reassure the reader that the books contain only field-collected material and ". . . do not represent reports from memory of white individuals . . . much of their value lies in the exact transcription of natural lines, words, and mixtures."[26] They pinpoint in this passage the difference between some of the assemblages from other already-printed sources and truer representations of the folk through actual field collections. They do also indicate that they are looking at the whole context of the songs and what they represent through the eyes of sociologists, not simply those of musicians or folklorists.

Thomas Talley was an African American collector who worked while keeping his day job as a chemistry professor at Fisk University. He wrote frame stories like Joel Chandler Harris with human beings as the tellers of tales and embedded the folktales themselves within that framework. His early collection was *Negro Folk Rhymes: Wise and Otherwise* in 1922, but his subsequent work lay in the attic for fifty years before being discovered and brought to light.[27]

In the same stream of publications from Chapel Hill, North Carolina, were the works of Claude Kiser and T. J. Woofter, which addressed the northward migration of the Islanders and the work world of the people of St. Helena Island. In Newbell Niles Puckett's work, *Folk Beliefs of the Southern Negro* (1926), he researched and collected amid practitioners of magical and healing arts.[28]

1930s and 1940s

During the Depression years, some churches and community institutions among African Americans turned to folklore to help sustain them. They collected their own material—such as old oral folk dramas, *The Devil Play* (Johns Island, South Carolina) or *Heaven Bound* (Atlanta, Georgia)—for purposeful community performance of folk drama in order to raise money. These plays and others like them are still performed.[29]

In the 1930s, Lorenzo Dow Turner, an African American linguist, collected field recordings of residents of various Sea Islands communities. The recordings, his subsequent publication *Africanisms in the Gullah Dialect* (1949), and numerous articles are invaluable resources for the linguist and the folklorist and are still being studied intensively.[30] A Mende song of Amelia Dawley (A256) has been traced to its origins in Sierra Leone, and the story of her descendants' return to Africa is told in the video "The Language You Cry In."[31] Certain songs demonstrate the creolization of African language and English sources of Gullah, for instance, A Mende-Gullah song (C256) and A Vai-Gullah song (E257). A Vai-Gullah song (D, 257) contains a line, ". . . eat some and leave some," which occurs in one of the games in Bessie Jones's book, "Josephine":

> Aunt Jenny's cornbread is sweet, sweet, sweet
>
> Take some and leave some, sweet, sweet, sweet.[32]

In the 1940s, results of the WPA team local history projects of the federal government were published, such as Georgia's *Drums and Shadows* (1940). Although the African provenience of African American tales had been discussed previously, *Drums and Shadows* collected personal life histories, which offered incontrovertible evidence of African influence. Alec Anderson of Possum Point speaks of the use of drums for messaging to other communities and performing the "Buzzard Lope."[33] Rachel Anderson remembered her mother praying at sunrise.[34] Stories, beliefs, genealogies, and artwork in *Drums and Shadows* all contributed to a portrait of the vanishing ways of a communitarian, African-influenced society.

Lydia Parrish, in *Slave Songs of the Georgia Sea Islands* (1942), collected material that reflected African influences on St. Simons and other Georgia islands. She recorded songs, spirituals, shout songs, children's games, and plays.[35]

The 1950s and Beyond

Richard Dorson, Director of the Folklore Institute at Indiana University, was a collector who worked using the Aarne-Thompson classificatory system of tale typing and motifing. Dorson utilized these systems to show what he perceived to be widely diffused elements in his *American Negro Folktales* (1968). He presented the tale-tellers giving biographic and stylistic data about them and their narrative art. Parsons, Fauset, and other earlier collectors had listed their informants but gave few details.[36]

After the 1950s and Beyond

Guy and Candie Carawan lived on Johns Island, South Carolina, and collected life stories and folklore, which have been published in *Ain't You Got a Right to the Tree of Life?*, a title taken from an island song. Song games of Johns Island children and statements by Islanders of all ages with accompanying photos give a picture of life as it was then in the 1960s.[37]

Johns Island also drew Patricia Jones-Jackson, a linguist, to do research on the Islands in the late 1960s and early 1970s and to write her book, *When Roots Die,* following the model of Lorenzo Dow Turner. She looked at her work as belonging to a chain of scholars beginning with Herskovits.

My study fills important gaps in history, confirms and expands the thesis proposed by Melville Herskovits over half a century ago of the rich African heritage of American blacks, illustrates the way it is expressed, delineates when and how African traits came to the coasts of Carolina and Georgia, and explains how they evolved.[38]

Bessie Jones of St. Simons Island, Georgia, and Bess Lomax Hawes collaborated on *Step It Down*, a compendium of island games and "plays" complete with music, words, philosophy, and instructions.[39] Ms. Jones was a member of the Georgia Sea Island Singers, who were encouraged to go on the road by Alan Lomax. They appeared at folk festivals, which had grown out of the Folk Song Revival Movement. Later, they convinced the Moving Star Hall Singers, of Johns Island, South Carolina, to go on the circuit as they had, and that people would be interested in their songs and lives. Thus, their music became known to many audiences.

Working toward the ideal of a person in the culture telling their own life and art as we see with Bessie Jones, Cornelia Bailey gives us the story of her early life with memorates, tales, and the state of the island. *God, Mr. Buzzard, and the Bolito Man* tells of life on Hog Hammock and Sapelo Island as the threat of state or corporate take-over looms. Suddenly, the land to which they had been marginalized had become valuable to the outside world. It is no longer a marginal area to which Americans can consign Africans to keep them out of the mainstream. To the contrary, it is coveted shore property, which oil-rich Arabs and newly prosperous mainlanders want to invest in or buy. Ms. Bailey and Ms. Jones show the traditional culture in context from the inside. It is that culture that is in danger of being obliterated by outsiders who understand nothing of its values.[40]

What began in the 1800s as an amateur preservationist pastime has expanded through an awakening consciousness of the lore of African Americans both inside and beyond the community. From testimony of Douglass and Kemble to Allen, Ware, and Garrison's recognition of the integrity of the songs of Sea Islanders, to Harris, Jones, and Christensen's "discovery" and sharing of tales, to Bessie Jones and Cornelia Bailey, this interest has been sustained. Parsons, Fauset, and Hurston recorded the folk culture from different perspectives and in varied styles, but each provided valuable documentation for the continuing life of Sea Islanders.

In a look at the overall picture, it appears that the emphasis in the works of these early collectors, confined as they were to the printed page, minimized the lively performance aspect, which is so much a part of the tradition. As the concept of documentation has enlarged from writing (Jones and Christensen) to sound recording (Turner, Carawan, and Twining) to film (Lomax and Opala), fieldworkers have been able to augment their documentary techniques to exhibit the complexity of folkloric events.

The collecting of aspects of folklore and folklife was the adventure of a lifetime for me among the gracious and welcoming people of Johns Island, South Carolina, and St. Simons Island, Georgia. They taught me so much of their culture and lore as well as life lessons. I did what I could to lighten their burdens, but the clothing I distributed, the pudding I made for Ms. Belle Simmons, the silver pieces I gave for communion to Wesley Methodist Church, were offerings far too small to ever match the friendship, spiritual gifts, and knowledge they gave me. I was walking in the line of collectors who had preceded me, and hoping not to fail in carrying forward an honorable tradition. I had to realize, as I voraciously read everything I could lay my hands on at the Charleston County Library, that well-intentioned people had been coming there for a hundred years. I wanted not to indulge in attitudes and mistakes they might have made, but by the same token, I wanted to understand what I could from their work and benefit from their insights. I hoped not to sacrifice my life as Colonel Shaw had done for the men that he led, but to live among the Islanders and know their life and culture as Charlotte Forten had done on Lady's Island as she strove to teach children and adults alike. I aspired to learn everything they were willing to teach me in my quest to collect the traditional songs and stories.

The collection of traditional lore has changed with the development of technology. The pioneering collectors worked with what they had, and they were foundational to our newer technological methods, which will take us into the future of understanding human expressive culture.

---

[1] William Smith, "The Persimmon Tree and the Beer Dance," in *The Negro and His Folklore in Nineteenth Century Periodicals*, ed. Bruce Jackson (Austin: University of Texas Press, 1967).

[2] Frederick Douglass, *Narrative of the Life of Frederick Douglass* (1845; repr., Boston: Bedford Books of St. Martin's Press, 1993), 47.

3 Ibid.

4 Fanny Kemble, *Journal of a Residence on a Georgian Plantation* (New York: Harper and Bros., 1864), 147.

5 *Music Quarterly*, 52.

6 Charlotte Forten, *The Journal of Charlotte Forten*, ed. Ray Allen Billington (1854; New York: Collier, 1953), 463.

7 William Francis Allen, Charles Pickard Ware, and Lucy McKim Garrison, *Slave Songs of the United States* (1867; repr., Freeport, NY: Books for Libraries Press, 1971).

8 *The Atlantic Monthly* 19, no. 116 (June 1867), 685–694; Thomas Wentworth Higginson, *Army Life in a Black Regiment* (Boston: Beacon Press, 1869).

9 Charlotte Forten, *The Journal of Charlotte Forten*, ed. Ray Allen Billington (1854; New York: Collier Books, 1953).

10 A. M. Bacon, "Proposal for Folk-Lore Research at Hampton, Virginia," *Journal of American Folklore* 6 (1893), 305–9.

11 Ibid., 305.

12 Bessie Jones and Bess Lomax Hawes, *Step It Down* (New York: Harper and Row, 1972).

13 Joel Chandler Harris, *Uncle Remus: His Songs and His Sayings* (New York: D. Appleton and Co., 1880).

14 Joel Chandler Harris, "An Accidental Author," *Lippincott Magazine* (April 1886), 417–420.

15 Heli Chatelain, *Folk Tales of Angola*, Memoirs of the American Folklore Society, Vol. 1 (New York: Houghton, Mifflin, and Co., 1894).

16 Alan Dundes, "The Making and Breaking of Friendship as a Structural Frame in African Folktales," in *Structural Analysis of Oral Tradition*, eds. Pierre Maranda and Elli Kongas-Maranda, eds. (Philadelphia: University of Pennsylvania Press, 1971).

17 Heli Chatelain, *Folk Tales of Angola*, Memoirs of the American Folklore Society, Vol. 1 (New York: Houghton, Mifflin, and Co., 1894).

18 Charles Colcock Jones, *Negro Myths from the Georgia Coast* (Boston: Houghton, Mifflin, and Co., 1888).

19 Abigail M. H. Christensen, *Afro-American Folklore Told round Cabin Fires on the Sea Islands of South Carolina* (Boston: J. G. Cupples Co., 1892).

20 Elsie Clews Parsons, *Folklore of the Sea Islands, South Carolina*, Memoirs of the American Folklore Society, vol. 16 (Cambridge, MA: The American Folklore Society, 1923).

21 Arthur Huff Fauset, "Folk Lore from St. Helena Island, South Carolina," *Journal of American Folklore* 38 (1925): 217–238.

22 Zora Neale Hurston, *Mules and Men* (Philadelphia: Lippincott, 1935), 18.

23 Ibid., "Introduction."

[24] Alan Lomax, *Georgia Sea Islands*, vols I and II (Folkways Records ca. 1950s), 33 $^1/_3$ rpm.

[25] Bessie Jones and Bess Lomax Hawes, *Step It Down* (New York: Harper and Row, 1972); See a fuller discussion of the games in "Cut a Step: Movement and Dance on the Sea Islands" in this volume.

[26] Howard W. Odum and Guy B. Johnson, *Negro Workaday Songs* (Chapel Hill: University of North Carolina Press, 1926), x–xi.

[27] Thomas Talley, *Negro Folk Rhymes,* ed. Charles K. Wolfe (Knoxville: University of Tennessee Press, 1991).

[28] Claude V. Kiser, *Sea Island to City* (New York: Columbia University Press, 1932); T. J. Woofter, *Black Yeomanry* (New York: H. Holt and Co., 1930); Newbell Niles Puckett, *Folk Beliefs of the Southern Negro* (Chapel Hill: University of North Carolina Press, 1926); Guy B. Johnson, *Folk Culture on St. Helena Island, South Carolina* (Chapel Hill: University of North Carolina Press, 1930).

[29] See "The Devil Made Me Do It: African American Folk Drama" in this volume.

[30] Lorenzo Dow Turner, *Africanisms in the Gullah Dialect* (Chicago: University of Chicago, 1949).

[31] Angel Serano and Alvaro Toepke, "The Language You Cry In" (Inko Producciones, 1998), Film.

[32] Bessie Jones and Bess Lomax Hawes, *Step It Down* (New York: Harper and Row, 1972), 59.

[33] *Drums and Shadows: Survival Studies among the Georgia Coastal Negroes* (Spartanburg, SC: Reprint Co., 1974), 140–141.

[34] Ibid., 27.

[35] Lydia Parrish, *Slave Songs of the Georgia Sea Islands* (New York: Lippincott, 1942).

[36] Richard M. Dorson, *American Negro Folktales* (Greenwich, CT: Fawcett, 1971).

[37] Guy and Candie Carawan, *Ain't You Got a Right to the Tree of Life?* (New York: Simon and Schuster, 1967).

[38] Patricia Jones-Jackson, *When Roots Die: Endangered Traditions on the Sea Islands* (Athens: University of Georgia Press, 1987), xix.

[39] See note 18.

[40] Cornelia Bailey, *God, Dr. Buzzard and the Bolito Man: A Saltwater Geechee Talks About Life on Sapelo Island, Georgia* (New York: Doubleday, 2000).

PART I

Talkin' Up a Giffie:
Continuity in Traditional Oral Lore

Residence of Laura Towne and Ellen Murray, who were among the teachers who came to the Sea Islands even before the Civil War had ended.

Talkin' Up a Giffie

Introduction to Continuity
in Traditional Oral Lore

> *Read um John an' ya read um*
>
> *Read um John an' ya read um*
>
> *Nobody read um like old John*
>
> *Read um an' let um go.*[1]

Listening to the McIntosh County Shouters sing the old shouts in bright sunshine and reconstructed surroundings at the National Black Arts Festival in 1994, I am transported back in time by memory to a dimly lit room on St. Simons Island, Georgia, with the old Georgia Sea Island Singers: Bessie Jones, John, Peter, and Ana Pearl Davis, and Henry Lucas. It is the charged atmosphere of the 1960s, and the singers are reaffirming their African past and preserving it for future generations. As some of the other singers died, Bessie Jones knew that the culture had to be kept alive. She worked with younger people in her family, her daughters Vanessa and Stella, and Frankie Quimby to pass on the stories of Ibo Landing, the songs that accompanied the "shout" (a religious dance from Africa), the Buzzard Lope, and the children's games.[2] It was through her devoted efforts and sense of heritage, as well as those of Janie Hunter of Johns Island, South Carolina,[3] and others that the present generation of singers, dancers, and storytellers have emerged.

The performing of songs, movement, and dance is so interwoven with every aspect of life that its pulse runs through such occasions as church services, informal get-togethers at home, a crab crack, hops at the club, or Saturday night at the juke joint. It spans the religious, spiritual, and secular spheres linking these social activities in a dynamic continuity of aesthetic expression.

There are songs such as "The Grey Goose," which celebrates the durability of African people; games like "I Come to See Miss Julianne John," where manners are taught; the lively, inspiring shouts such as "Walk Believer, Walk Daniel," where models of courage and endurance are provided; and the spirituals like "Ain't You Got a Right to the Tree of Life?" On Johns Island, South Carolina, a great natural wonder known as "Angel Oak" might be symbolic of the steadfast nature of the Africans who were brought here when the tree was just an acorn. Its huge, spreading limbs recall the large trees in Africa under which their forebears and contemporaries sat in council meetings.

The Sea Islands region of South Carolina is part of a coastal area which extends for almost four hundred miles, from the southern border of North Carolina to the northern border of Florida. Separated from the mainland and from each other by a number of streams, riverine waterways, and brackish marshes, some of the Islands are located far enough out into the ocean as to require boats to reach them, while others are, since the 1930s, only accessible by land vehicles by means of bridges and causeways. Because of this geographic isolation and the social circumstances attendant on their arrival in the early 1700s, the Africans have kept hold of so many elements of their ancestral heritage of language and culture. The Sea Islanders of South Carolina and the adjacent mainland area and their culture are known as Gullah, a term thought to refer either to the country Angola or to the Gola, an ethnic group in Liberia in West Africa.

It is not, however, only from these two localities in Africa that the Gullah people originate. Evidences drawn from their quite distinctive language and culture indicate that among the ancestors of present-day Sea Islanders were speakers from over twenty different linguistic communities involving an expanse of territory that embraces some eighteen presently independent nations of West and Central Africa. Sea Islanders in one way or another exhibit their consciousness of and pride in their African origins and cultural heritage. For instance, Frankie Sullivan Quimby, a member of the present-day Georgia Sea Island Singers, traces her family roots back to the Fula people of the Kingdom of Masina, which flourished in what is today the West African Republic of Mali. In the films *Family Across the Sea* and *The Language You Cry In*, one can see the language, cultural, and historical linkages demonstrated as Sea Islanders visit Sierra Leone.[4] The McIntosh County Shouters perform "shouts" and songs in the manner in which they were performed by Africans who arrived by ship in Virginia in 1722 en route to the rice and cotton plantations on the Sea Islands of Georgia and South Carolina.[5] The term "shout" in the Sea Islands context does not signify, as it would in English, a loud vocal utterance, but is an Afro-Arabic expression meaning "dance." The songs to which the shout is danced are in the Gullah and English Languages, in keeping with the authenticity which the contemporary performers seek to maintain.

Gullah, or as some linguists call it, Sea Islands Creole, is the Sea Islands form of a blending of English with words and grammatical features of the West African Languages spoken by the captive African people brought across the Atlantic for forced labor on plantations in the English-speaking Americas. The same process, usual to intensive contact between speakers of two or more different languages gave rise to the Afro-French language spoken in Haiti (Kréol) and the Afro-Portuguese language, Papiamentu, of Aruba, Bonaire, and Curaçao in the Netherlands West Indies. Visitors to the Sea Islands from Jamaica and Barbados in the Caribbean have little or no difficulty in understanding Gullah, because Jamaican and Barbadian (or Bajan) also originated in the same African-English language contact first in West Africa and, more intensively, in the English-speaking colonies located in the Caribbean and on the American mainland.

It is neither necessary nor appropriate here to enter into a technical discussion of the sounds system, the grammar, and the syntax of the Gullah language. A look at a few features found in Gullah songs will give some idea of how Gullah speakers used ostensibly English words, in accordance with specifically Gullah pronunciation, sentence structure, and meanings. (It should be borne in mind that Gullah utterances, as transcribed by speakers of English, are usually recorded according to English spelling.) Thus, in the song "Ain't You Got a Right to the Tree of Life?" the word "born" is transcribed as rhyming with "gone" and "down" as rhyming with "ground." Actually in Gullah speech (as in Bajan and Jamaican), both "born" and "gone," the sound after the initial consonant sounds "b" and "g" would be

like the sound following the consonant sound "a" in the English pronunciation of "dawn." The Gullah "down" and "ground" would rhyme with the
English pronunciation of "hung."[6]

There is a Gullah song in which each verse ends "I done done what
you told me to do." Here "done done" corresponds to the English "have
done," and is in grammatical accord with "I done pray," "I done sing," and
"I done shout" in Gullah.

In the song "The Grey Goose," as Bessie Jones has pointed out, the
"grey goose" refers to the African, his longing for freedom, and his ability
to endure harsh circumstances. The grey goose sets out across the Atlantic
Ocean in the last verse of the song with a "long string of goslings," emblematic of the flying back to Africa tale theme and the African family's
viability in spite of all. Here is an example of the "double entendre," the
hidden meaning of a Gullah expression. A certain mischievous rebellion is
to be observed in the Sea Islands song "In the Grass, in the Grass," which
is a ribald parody on a favorite hymn "At the Cross, at the Cross." These
commentaries are comparable, in a sense, to the subtle dissidence of schoolchildren in Jamaica, before it won independence from the British, when they
sang "Roll Brittania, Britannia roll away" instead of "Rule Britannia, Brittania
rules the waves." Such ridicule and double meaning were found in the songs
of captive laborers who appeared to be singing praises to the master.[7]

Important scholarly investigations continue to be done on the language
contacts, which have produced such viable Afro-European languages over
the past five centuries in other parts of the Americas. A fruitful field for
further research lies in the study of Gullah as a language, which is an
important United States example of the results of language and culture
contacts between speakers of African languages and speakers of English.
The songs, games, and folktales of the Gullah people can contribute much
to this culturally enriching endeavor.

The Islanders have been invited to the folk festivals at Newport in
Rhode Island, California, and numerous college campuses. The Sea Island
Singers from St. Simons Island, Georgia, with Bessie Jones and the Moving
Star Hall Singers from Johns Island, South Carolina, with the Bligen family
were known as the keepers of the Island culture. It is against this backdrop
that the younger generation of cultural conservators have come into their

heritage, which is much treasured far and wide as people have come to know the Sea Islands culture and history.

It is through the language of the songs that much of Sea Islands culture has been spread. Pete Seeger made John Davis's song "Pay Me My Money Down" popular. The Kingston Trio popularized "There's a Meetin' Here Tonight" and "Michael Row the Boat Ashore," both from Johns Island, South Carolina.[8] These songs went into our popular and folk revival culture because of the efforts of those who recorded them in books and on records.

The Gullah language has held a fascination for African Americans seeking greater affiliation with a sometimes elusive past. It has also intrigued people from all around the United States because of its seductive climate and interesting culture—past and present; Sidney Lanier, the famous Southern poet, wrote "The Marshes of Glynn" about the natural beauty and atmosphere of this region.[9] The genius of this creole language is demonstrated in the songs, games, sermons, prayers, and other utterances of the people. The texts of the "shouts" performed by the McIntosh County Shouters contain some of the oldest traditional song texts in the United States.[10] The language in which they are sung is a mixture of English and African contributions.

The performances of the McIntosh County Shouters are close to a true recreation of the actual practice of these songs/dances. They have brought forward the spirit and cultural reality of their African past in a reaffirmation that is organic in the culture, not part of a revivalist movement. There is significant information that Joseph Opala has been lecturing about which includes a gripping tale of a funeral song, originally from Sierra Leone, sung in Harris Neck, Georgia, for generations and then brought back by the Moran family to Sierra Leone.[11] Since funerals, respect for the ancestors, and the transition between this world and the next are of paramount importance to African people, such ceremonies are the most likely to be remembered. The Home Going section of the Hallelujah Singers' presentations at the 1998 Spoleto Festival, Charleston, South Carolina, is of tremendous importance in understanding this culture, the meaning of home, and its Africanity. It is also why a funeral song would be the survivor for people in a community so far separated in time and space from their ancestral home.

The Hallelujah Singers follow the life cycle of the Islanders for concert audiences: church, marriage, children, work, and death are pillars of human societies, interpreted through the spirituals, blues, work songs, mourning songs, lullabies, games, storytelling, and preaching. African societies value verbal art and ability, and those also were brought from Africa to the Sea Islands and beyond to communicate worship, joining, the future, what brings joy, what must be done, the agony of parting, and the longing to connect over long space and deep time.

---

1 I was a witness to the old Georgia Sea Island Singers singing this song in the 1960s. They called it "John the Revelator and the Letter."

2 Bessie Jones and Bess Lomax Hawes, *Step It Down* (New York: Harper Row, 1972).

3 Guy and Candie Carawan, *Ain't You Got a Right to the Tree of Life?* (New York: Simon and Schuster, 1967).

4 Joseph Opala, "Family Across the Sea" and "The Language You Cry In," Films at California Newsreel.

5 Mary A. Twining, Fieldwork, 1970s.

6 Louise Bennett Coverly, Personal Communication, 1980.

7 Roger D. Abrahams, *Singing the Master* (New York: Pantheon Books, 1992).

8 Lydia Parrish, *Slave Songs of the Georgia Sea Islands* (New York: Farrar, Straus, and Co., 1942).

9 Sidney Lanier, "The Marshes of Glynn," in *The Literary South,* comp. and ed. Louis Rubin (Baton Rouge: Louisiana State University Press, 1979), 392–395.

10 William Francis Allen, Charles Pickard Ware, and Lucy McKim Garrison, *Slave Songs of the United States* (1867; repr., Freeport, NY: Books for Libraries Press, 1971).

11 See note 4.

The Devil Made Me Do It

African American Folk Drama

African American folk drama is a lesser-known field, but three productions of "The Devil Play" have survived in different performances to exhibit an historical perspective as well as a continuing modern vitality. These three Afro-American folk dramas take place in one rural and two urban communities. The musical styles, the costuming, and the general setting of the productions reflect the aspirations and socioeconomic status of the members of each group.

Munro Edmonson introduces the subject of drama and dramatic play in *LORE* in the following quotation:

> The essential features of dramatic literature constitute a configuration of roles, rules, action, and symbols also present in rudimentary form in ritual, in games, and in children's play. In fully developed drama, these elements may be further elaborated by compounding with other forms of expression: masking, costuming, and setting, the dance, vocal and orchestral music, prose and poetic dialogue. But these elements are of variable occurrence, while the more nuclear focus of the dramatic (the seemingly essential core) is a pattern of roles.[1]

Certainly, there are dramatic elements in the church services, which often culminate in one or more persons in the congregation experiencing possession, providing a dramatic climax for the services. The children's games in the Sea Islands area also contain dramatic elements. Often called "plays," the games involve enactments, which are part of the whole complex of dance and song, prose and poetic dialogue mentioned in Edmonson's quotation. Furthermore, it is the pattern of roles, within and outside of the game world, that is the chief significance of these games.[2]

In the section on "rain gods," he says, "They are also mythologically commemorative, for the gods (characters) represented are the figures of myth. They are not ancestors but are associated with the ancestral spirits; they are not creators but are associated with the creation."[3] Though this statement is intended to refer to Pueblo Indian drama, it has relevance for the African American folk drama considered here.

In the Sea Islands area of South Carolina, there is a great deal of dramatic expression, not only in the form of plays per se, but scattered throughout other genres—such as storytelling, rapping, the dozens, and all other forms of verbal expression. Chief among these types of oral art is the sermon, where religious encounters and feelings are acted out for the edification of the audience. With the congregation gathered around on Sunday when work is proscribed and with the need for relaxation and catharsis focused on this time period and place, we see the New World adaptation of the West African storytelling session. The Yoruba say that "If you tell stories in the daytime your teeth will grow crooked;" in many other African groups, the expected time for storytelling is after the work is done in the evening.[4] In both the African secular sessions and Afro-American religious sermons, the stories themselves are accompanied by dramatic gestures, which amplify the verbal narration. The audience/congregation participates in the occasion replying and rejoining to the sentiments expressed, interweaving musical phrases and verbal outcries into the main body of the oration. When called upon to do so, they sing songs/hymns or spirituals, and thus, carry the action forward. Elapsed time is important in both situations as the people involved expect to be engaged for a certain length of time in this activity—somewhat on the order of our watching a television special knowing it will be an hour long.

The sermons tend to follow the formulaic pattern set down by Parry and Lord, whose theory was later applied by Bruce Rosenberg to the folk sermon.[5] The episodic narrative, told in a combination of formulas and spontaneous phrases, uses themes from the Bible and from the preacher's own conversion experience. The telling is dramatic, and the actions specific. The teller must be skillful verbally and emotionally, giving the audience the catharsis they expect. The Sea Islands community holds "Seven Speakers," occasions that are preaching contests. Each person does his talk or sermon and then literally receives the payoff. A collection is taken up after each speech and the best speaker in the estimation of the group is quickly revealed according to who raises the most money. Rewarding the skillful speakers both with money (which is actually donated to the worthy cause that occasioned the speakers' contests) and adulation indicates the high value placed on these skills.

Of course, stories and jokes are told in other contexts with accompanying paralinguistic gestures, mime, pantomime, invisible props, and all manner of facial expressions, which add a definitely dramatic air to any performance no matter how casual its occasion.[6] Some examples of this accompaniment, along the parallel gestural channel, would be found in such dances as the Buzzard Lope; the opening is dramatic as John Davis of St. Simons Island stomped around preparing himself and shouting at the others to fall in formation. The other Sea Island Singers from St. Simons Island begin to sing "Throw Me Anywhere, Lord, in That Old Field" and keep rhythmic impetus going with their feet tapping and hands clapping.[7] The "buzzard" circles a handkerchief, which represents a corpse, pecking at it and finally making his pounce. It is a pantomime and small representation of a cosmic drama.

The religious shouts, also done by the former Sea Island Singers and the present-day (2000) McIntosh County Shouters, are also dramatic in the way that they build up the emotional intensity. The singing begins quietly enough, but soon the singers build the sound and movement, bringing the song to a dramatic climax. These examples of theatrical behavior occur within the framework of other culture traits.

Religious and secular dramatic behavior, including the use of masks, exists as a strong tradition in West Africa and has appeared in some form in African American culture. The tradition of masking the human form did come to North America with enslaved Africans, often though not exclusively in verbal form. There are a few scattered examples of masking and costuming to be found in North America, although according to Herskovits, the Sea Islands have the lowest retention of "Africanisms" in the Americas. Suffice it to say, however, they are there to be seen.[8]

On Johns Island, South Carolina, the members of a Presbyterian church enact a folk play entitled "The Devil's Funeral." It is a play with broad satire of human failings—such as greed, envy, and lust. The men, who play all the parts, rollick about dressed as women with overexaggerated bosoms. They wear rural clothing and seem to be making up the dialogue as they go along. It has African traits as it ridicules people in an open performance, just as "Heaven Bound" does in Atlanta. Men play the women's roles and the play is very much a function of the community.

The players go around to schools to do performances and make sure the Devil and everyone else gets his or her just deserts in the end for the instruction of the children. These examples of the actors wearing masks demonstrate some of the African traits that have been submerged in isolated African American communities; others have been right out in the open but are often misunderstood by the dominant culture group as disruptive or unacceptable social behavior. The whole tradition and use of masks, physical and attitudinal, in African American communities has been in response to the repression and willful misunderstanding of the surrounding Euro-American group. Paul Lawrence Dunbar's "We Wear the Mask" is a very poignant expression of the need for dissembling one's feelings in order to survive in an alien land. The tradition of masking does, however, have roots in the West African experience, where the use of masks in verbal and plastic art forms is well known.

Masks in West Africa are an expression of abstract forces within the communities who use them as agents of social control. They mask not only the face, but the entire body of the person wearing the mask. This masking disguises his human shape purposefully as he often embodies the will of the society meting out justice, expressing religious feelings, or otherwise focusing emotions of the community through ritual expressive behavior. Masks have not been found very often in African America but, no doubt, some were used in the African manner in the early days of the enforced immigration of African Americans.

A mask has appeared in another folk play on Johns Island, South Carolina, called "The Devil Play" or "The Devil and Angel Play." The Devil himself is masked and costumed humorously, although none of the other characters in the play are similarly masked. Most of the people in the play are dressed in ragged plantation-style work clothes, except the Angel, the Devil, and the Wise and Foolish Virgins.

The people who played the characters were close to their own roles in real life and lent a certain lifelike quality to the play. The Devil was played by a woman costumed and acting humorously, not at all a threatening figure. She bustled about contending with the Saving Angel for the souls as they appeared and showed evident satisfaction when she triumphed. She did not sing or speak except to engage in mock arguments with the Angel, which were mostly pantomime punctuated by high-pitched gabbling. Many people went to Hell in this production, which seemed to signify a certain raucous fatalism on the part of the Islanders, who have few illusions about their lot in life. The Islanders' participation in the play in roles which suited or reflected their own inclination or weaknesses, coupled with the realistic costuming from the era of plantation servitude, showed their pride in their heritage and acceptance of themselves as they are. As in West African drama societies, the actors/persons in the culture can laugh at themselves and others caught in similar traps created by their own besetting sins.

Cast in the Christian framework of the morality play, the Devil triumphs over frail human nature; meanwhile, however, the community has had a good look at itself in the mirror of art. The African secular drama societies and the Afro-American religious plays both accomplish essentially the same function in airing certain social behaviors with an eye to controlling them. The play also provides a socially acceptable outlet for people's opinions of each other's actions.

The plays are expressive of values in the society; the temptations are referred to in the segment called the Wise and Foolish Virgins. Gambling and drinking are the men's temptations; dancing and using up all the oil in your vessel before the bridegroom comes, so to speak, are the women's temptations.

The music was supplied by the actors and the congregation/audience. The Angel was played by one of the strongest singers on the island, and she led most of the old traditional spirituals and songs. The congregation joined in lustily, springing to their feet and surging forward in response to the appearance of the characters to celebrate the dramatic action with their participation. The music is leader-and-chorus style using the call-and-response so typical of West African music. The singing is spontaneous, sung by whoever wishes to participate, with accompanying body percussion consisting of hand clapping and foot stamping.

Movement and dance were prominent features of this play. The characters entered at the back of the church and moved up the aisle, dancing, gambling, singing, or whatever they were required to do by the action of the play. the Angel stayed at the front of the church just in front of the pews, moving into the aisle and along the corridor in front of the altar as the action demanded. When the rhythm change for "shouting" came, she danced with the singing. The Devil moved to and fro as her efforts to capture the souls increased; her movements were stylized in order to get a humorous effect, waggling her head and posterior in gestures meant to mock the Angel. The dancing ladies and their guitar-playing gigolo danced down the aisle to a popular jukebox tune, straight to the choir stalls designated as Hell, stopping only for a short struggle to get into Heaven by the dancer in red lace. She later begged the pastor of the church to release her from Hell, as it was too hot!

The congregation moved as a whole all through the production; they went forward into the aisles to dance during the shouting, they lurched back into the pews to await subsequent developments; the people rose to their feet in approval of the events, some standing on the benches in order to get a better view. They rose and fell like the waves of the sea, emotionally responding wholeheartedly to the proceedings. They laughed and sang and danced, saluting their friends and neighbors in the play and contributing to the artistic picture of aspects of their own lives.

In times past, other skits and plays, such as the "Indian Wedding," were enacted as entertainment and served the same mimetic and cathartic function as this "Devil Play," but this and "The Devil's Funeral" are the few performed in recent times.[9]

In Atlanta, Georgia, there is a play adapted from one of the old oral devil plays. In response to the needs of an upwardly mobile, urban Afro-African population, the play has a somewhat different emphasis; it is called "Heaven Bound." The massed heavenly choirs, the saved souls (of whom there are twenty), and St. Peter are all dressed in white; the decor is chiefly white, including the pianos prominently displayed in the foreground. The cast of characters is quite large, which gives ample opportunity for well-prepared solos interpolated with the heavenly choirs from time to time. The audience used to sit throughout the production applauding at the end to show their appreciation. Now, however, they join in the singing as they can and thoroughly enjoy the parade of characters.

A few characters are costumed in street clothes, which signifies their damned status, and the actor who played the Devil was most spectacularly attired in a red satin bloomer suit with a close-fitting hood on his head, leaving only his face exposed. He carried a pitchfork and never made a sound during the whole production. He mimed and pantomimed quite cleverly, gesturing significantly toward rich donors to the church when the character of the rich man appears, clutching his moneybags. He danced derisively with the hypocrite who comes on the scene in four-inch high heels and a red lace dress singing "I Shall Not Be Moved." The surprise came at the end of the play when he whipped off his hood, revealing snow-white hair, and led the singing of "Hand Me Down My Silver Trumpet, Gabriel" in a rich baritone voice.[10]

The production has many of the elements of the folk play, but it has been smoothed out and follows a written script. The music has obvious Euro-American influences in its harmonies, but it has a strong style and delivery. An organ and two pianos were used to accompany the singing and action. Two well-trained choirs sang throughout the production, and the audience was only asked to join in the spiritual singing at the end. No face masks at all were used. The players, however, were presenting as fully costumed characters, hence they were analogous to their African cousins in their full-body, masked appearances. The Devil in the Atlanta production used his face gesturally as well as his arms and legs. The Johns Island Devil had to rely more upon her movement and gestures because of the mask concealing her face, in the manner of the people wearing African masks who have to rely upon body gestures and context rather than facial mime to convey the meaning. The presence of the mask on the person conveys a certain message in itself. The masked or costumed characters represented certain aspects of Christian teaching and duly presented personae different from themselves.

The two plays deal ostensibly with the same subject, the progress of the human soul between good and evil. The dichotomous predicates of Christian morality function to balance the world, as do the masked figures of West African societies. Voyaging uncertainly among many temptations, handicapped by certain besetting sins, the Christian soul tries for Heaven and approval, which shall be everlasting. He/she strives to make it, and in the play "Heaven Bound," their arrivals are celebrated by harmonious choirs singing praises while the Devil lashes his tail in frustration outside the pearly gates. The drama of the soul traversing life's journey, harassed by temptations, is the same in the Sea Islands version, but the hapless sinners receive as much recognition for their struggles as do the saints who march into Heaven in orderly fashion. In the Atlanta play, Hell is a fearsome place into which a few sinners disappear among lightning flashes of doom and destruction. In contrast, the Sea Islanders sit up in a Hell, designated by a drawing of the Devil, in full view of the congregation, who probably recognize little difference between some other hell and the one they have. Dramatically, approval and support of the community is shut off from sight by the entrance-to-hell scenery of the urban version of the play. The rural version, however, lets the sinners remain within the community, still able to draw on the emotional sustenance they need to survive.

Other social commentary shows up in the play too. One of the gamblers appeared in whiteface. When asked about it, he remarked, "I just wanted to make sure that one of you all was in the play too." He also added that he did not want people to think white people were not sinful. The attitudes of the people toward their own weaknesses also showed up in the play. The drunk was played by a man who was lame and tended to have a staggering walk anyway. Nothing loath, he happily staggered up the aisle as the drunk, enjoying a moment of glory in a life that offered him little adulation otherwise.[11]

In the Sea Islands, we find that drama reflects and enhances life as these people live it. In their picture of themselves, they accept their personal sinful nature and poverty with a certain playfulness. Their ability both to laugh at themselves and to share their sorrow are not only saving virtues and graces, but also safety valves in an emotionally loaded situation.

Clearly, the urban version is closer to a Euro-American Christian morality in its ideals, which may partially be due to the sentiments of the ladies who undertook to formalize the play script. The characters in the Sea Islands version seek to survive in an isolated situation where their value system has not had to respond to the value system of the dominant society to the same extent as that of the Atlantans. The urban group, surrounded by the whites who were often critical and hostile to Afro-American morality, strove to show their ability to conform to the standards of the dominant group in hopes of insuring survival and upward mobility to a certain extent. The music, the costumes, the characteristic coloration, and general cast of the two productions all point to these differences; each play gives us a dramatic enactment of the values of the group.

The Church of the Living God, No. 18 in Indianapolis, Indiana, has been involved in filming a version by William Wiggins of a musical drama called "In the Rapture." It belongs in the same group as "The Devil Play" of Johns Island and "Heaven Bound" of Atlanta. To almost operatic accompaniment of singers in gospel style, Everyman sees people struggling with their burdens and triumphing because of their spiritual rebirth. The literal enactment of finding the Savior characterizes the triumph of the spirit and the foiling of the ever-present Devil.

In this production, Jesus is actually represented by an actor who silently takes up the cross to the accompanying moving, melismatic rendition of "Calvary" and a poem about his crucifixion. He reappears dressed in purple robes with a long dark wig and a crown made of silver-gilt tinsel. He interacts with the Devil, Everyman, and the other actors and singers as they appear, but the main dialogue is carried on by the Devil and Everyman.[12]

Like the other two productions, the temptations of money, flesh, power, and worldly goods are offered as reasonable alternatives to peace of mind and tranquility of spirit. The forces of good and evil are represented by the Devil and the Angel on Johns Island, St. Peter and the Devil in Atlanta, and Jesus and the Devil in Indianapolis. The first two pairs contend for each of the souls that come along and so it is in the Indianapolis edition, but the main object of the conflict of wills is Everyman, gullibly believing the Devil's tempting schemes while suspecting that Jesus's power might be worth his allegiance. Torn between the two, he vacillates until he finds out that the wonderful-looking temptations of the evil one turn out to be dross. Jesus heals his broken heart and the grand apotheosis is celebrated in the singing of "O Happy Day."[13]

All three productions feature music as the connecting thread because the dramatic vignettes are strung together by its emotive and moving force. The styles of music are quite markedly different though much the same in their power to move and engage the audience. On Johns Island, the singing was unaccompanied and consisted mainly of old style spirituals and "shouts" except for the entrance of the dancing ladies and their guitar-playing escort. The Atlanta production was as described, characterized by Euro-American harmonies and careful arrangements of the spirituals, somewhat in the manner of the Hall Johnson choir. The Indianapolis production was highly instrumentalized with organ and drums. The gospel was jazz gospel at moments and some of the singing performances were pyrotechnically brilliant, certainly emanating from the more recently established gospel style of composed music, which originated in the 1930s with Thomas A. Dorsey.

We can see the differences among the three productions due to stylistic variations, responses to movement in time, movement along the rural/urban continuum, and the acculturative influences from the dominant society. The question is then: How many of these three may be considered folk drama? They are transmitted orally and conceived in visions and dreams, a source often cited by traditional artists. The woman credited with the vision, which resulted in the production of "Heaven Bound," was a laundress from Jacksonville, Florida, who communicated her dream to Nellie Davis. It was written down, clearly composed of many Afro-American cultural elements. Popkin writes in a patronizing tone about the performances in Atlanta, Savannah, and Macon, but she does give credit to this play as America's "first great folk drama" and predicts that Atlanta would become as much a pilgrimage as Oberammergau in Germany.[14] Suffice it to say that the Devil, who played in the production from 1944 until 1976, packed them in two nights running every year at Big Bethel Church.[15] Furthermore, the church has occasionally scheduled a second semiannual performance in July and played to standing-room-only-capacity crowds then too.

Gertrude Shelby indicates that the elaborate and gripping production in Brunswick, Georgia, was done with a two-page minimal script, which brought her to the conclusion that the drama was all generated out of the minds and culture of the actors.[16] This factor of what Ms. Shelby calls "free-hand" performance is the link between each of the productions, for they are truly passion plays in that they are representative of the emotive force of the people whose reactions to life's trials and tribulations are honestly manifest and call forth ready and recognizant response from the audience. All of the foregoing proves Edmonson's points that the expressive forms and styles may be different, but the core is the dynamic interplay of the roles.

Margerine Hatcher, who had the vision which inspired "In The Rapture," apparently went to bed and dreamed the play. Disturbed and awakened, she came down to ask her husband how they might do such a thing. They have been doing it for many years and the vitality is, if anything, stronger as the years go by.[17]

American folk drama is sparsely represented in the literature by some accounts of mummers' plays in the memory culture of certain groups, Native American rituals, the plays of the Spanish speakers of the southwestern United States, and these few references to African American folk drama. It is evident that the Johns Island "Devil Play" and "The Devil's Funeral" represent earlier more original renditions of which "Heaven Bound" and "In the Rapture" represent more modern versions. Clearly, Afro-American drama may be less neglected and more honored than it has been in the past for its continuing *élan vital.*

[1] Monro Edmondson, *LORE* (New York: Holt, Rinehart, Winston, 1971), 165.

[2] Twining, Fieldwork, 1970s.

[3] Monro Edmondson, *LORE* (New York: Holt, Rinehart, Winston, 1971), 175.

[4] Ojo Arewa, "Story Telling Among The Yoruba," paper presented at the American Folklore Society Conference, Austin, TX, November, 1997.

[5] Bruce Rosenberg, *The Art Of The American Preacher* (Oxford: Oxford University Press, 1970).

[6] Twining, Fieldwork, 1970s.

[7] Ibid.

[8] Melville Herskovits, *Negro in the New World* (Bloomington, IN: Indiana University Press, 1970).

[9] Janie Hunter, Personal Communications, 1970s.

[10] Gregory D. Coleman, *We're Heaven Bound: Portrait of a Black Sacred Drama* (Athens: University of Georgia Press, 1994); "Diabolical Doings in Atlanta," *Life* 26 (January 1953), 55–58.

[11] Twining, Fieldwork, 1970s.

[12] Ibid.

13 William Wiggins, "In the Rapture," (1976), film available through Indiana University Audio Visual Department, Bloomington, Indiana, 47401.

14 Zelda Popkin, "Heaven Bound: An Authentic Negro Folk Drama Out Of Old Savannah," *Theatre Guild Magazine* (August 1931), 14–17.

15 Gregory D. Coleman, *We're Heaven Bound: Portrait of a Black Sacred Drama* (Athens: University of Georgia Press, 1994).

16 Gertrude M. Shelby, "Heaven Bound Soldiers: A Negro Green Pastures," *Theatre Arts Monthly* (October 1931), 855–861.

17 William Wiggins, "In the Rapture," (1976), film available through Indiana University Audio Visual Department, Bloomington, Indiana, 47401.

Telling Lies

Adult Stories of the Sea Islands

O ral transmission on the Sea Islands is vital to the exchange of information, doing business, education, and settling down to a good session of drinking and talking.[1] If you inquire what people are doing in these gatherings, they cheerfully remark, "We're just telling lies." This characterization does not reflect on their honesty or veracity; it is a recognition of the fact that the stories are fiction, made up by the participants from tradition and the exigencies of life. These communication events are not performances; the fluidity of movement and contacts, the ever-present pints of liquor in the car trunks, and the easy flow of conversation make for a quick coming together just about anywhere. In a culture that is oral/aural, a good command of language and expression is invaluable. Their authority of speech and expression came with their ancestors from Africa during the otherwise disastrous voyages. The persuasive sermons of the preachers, the hilarity of the well-told story, the riddles and jokes on which the children practice, and the courtship suasions of the young people all contribute to the richness of life, the beauty of the church services, and the relief offered by humor. William Pipes, William Wiggins, and Bruce Rosenberg have all demonstrated the structural framework of oral sermons.[2] Alan Dundes has analyzed how the tales were devised by showing the underlying structure.[3] The composition of the songs and spirituals with alternating verse-and-chorus pattern performed in call-and-response style demonstrates the Africanity and artistic ability of the Islanders in handling the "word." The communication events taking place within the community, which are represented in tale-telling sessions, church services, educational instructions, business dealings, and joke telling, are intricate exchanges that are woven into the fabric of everyday life and normally consist of many face-to-face encounters. Contacts with the outside world, which they seek in Charleston, Savannah, or beyond, provide stressful occurrences that build up and which the individual must relieve in various ways. Formal church services, "stump knocking" preaching, and praise-house services are some of the religious outlets. Higginson describes such a variety in the sessions among the soldiers in the unit he commanded during the Civil War:

> —beside others telling stories, shouting with laughter over the broadest mimicry, in which they excel, and, in which, the officers come in for a full share. . . . Then there are quieter prayer-meetings, with pious invocations and slow psalms, "deaconed out" from memory by the leader, two lines at a time, in a sort of wailing chant. Elsewhere, there are *conversazioni* around fires. . . . Sometimes the woman is spelling slow monosyllables out of a primer, a feat which always commands all ears . . .[4]

Folklore is often thought to be suitable for children, and there certainly are many games, rhymes, jokes, and stories for and by the children.[5] These counting games, dances, "plays," jokes, and storytellings are similar to what the adults do, but with different subject matter. The "plays" involve sympathetic movement, emerging leadership patterns, small dramatic enactments, and other devices to teach them language, song, manners, and social interactions of all kinds. The children's games function as part of the socialization and education process and provide child-to-child communications that are independent of the adult world. They provide some of the first literature that they know.

As the young people grow up, they begin to sense the wider adult world just beyond their reach and want to imitate and partake of it before they are really ready. They make up parodies of the hymns and otherwise innocent songs substituting quite raucous words and verses for the originals. By demonstrating their ability to handle adult topics, as they suppose, they are showing their readiness to enter adult life. The young women exhibit their preparedness to take on adult experience and posture by dance and acceding to the blandishments of the young men. They have hardly stopped playing

"I Come to See Miss Julianne John" before they are moving seductively on the dance floor with young men dancing admiringly around them. These passages into adulthood take them along another path, leaving childhood things behind.

The life of traditional expression continues and wanders over the border of popular culture. Recently a popular music television outlet featured a group of young African Americans more used to doing the Electric Slide than traditional games. The dance they were doing was a more modern edition of "Shout, Josephine, Shout, Shout!"[6] The tradition of innovation of verses among known choruses is still present, any of the old games, songs, and stories can be updated and find new uses and expression due to the combination of repeated refrains and improvisation.

Spontaneous eruption of storytelling was more prevalent in times past before television, radio, and internet. In rural situations in Africa, storytelling sessions were for after working hours, and the same restrictions applied in rural African America. Aggregations of people in "piccolos" and "grab-alls" told stories, listened to guitar music and jukeboxes, and shared the day's events. Juke joints were favorite places to let off steam in various ways. Since "juke" has a number of meanings—fighting and sexual exertion among them—the activities were many and varied. Zora Neale Hurston describes such times in her own old hometown of Eatonville, Florida, sitting on the front porch telling tales with religious, secular, and scatological themes. Uses of mojo hands in poker games, drinking bouts after work, and venting about jobs, families, natural and manmade disasters are all grist to the mill. Daryl Dance's *Shuckin' and Jivin'* and *From My People: Four Hundred Years of African American Folklore* describe such gatherings and the tales which emerge from them, spanning deepest sadness, obscenity, and hilarity.[7] Life in America demands well-functioning escape valves and opportunities to vent frustrations, sorrows, and a chance to see the funny side of their encounters with racism, poverty, and the uphill struggle to achieve and maintain:

> Times was so hard that when the rat came into the kitchen
> to raid the pantry, all he could find to eat was an onion.
> When I came into the kitchen, he was sittin' in the corner
> eatin' and cryin' and eatin' away on his onion and cryin' his
> eyes out.[8]

Although the tradition as it once was known may have substantially altered due to the passage of time, technology, and social customs, people still carry on the oral literature in a number of ways. One is the revival of storytelling as a subject of meetings, regionally and nationally. In less formal circumstances, people gather spontaneously to "tell lies," "shoot the shit," or reminisce about their own or friends' experiences, generating an atmosphere of belonging to the community by entertaining with shared ordeals or escapades. Jokes, urban and rural legends, and memorates often comprise this evanescent, unpublished body of lore. Keith Cunningham's *American Indians' Kitchen-Table Stories* celebrates the commonplace of the setting, the importance of the communications, subject matter, and the depth of their connection to deeper issues and values.[9] The issue is not to focus on forms and subject matter of the past exclusively, but to recognize the validity of the continuing tradition, whatever form it takes.

Needless to say, exchanging perceptions and experiences will reveal certain universalities among all groups, but the culture specificity will also disclose encounters and trials which belong only to the in-group.

The stories adults tell on the Sea Islands have certain themes which are not suitable for children, such as violence, murder, adultery, and deception. "The Partridge and the Rabbit" features violence, murder (though unintentional on Ms. Rabbit's part), what may look like adultery from a Euro-American standpoint, deceit, and a certain cannibalistic episode as the Partridge family eats the unfortunate Mr. Rabbit for dinner. "Gorm the Giant" also has cannibalism in the story, violence, and a monster child molester. The story is an example of a *cantefable*, which is a tale including song intervals. The song refrains may be typical of a character and herald his or her appearance in the story. In African storytelling sessions, the audience may be instructed by the narrator to know the words and sing along with the refrain.

"Dividing Souls" has hilarious aspects as the two "noodles" count the potatoes with the two men outside listening and drawing the wrong conclusions. Ghost stories including dogs, cats, people, and shapeless horrors abound in the South. "Tom Wasn't There" has a wistful side to it as the narrator tells of seeing and not seeing her cousin, Tom. "Enoch Meets Gawd" is a humorous telling of an attempt to deceive on Enoch's part, which is met and trumped by the machinations of his boss. Enoch's passive resistance and malingering finally has a very active denouement. "The Leg of a Rabbit" has a poor but worthy hero, courting behavior, and a turnaround of their lives through the redeeming quality of love. "God Scay de White Folks Too" tells a story that could be of comfort to one done wrong by the more powerful boss. The two stories "I Come From Heaven" and "The Husband Didn't Go Out Because of the Rain" deal with adultery, plain and simple. It is not the situation of the Partridge and the Rabbit, which reflects polygyny (a still viable cultural phenomenon in the Sea Islands in the 1970s). The man-up-the-chimney motif is an old theme of the lover hiding as the husband approaches, with hilarious results. The husband being at home unexpectedly provides the drama of both stories. The husband-didn't-go-out story is called "The Moon is as Bright as Gobach'e deh" (go back he's here) in Barbados, which is what the wife calls out to warn off the lurking lover. The tale type and motif numbers in some of the headnotes to the stories demonstrate the codification of the universality of the tales whose themes may be found in many cultures. They are based on the Aarne-Thompson Tale Typing and Motif Indexes, which are a catalog of such themes as they are found in different societies.[10] Certain tales may be culture specific and so have a limited provenience.

These stories are clearly not suitable for young ears, except possibly where a moral lesson at the end occurs, which tells the listener not to let himself be duped because he might lose his head. Adult tales fulfill certain functions of folklore, especially to amuse, to expose possibly socially disruptive behavior, to warn of consequences of misbehavior, and to make people aware of community observation. Only honest representation of human frailties will pass muster in the African American communities, both rural and urban, where proximity to the boundaries of life and death is all too apparent.

The following tales illustrate certain aspects of Sea Islands culture and the richness of the expression, which belies any underestimation of this group of people, its artistic output, and its relationship to African cultures.

"The Partridge and the Rabbit"

Told by Janie Hunter

The story shows an example of the de facto *polygyny that exists on the island. There are very few places where it shows up on the surface level of the Sea Islands culture. Needless to say, it is against American law to have more than one wife. Customary law of African cultural provenience, however, provides for men having more than one wife. The status of marriage and wife, as opposed to looser intimate arrangements, could be defined by co-residence and the raising of children. There are several such marriage situations on the Islands.*

This is type 1535 called "Fatal Imitation" by Parsons : 33–35, I, II, III, and IV. It was told by the late Mrs. Janie Hunter on Johns Island, South Carolina. Mrs. Hunter's style was quiet and soft voiced. She often opened with a question in order to begin the process of engaging the audience's attention so they entered into the world of the story.

Though the partridge and rabbit story depends on the peculiar animal characteristics of the two protagonists, they are obviously humans.

The partridge or the rabbit, which suppose to have more sense? Everybody say the rabbit is a very sensible animal. So, partridge and rabbit, they was two very close friend, so one day the rabbit take a walk to the partridge house. Partridge settin' in the sun. The rabbit say, "Old frien', I going home to have dinner, I'll be back later." And then the partridge get home. His wife didn't cook dinner yet, but partridge very much in love with Mr. Rabbit wife. And he have to see about a plan. Rabbit have a very beautiful wife. He tell his wife say, "You go on and make dinner I'll be back later." When the partridge get about a mile from the rabbit house, the partridge take he head and stick it way under his wing. When he get to the rabbit house he say, "Wha' you doin' old friend?" The rabbit say, "My goodness, you have dinner already?' "O no, my old lady ain't cook yet, so I thought I'd take my head off and leave 'em home for she to shave until I get back." All that time he have his head under his wing. So when he get in the house he say, "I ain't gon stay. I'll see you later I think I goin back." Partridge went back. Rabbit say to her, "Old gal cut my head off!" You ain see that partridge lef his head off for he wife to shave? He say you could take off mine for shave em too." She worry bout it. She went and got the big butcher knife and chop the rabbit head off. The rabbit jump way yonder and die. The partridge get the rabbit they cook em have a big dinner say. When they no fooling, there's no fun;' whey they no loven, there's no getting along. Partridge have his wife and the rabbit wife and the rabbit for dinner. The partridge have the sense that's right—no sense rabbit.

"Gorm the Giant"

Told by Bessie Jones

I have spelled the name of the man-eating giant in several ways because it seems unclear in the story. It may be related to a word, "Gaum" or "Gorm," found in a section on archaisms in Reed Smith's booklet "Gullah, Bulletin of the University of South Carolina on November 1, 1926." It means to daub or smear with spilled victuals and grease so the giant would be repulsive, like a booger man, covered with old food because of his greedy behavior. A man or child-eating person occurs in Parsons no. 74 on page 83; it has some elements in common with tale type 327 and involves motif 3524.1.2 among others. The giant sings his song while he sharpens his knife, which echoes motif G83.1, Ogress whets teeth to kill captive. The story also includes a small version of "The Obstacle Flight."

This remind me once there were some bad lil children—lil girl and lil boy, they was really hardheaded. They would go way out in the woods and play every day, go way out so their mother tell them say, "Don't go so far out in the woods you'll get lost out there." In this country, they had a thing out in the woods they call old Goff, who catch the children and eat them up cut their head off, and cut their head and suck the blood—you know they didn't want the meat, but the blood. He was a blood eater. So these children, they went out in the woods one day and they was ramblin' around, they was playing and they get some flowers for the girl and boy and they go for a stroll and they finally get lost. And dark come on before they know it. They lost their way home. They went to walking there was a little path they could see in the woods carried them further and all like that. Finally, they heard a great trump and walking TRUMP TRUMP TRUMP and they wondered what in the world could this be? They stopped say, "Somebody a comin?" and they stopped. Come a great big giant, and he said, "CHILDREN, CHILDREN Y'ALL LOST?" "Yessur, we lost our home we can't find our path." Say, "ALL RIGHT COME ALONG WITH ME AND TO-MORROW YOU CAN GO HOME." Say, "Yessir." So they walked on, the girl was older than the boy, and walked on and walked on and came to a house, an old piece of shaggy thing made out of sticks all kind of hair and old grass up there for him to sleep on an old bunk bed made out of grass you know out of sticks and things and grass on it and he had a stove. The child ran looked at it and so one thing the girl said she'd been reading about it when he got in there. He went up to the bed and said, "I'm goin to bed." There was a funny lil old step made out of round wood on up there the girl told the boy say, "Let's don't go to sleep here." "This old Gart house Mama done told me about it, Mama used to read to me about it." Say, "This is him." The boy, he was so tired till finally he did drop to sleep sho nuff and so he hurried down there down the stair. He was getting ready for his long knife, he was getting ready to kill 'em, cut they head off so he could suck the blood. He sing this song as he sharpen the knife [singing]

> Dang a dang a dang danga deellah deelah
>
> I'm going to throw this skin away
>
> Dang a dang a dang danga deelah deelah
>
> I'm going to throw this skin away

They heard, and the brother, he got wide awake then and knew his sister was right. He said, "CHILDREN, CHILDREN TO GONE TO SLEEP YET?" They said, "NO, suh. Mama say we musn't go to sleep in your house until you go down and bring me a sifter full of water." You know what a sifter is? [To the audience] What you use to sift your flour and meal in, sifter—and so he went down he was getting madder and madder then he'd go on down he go out to his old fury. Well you know he'd get the water up and he'd start out and all the water would go out the sifter. He'd try it again he did it for bout two, three hours. He got completely mad he could never get a sifter of water. He got real mad and so she put, they put the two pillows in the bed and the cover curled with an old bag and sheet you know they went on out they ran they ran they ran about five miles. The lil boy had a little knife he sharpen a stick you know and he put the stick right in the middle of the road. And they run they run they run and found a road didn't care where it go, they was going out of the woods, they run. Finally, he come back in where he walked around, "I'm going get them children." Walked up there he call, "Children, children." Nobody answered. "Children, children," went back down and get his old knife come back up there he was so mad he was going to cut 'em in two you know half in two. He pull that knife right down across them big pillow. WHAM! And all that hay and grass and stuff flew up in his eye, and everything he was raving, he was mad then sure enough he romp and he stomp. There was no children and he ain't had nothing there to eat down the road, and he got the trash out and he run he run he run try to catch up with them. He say, "I'm getting my five mile boots." He could step so far OO BOOM OO BOOM. He done got his five mile boots well see the child knowed it and his last step he made it he step right in the middle of that big stick and it stuck up in his stomach he know his search out, 'bout that time I left and he went back to sew it up.

"Dividing Souls"

Told by John Davis

This is no. 49 in Dorson, American Negro Folktales.[11] *This variant includes the two being unable to count and the soul dividing, but not the subsequent death and talking-skull motifs. The present text has the lame master beating John back to the house.*

Another version of this story appears in South Carolina Folktales: *104–106. It is classified as a ghost story; actually, there are no ghosts involved, but only people staring at each other. Parsons lists two versions in* Folklore of the Sea Islands, South Carolina: *68, no. 58. It is type 1691, motif x424.*

One night a fella steal some potatoes. That must have been right after slavery cuz they couldn't even much count. Bad counting. Well, anyhow they didn't want nobody to disturb them while they was dividing the potatoes, so they went over in the graveyard. So when they jump over the fence they go in the graveyard, they drop two potatoes but they didn't want put back the sack. They say, "We get that on the way back." They went on in the graveyard. They divide the potatoes, "You take this and I take that, you take this and I take that . . ." One marse and he fella he come by there and listen at that "Marsa," you know God and the Devil in the graveyard dividing souls. "You go way from me with that line." "Marse, it is!" Marse never did walk. "Say, I'll tote you down. I give you leave to kill me if it ain't so." Marse say, "It sho is" and they sit there listening. "You take this I take that; you take this, I take that." So they got through dividing the potato fella say, "Well thas all," the other say, "No, we got two at the gate and [hand slap] GOD AWMITY." So, when he got home then he thought about his boss man couldn't walk. So he say, "Lawd God gon git boss man." His boss open the door, he say, "You best come on in' fo I shut this do' on you."

"Tom Wasn't There"

Told by Sister Bessie Burkes

Ms. Bessie Jones and I, with assorted grandchildren and students, went to Ms. Burkes's house on a rainy, rainy day. We could not go out, so we settled in for a storytelling session. Ms. Burkes told us this supernatural memorate.

We were living on a farm place out to Albany, Georgia, out in the country and we were chopping cotton and I was the leader, and so we had to work from sunup to sundown. We were getting fifty cents a day, now you see how that were that time back dere, and so I always like to go to church, and when we knocked off at sundown I had to run home and cook my husband supper and then I had went to church I had walked about seven mile I thought by the time I get cross Mud Creek that I would ketch Belle and them and gwine cross that creek everything down there kine of lost, you know, and I was scared and I hear the bushes was rustling behind me and I say, "Have mercy, Lord," and it were raining and drizzling just like it is today, so when I got through Mud Creek then I had to go cross Duckfoot Creek and then when I got cross there I say well I get cross there I would see Thomas, that were my cousin, and I saw a tall old man were standing in the road and I said, "Wait, Tom," for and just kep on going further and keep on going further and I got so scared I could hardly walk. I said, "Wait, Tom; wait, Tom" and the man kep goin further. Finally, he just stood up, he growed so taaall, and I gwine round there I say this ahere ain't no Thomas ooh I go so scared ay "Have mercy, Lord. Have mercy, Lord. Have mercy, Lord." And then I went round the man again I didn't see no man so I kept on going to the church and when I got to the church I fell and fainted at the door. I was so scared that was a true story.

"Enoch Meets Gawd"

Told by Bessie Jones

Cf. Dorson, American Negro Folktales, *no. 54 on page 153, "Old Boss and John at the Praying Tree," which shows a reversed situation to the one in this story of Bessie Jones. Dorson cites motif 1971, "Man behind the statue (tree) speaks and pretends to be God (spirit)." However, motif 1971.8 seems closer in this story. "Hidden man behind image gives unwelcome answer to supplicant: image blamed." Mary and Enoch are deceived into thinking the boy, masked in the white suit, is indeed God and deal with him on those terms. The people on the Islands talk to God in many forms such as prayers, in stories, etc. The Holy Family is also represented in their world view as persons close to them and people with whom they can communicate. They see Joseph as a person who was being very nice to Mary, considering his generosity in accepting another man's child; they sustain a sense of injury from the adulterous act and felt that Joseph might too. Enoch is a perfect example of the passive resistance that was a common weapon against slavery.*

Once upon a time—this is a short one—there always has been lazy peoples you know in the world, some don't want to work. This man, back in slavery, say he didn't, he really didn't want to work. He learn a way to keep from work, he say he was sick. He found that out; they didn't want to work him sick. They let him stay home, he stay sick so long, so long. Enoch and his wife were name Mary, and she would cook. You know she had to cook on the fireplace. She'd cook food for him and leave it there, and she'd get back there and Enoch done ate up everything. He always eat up all the food, you know. I don't care what she cook, he eat. Anyhow, tired people coming from work at night—they had to go from sun to sun you know—and after they go in and eat and then they come and see about Enoch, want to see how he getting' along on the plantation. "Les go see how Enoch getting along." Doctor don' know very much. Know more than they know they were studying about it, but they couldn't see why this man stay sick all the time he were sick. Go there at night, "How you feeling, Enoch?" "Oh, so sick I'm just waiting on the Lord to come git me. I'm so sick I don't know what to do just waiting on the Lord. Po thing just sit there eating gravy and all I'm just waitin' on the Lord." So he stay like that two years. They ask Mary, "Mary does Enoch eat?" "Yes, Enoch eat up all the thing we cook for Enoch, eat everything." "Awright, went on study a plan we gon see if he is sick." See on that plantation they didn't have any white horse neither, neither white mule old grey mule so they went to another plantation far away and borrowed a white horse and in that yard they had a sycamore tree; you know how the sycamore tree are, and they got a white horse—borrowed from another plantation and they got a white boy off that plantation over there somewhere and also they got flour sacks. In those days, we bought flour in twenty-four-pound bags, you know cloth bag. She wash one of them flour sacks and starch good and stood it straight, and it were real white and put it on this boy's head like a crown. He had on a white suit all over had a white horse. Well, they knew there was no white horse on that place, and so this particular night, the moon was shining very bright they's gonna see is Enoch sick. Set this white boy down there dress this way. Mary, she's settin' down there, Enoch laying on the bed, she setting down patching up a quilt. Somebody out at the door there, "Who a hellow hellow" [drawn out]. The folk generally come to the door you know. She said, "Who dat?" Say, "It's the Lord, Mary. I come for Enoch." He heard it [meaning Enoch]. He said, "What he say, Mary?" She was tired of waiting for it. She said, "Enoch here Gawd. Gawd gon come at you, Enoch." Enoch said, "Mary, tell Gawd I ain't here" [whispering]. So he got underneath the bed you know, so if he did come he wouldn't see him. He got underneath the bed and Mary she say, "Gawd, Enoch ain't here," cause she was skaid. He said, "Mary, I can't go back devoid I got to have somebody. I guess you have to go with me." "No! No! Enoch come out from underneath the bed and go with Gawd. You are ready, I ain't ready yet, come and go with Gawd." He said say, "Mary, get back out the door I'm goin out by God tonight," He did it, and ran by that boy sitting on that horse. And that man run to freedom—ain't see him since. That is the last of him. She say, "Run, God, run, you have a footrace to catch Enoch tonight.

"The Leg of a Rabbit"

Story from St. Simons Island, Georgia, told by Bessie Jones

This man here met a lady here in Brunswick years and years back on the waterfront, and he was po and she was po they was very po both of em, but the girl was nice to the man, she follow him day after day around and looking after him. He was raggedy and patches everywhere his clothes was very patched up so they met on the dock and was talking out there on the dock so she liked him and he found out and he asked her would she be hisn' and she say yes she would marry next Sunday so anyway . . . he told her his job. He only was hauling around kindling wood you know lightwood lighter you know kindling lighter but its kindling wood and so when he was setting out to make a living and he wanted to let her know he didn't have no big job with nobody but she didn't care about that she liked him just for himself and so she just let him know that she really like him. After they had got married . . . you know how folks got to talk about people if we was to hear and now all that folks say that you took it. That's our motto you know they say if you're crooked you got roots and you are a hoodoo man. That's what they had thought about them. They got up and got themselves a car they got theyself a nice little home and they just saved together. You know now they got it? He told her he sold kindling wood for his living she say "Kindling wood." He say, "Yes, kindlin' wood." They sell the kindling wood on each side of town every day for a long time probably a year or so begin to see no more ragged folk no more street walking. Things began to change up; begin to look good had a nice home and everything. They said, "ununh" they didn't make that money that way. They got a rabbit foot for luck. They put out a song about it 'bout the rabbit foot.

Will you be mine? Oh yes

Will you be mine? Oh yes

I will marry you next Sunday after noon

My name is Robert Johnson all the way from

North Carolina

I am selling kindling wood to get along

Kindling wood kindling wood kindling wood

Kindling wood

I am selling kindling wood to get along

Yes I got the luck by the leg of a rabbit

All I got to do is just to reach out and grab it

Things are coming my way

Oh me me oh my I stay happy all the time

I don't have nothing to worry about cuz things

Are coming my way

I got luck by the leg of a rabbit

Things are coming my way

All I got to do is just to reach out and grab it

Things are coming my

Oh me me oh my I got such an automobile

And I can eat chicken and don't have to steal

Things are coming my way

I got the luck by the leg of a rabbit

Things are coming my way

All I got to do is just to reach out and grab it

Things are coming my way

"Gawd Scay the White Folks Too"

Told by John Davis

The late John Davis was a fine raconteur. He kept a straight face and thoughtful expression when he told a story, as though he were thinking something over. After he told a story through to the punchline, he'd laugh and repeat it over until he was through enjoying it himself. This story recalls the story in Dorson, American Negro Folktales*, 309, about the African American who justified his having run a red light by saying he thought red must mean for black folks to go, because green was the signal for the whites to go. This story also reflects closer parallels to the praying tree (see headnote to "Enoch Meets Gawd").*

Sharecropping you get the share and the old man get the crop. So a fellow was sharecropping, he didn't make nothing too much for 'bout two or three years. He had some good mule, good cow, a good horse, chicken. When he did made, he got the share. So, the boss man say, "Well, I'm got to have somepin' for the year of work, the money I give you. I'm coming in to take your cow, hog, chicken," so he didn't know what to do, he couldn't go nowhere else to get no money cuz he didn't know where no money was. So, he say he come in the next day, he say to his old lady, say, "You stay out and watch now. I'm goin' out in the woods and I'm a gon' to pray to God, maybe God will help you. I'm gon' pray to God for *my* stuff." So, he went down in the woods and kneel down and pray, "Oooh Lawd, please, I don't have nothing," He were down there praying so much. Get up and come tell him, "Let me show you something." Whole hosts going down there—chicken and cows, horse, and everything. He say, "You know one thing." She say, "What?" "I ain't know dat Gawd scay the white folks, too!"

"I Come from Heaven"

Told by Bessie Jones

Ms. Bessie Jones's style of performance was strong and vibrant. She stood to sing and tell stories, playing her tambourine and moving about in whatever space had been provided. She was a very engaging performer and pulled people in with her whenever she could. Ms. Jones tended to include more songs embedded in the stories, cantefable style, and more movement.

In her narrative style, she would stop to explain something as she told the story to make sure the audience understood what she was talking about and, at moments, to bridge the cultural gap, which was only recently opening up. Some of the stories were funny, some romantic, some risqué, some more serious, but she was an entertainer of high skill.

This is a story 'bout a stumpknocker preacher. Maybe you don't know what I'm talking about, he didn't gather no stump out in the woods. He is a man who have a lil church of his own, he's going round and preaching in different people churches; he ain't organized to a church, he just preach. Stumpknocker, he preach here then knock around there and he knock over yonder, he jus ain't got no regular place to preach. He will preach if you 'low him a chance if you got a big church to go to somewhere you can let him carry this meeting here today a few block? Anyway, this particular preacher that's what he was. He was real light-skinned fella, so there was another big deacon man there, fine peoples as they thought. He was corresponding with this man's wife this stumpknocker preacher was. But this man was a huntman he would go and hunt, he loved to hunt. He would go hunting; when he went hunting, he had a horn so they know he in the woods by that horn—they know how far he is by the sound of the horn. they know where he at and how far he is and when he coming in so he could steal all the stuff he went out. Well, in those days, mens wore BVDs. You all know what that is? They wore them BVDs, and he was a real light-skinned guy. He was in there him and this one man's wife they knowed the man be gone at least till one o'clock. After a while, the man knocked on the door not a horn blowed nothing! Just knocked on he door. It's you—quite naturally she slowed around bout letting him in because she "It can't be you who is that" [high voice]. "Open the do', it's me, open the do'." In those days, they had stick and dirt chimley. You know what a stick and dirt chimley are? Clay chimley made with clay and sticks and things. We used to have to stay in that kind of house the fireplace so long you could put half a rail on there long wood you know on the fire. That's the kind of fireplace they had. So anyhow, that's the kind of fireplace a wide fireplace the preacher had to go up the chimney that the best he could do he grabbed his clothes and went up the chimney, you know his shoes and his pants and went up the chimney. He goin to stay up there until the man go to bed then he say I can go home and it the best he could do. And so, she opened the do' for him after the preacher got up the chimney. She said, "I didn't know who you was. What you doin' home so early?" He said, "I got a what you call it cold trail my dog got a cold trail and I ain't got but one possum and I just got tired and come on home that was all of that." So, she went on to bed the bed was in the same big room near the fireplace there he went right to the fireplace and sit down. So, he sit to the fireplace and start to make a fire. She say, "Why don't you put your possum up and clean him in the morning." He is very—he mean what he say and he say what he mean. He say, "I'm gon clean my possum now." She said no more to him. She studied now he got to go out to there to do the best he can cause he got nothing to do with that you know was all she could do—ask him to wait till the morning—so he started raking on his side of the fireplace he rake the ashes back and get them hot and put that possum in there and get that hair burnt and scrape it that's the way they cleaned the possum, so he was getting it hot the smoke begin to go up the chimney it got too bad. He turned his head so all the way he could he couldn't do anything it got too bad on him up there so finally after a while he know he have to call or do something. So he decided that if the man catch him he knew that he was a stumpknocker preacher. He knew he call to a preacher. He decided to say something or another in the Lord's name because the man gonna kill him anyhow. He figured to his self you know. So he have them BVD's on and them great big knees and he was real, real fair-skinned man and he come down and started to study something to say and he come down and he just showed along here just at the top of his knees and a great big foot real light skin. He fell down there and he said, "I cum from Heabn" the man ain't see nothing but him all he seed was them big foots and them knees he looked up the chimney. "I didn't care if you come from Heabn, you can't get *my* possum!" And he run in the kitchen and that man run out well that preacher went on he knocked out a tree that night he knocked out a lot of stuff and he was gone and that was the end of him too, Lawd!

"The Paternity Fight"

Told by John Davis

You know, I remember when I was a boy, we just go miles and miles to church. Sometime we get off the train and we had to go ten miles to get to the church. So one preacher said he set out to preach at a church somewhere in the country. He thought he walk and get to the closest house to the church. When he woke up the next morning, he would go on to the service. The house settin' up on a hill just as he got started up the hill, he hear a boy come running down the hill, "Oh mister come and stop him, come and stop him. My daddy up there fighting." He run up there, and two men fighting sure enough. He turn to the lil boy, "Hey, hey, which one of them men your daddy?" He say, "That's what they fighting bout now."

---

1 These stories were told to me on Johns Island, South Carolina, Charleston, South Carolina, and St. Simons Island, Georgia, 1969–70, and were part of the collectanea in my PhD dissertation, "An Examination of African Retentions in the Folk Culture of the South Carolina and Georgia Sea Islands," Indiana University, 1977.

2 William Pipes, *Say Amen Brother!* (1951; repr., Detroit: Wayne State University Press, 1992); William Wiggins, *O Freedom!: Afro-American Emancipation Celebrations* (Knoxville: University of Tennessee Press, 1990); William Wiggins and Douglas DeNatale, eds., *Jubilation! African American Celebrations in the Southeast* (Columbia: University of South Carolina, 1994).

3 Alan Dundes, "The Making and Breaking of Friendship as a Structural Frame in African Folktales," *Structural Analysis of Oral Tradition*, eds. Pierre Maranda and Elli Köngäs Maranda (Philadelphia: University of Pennsylvania Press, 1971).

4 Thomas Wentworth Higginson, *Army Life in a Black Regiment* (Boston: Beacon Press, 1869), 47.

5 See "Cut a Step: Movement and Dance on The Sea Islands" in this volume.

6 Bessie Jones and Bess Lomax Hawes, *Step It Down: Games, Plays, Songs and Stories from the Afro-American Heritage* (New York: Harper and Row, 1972), 52.

7 Daryl Cumber Dance, *From My People: 400 Years of African American Folklore* (New York: W. W. Norton, 2002); Daryl Cumber Dance, *Shuckin' and Jivin': Folklore from Contemporary Black Americans* (Bloomington: Indiana University Press, 1978).

8 "Al," Personal Communication, 1977.

9 Keith Cunningham, *American Indians' Kitchen Table Stories* (Atlanta: August House, 1992).

10 Antti Aarne and Stith Thompson, *Types of the Folktale* (repr., Bloomington: Indiana University Press, 1995).

11 Richard M. Dorson, *American Negro Folktales* (Greenwich, CN: Fawcett, 1968), 146–147.

"A Weapon of My Song"

Two Sea Islands Poets

This chapter is a brief comparison of Léon Damas and two Sea Islands poets in the light of the philosophy of *négritude*. The two poems that are the focus of this chapter were written as a response to the pressures of imperialism felt by people of the African World. With the message of Langston Hughes in mind from his essay "The Artist and the Racial Mountain," one understands that the Euro-American populations may or may not be the intended audience.

The theme of beauty is found in the poetry of négritude, but with a twist of wryness born of the dislocated sense of self, a self acculturated by people who are morally convinced that they alone know what beauty is.[1] Having mastered the techniques and expressions of the European, the poet of négritude lashes out. The terms of the discourse are European, but the expression is African. Wilfred Cartey wrote:

> Necessarily, the tone of much of this poetry is condemnatory, the mood harsh. The poets catalogue the extent of the losses suffered by the black man through the exploitation, degradation and cruelties that brought about a diminution of forces and a decimation of peoples.[2]

Léon Damas, one of the fathers of négritude along with Léopold Senghor and Aimé Césaire, makes a statement in "Si souvent" (So Often),[3] which clearly describes his feelings of rage and frustration. He tells us he is suppressing his feelings, which might be assuaged by actually taking violent action. The poem evokes the city scene (if something heard can be a "scene") in which one hears all the cars skidding and skidding, but only occasionally the satisfying crash. He feels the rage, which leads up to violent anger over and over, but does not take the chance for a bloody catharsis. In "Savoir-vivre" (Good Breeding), he finds a falseness in the suppression of real emotions and being, symbolized for him by the necessity of covering the "yawning" chasm so as not to horrify anybody with a view of things unmentionable.[4] It all seems silly and vain to him, for the rest of the scene and culture surrounding him seems not to have much reality in contrast with that of his home. The yawn in the last section seems to be an almost regretful sigh, as deep as a yawn, for the life he left behind. He cannot participate with a whole heart in the existence of the cold place, cold in weather and feeling, nor can he deny that he came away, severing ties with his other environment.

"Sur une carte postale" (On a Post Card) stresses again the futility of the clash of alien cultures, both of which seem the same to him.[5] Someday, while they are too busy haggling over minutiae of provincial pride, the whole thing will self-destruct. The basic sense of alienation pervades these poems of Damas. He knows the world, for which he has such a distaste, well. His heart does not make a willing subject and the futility of European concerns turns him off. The poem "Solde" (Bargain) conveys the embarrassing situation of feeling discombobulated by culture shock in an alien environment with different food, clothes, manners, etc. The last verse communicates the deep passion that underlies the sense of foolishness with a nightmarish horror:

> I feel like an awful fool
>
> Accomplice among them
>
> Panderer among them
>
> Cutthroat among them
>
> My hands hideously red
>
> With the blood of their ci-vi-li-za-tion[6]

Here is an expression of the wearing of a mask which dissembles the depth and strength of the writer's shattering anger at what has happened to him and his people.

There are some similar poems that come from the Sea Islands of the United States. The poems do not match in artistic beauty the European elegance of Damas's unwillingly acquired command of French, but they do match, fiery syllable for fiery syllable, the honesty of the revealed feelings. Furthermore, we find a parallel to Senghor's threefold development, that is, the process of cognition or recognition leading to acceptance which leads to responsible action.

James Jenkins is an artist, not a poet, by profession. He is a musician and has been writing poetry off and on for some time. He went through the demonstrations in 1963 in Orangeburg, South Carolina, believing, as many did then, that showing people what was wrong would take care of everything. He was angry, but still talking to whites. Come 1968, the shock of the massacre at Orangeburg and the slow process of change, came realizations of how serious the situation was through contact with Stokely Carmicheal and the speeches of Malcolm X. This acceptance led to "the moment of truth" when it all boiled over and the poem "What is de Hour?" resulted. In the beginning of the poem, he shows the attitudes of those who do not realize the situation clearly enough to accept it and act without fear. He begins to define his own existence as black by the positing of white hypocrisy. He rejects the nonviolent philosophical position (Section VI) put forward so urgently in 1963. He determines near the end (Section IX) of the poem that the time has come to put into action/expression all the violent feelings he has been having over time, like Damas in "Si souvent."[7] For Damas, the time never comes to use the cane knife. For Jenkins, the moment for responsible action for his hero seems to have arrived. The ego of the poem is a man of middle or late age who decides he's seen enough to be able to judge for himself. This person, among the black militants of the 1970s, who were quite young, does not generally get credit for such a development taking place. He is in the age group accused of being "Uncle Tom." He says don't rock the boat, but it becomes clear that he is tired of being told that rewards and restitution for present pain will be forthcoming later in heaven by the reverend. At the end of the poem, the central character, the persona of the author, articulates his intention to take action.

The poem is written in a creolistic style, which is partly the Gullah language of the Sea Islands and partly Afro-American English (sometimes called Black English). The principles of négritude are operative here—the rejection of the cold, hostile, hypocritical, imperializing Euro-American is juxtaposed with the victimized, imperialized, sensitive, liberty-loving African man.

James Jenkins's poem "Orangeburg Massacre" is by a man who does not write at all. His letters are closer to written creole, measured by standard, edited English. His education stopped after high school, unlike Jenkins, who finished college and one year of graduate school. This poem was an articulate result of the horror of the Orangeburg Massacre,[8] for this man was one of the ones "they" wanted to catch in the trap. He was forewarned and escaped. The poem suddenly emerged as a cry of anger and anguish at the open demonstration of the white-imperialist supremacy.

The poem, even more than "What is de Hour?" shows négritude's contradistinction of the unfeeling white man as opposed to the warm, human nature of the African American man limited in education for centuries without even his history for comfort. Pinned down, then smacked in the face with the open, brutal exhibition of hostility and hate shown in an overkill situation, the author shows how their own violence and hatred blows back in their own faces and the Euro-American men will succeed only in destroying themselves and killing all the others. The poem tends to be somewhat open in style; it does not follow any verse pattern as the Jenkins poem does. It seems to be closer to the more open form of the French négritude poems of Damas.

For this author, the transition between the stage of acceptance of his own Africanity and the decision to take responsible action as a consequence of that acceptance was a rather long and very painful one. The realization of the sentiments found in this eloquent poem was a long time in coming, but the narrow escape and trauma involved with Orangeburg brought forth, in verbal form, the feelings that had not expressed themselves in action before.

The contrast stylistically in these six poems is obvious. It would seem that the sentiments, however, are similar and the frustrations congruent between African people wherever they may be, though their modes of expression may be different. Each is attuned to the culture that oppresses them, and so is forced to use the tools of that ambiance to fully express their feelings against that oppression. The philosophical position of négritude amongst French-speaking Africans was part of a movement that eventually led to freedom and self-government, more or less, or possibly only to a more subtle kind of neo-imperialism. The philosophy of négritude, if such could be called in this context, among Afro-Americans can never lead to such an autonomy unless Maulana Karenga could realize his dream to establish the five Southern states as a separate nation. Therein lies the greatest frustration of all for African Americans; they are more truly separated from their native area than continental Africans ever were and never felt genuinely a part of the alien society in which they live.

Two options are open on either end of a scale of conceivable action: to die bravely and at the expense of the other side or not to participate in the game by the other man's rules (or "the man's"). Homeless men who would rather be street-corner men than work for pittance wages choose the latter.[9] Some, like the Prosser brothers and the Black Panthers, choose the former.[10] There are fighters, however, who wish to stand and fight with socialized tactics rather than revolutionary. It is this frustration-loaded, ulcerative, heart-stopping middle road which our two Sea Islands poets have chosen. They continue to move with firm social and economic action, hopefully looking toward significant social change. It does not always come as a result of their planning; over time their seeds will bear fruit, but that does not seem clear compared to the immediacy of the sentiments of "Freedom Now" and "Black Control for Black Communities." The revolt at Attica was dashing to the hopes of the future,[11] so was Orangeburg—their action was not enough, the mountain high and obdurate, their enemy stubborn and implacable. Hence, the poems burst forth as an extension of the hope their road of action implies and concrete realization of themselves and their frustrating battle—the battle for life itself.

"What is de Hour?"

I

Dem white folks and dey niggers always say

"Prayin' Time!"

When talks 'bout freedom for people of

my kind.

But when dey talks 'bout dem

Cussed White,

Dey give all dem black boys

guns fo' fight!

II

Now, reverend do you think

dis is right,

To teach our chullan

day en night:

"Turn de ot'er cheek and Thou

shall not kill?"

Then when they gets old 'nough

to climb dem hill,

These durn blesses Crackers teach dem

to kill at will.

Innocent dark people in dey

Native land,

And lies 'bout "Democracy and

Freedom demand—"

To burn de baby, de chullan, de women

and butcher-up de man for dey land.

Reverend, look at this in a

bigger span,

Since you claims to be a

"God sent man—"

Who got all dem wisdom to get 'round

de devil in the sky,

Then tell me how to get 'round these

White folks' lie.

III

You know that talk 'bout "democracy"

Ain't true,

When dem crackers can't make thing work

right-yah for me and you.

Talk! Reverend and stop scratchin'

yo! head;

No sir! don't you start that lie 'bout freedom

for me when I is dead!

Cause if you can't help me get freedom

on dis earth,

I is surely not goin' to let you talk me to wait 'til

I is covered-up under dem dirt.

In de fuss place I don't see how

When I is buried in that ground—

Goin' fly out that deep hole to heaven

to get me a Freedom Crown.

IV

Hold it Reverend! don't tell me de Bible talks 'bout Wars

'cause white folks dun fool wid that Bible too,

And they just use that to butcher folks

like me and you.

But on de ot'er hand if you obey this Command,

Then why not start a war right yah

for our freedom in this land?

Dem folks over yonder didn't bo'er

us!

Dem white folks dun gone over there and start pickin'

fuss!

And we is so fool! Jus' runnin' over there

under dese Crackers' command!

Killin' dese poor people for their

own blesses land!

V

And de blasted thing that gives

me such a fit!

Is when dem niggers come back home

talkin' bunch of shit!

(dun been all over de world killin' folks dey

don't even know,

fo' dese same old crackers who's bringin'

hell! right in their door)

Got de nerve to say: "Shootin' and lootin' and burnin'

and all de ot'er mess!

Is de wrong way to get freedom fo' black folks—

Nonviolence and prayin' is de best!"

Now, what kind a shit is this

Brain washed I guess.

VI

Stop cussin!? huh! . . . This talk, talk, 'bout

nonviolence and prayin' ain't worth a cuss,

'Cause when dese crackers talks 'bout freedom—

fight or die we must!

Come on Reverend tell me what kind a

shit is this!

Oh, you done got mad 'cause you too

tied up in this myst.

Well, I, fo' one, never been quite that

bigger fool!

To let dese-yah Crackers use me fo'

Their wicked tool,

To shoot and loot and burn our friends

And come back home 'mong enemies talkin'

nonviolence and callin' on de lord.

VII

Don't call on de lord—he's sick of us

dumb folks now,

Let de Crackers used us to kill fo' their freedom

but fo' ours we ready fo' bow.

What we really need to do is use

Our blasted Mind!

To see that it's right to kill dem folks

who done rob us fo' every dime.

And cram us in dese nasty place to

live in Modern Time—

Dyin' from de starvation, de liquor and de wine.

VIII

But if we ain't a bunch of fools Reverend—

What else can we be?

No Reverend! don't you talk that religion

talk to me.

Y'all kinda religion Reverend jus'

Ain't worth a damn!

See I believe in freedom on earth

for every livin' man.

Look at a not'er thing Reverend

how dis Johnson man stand,

Jus' done told dem boys keep burnin' and bombin'

and lootin' and shootin' in foreign land—

Had de nerve to stand on TV wid

his religious sham,

('Cause he been gettin' doses of his medicine where

he got dem niggers Cram)

To tell all America to set a day of

worship for de Supreme Man.

You know dese-yah White folks wid that

religion been foolin' us too long.

So some of us you call non-Christian

goin' to have to stop this wrong.

IX

But de fuss thing we goin' have to know—

What Is De Hour?

Is we gonna still fool 'round yah like little boys

or gonna fight fo' "Black Power"?

I may be pretty old and ain't been

to de school,

But let me tell you right now Reverend,

I ain't that bigger fool!

To think that dis is not de proper time

and de proper hour—

When we black folks gon' have to stand up

and fight fo' some Power!

Dem White folks dun got so much power

they stand over we like a tower,

Keepin' us down and kicking' us 'round every day

On de hour.

X

Well good night Reverend—I think you got

a mind full to think over,

And don't keep dem black folks in that Church

fo' feed you and wait fo' Jehovah.

When dem smilin' sisters ask

"What Is De Hour?"

Say: "Baby! God done told me—

We must stand up fo' Black Power!"

"So long, brother Mose, I'll begin

The next hour!"

"Orangeburg Massacre"[12]

White people cried in the night for fear

of what is written in history books that

might they

did.

Fear, afraid for their lives—

never lived

like their victims did,

Their brothers, so tired

of trying

to just tell something.

The Indians tried too (for longer even

from the beginning of the invasion

the white horde)

And they gave up.

Black people without even the crumbs—

the reservations—

to go to and drink and forget,

and remember and tell and retell

the old history—the beautiful thousands

of years, of living, of letting live

and being, with everything living

being God

NOT PLAYING GOD

The black man, even denied telling his history . . .

White man, he could of been more a brother

to you than your own twin.

But you still don't hear,

just kill.

Can't get enough of your own fear

Your history is fear . . .

Black men aren't in your books

but you can't stop men from being

their own history.

You could be men any time, you know,

but you save face in flurries of a go

and send in the troops,

surround the campus,

begin the massacre.

Listen! You are killing *yourself*.

You've done it for so long.

Our brothers are dead now

lying in white porcelain morgues

waiting to be taken back

to the rich black

soil—where more will follow.

You! Don't cry for fear. Cry for hate!

Bullets and words will not swallow

but only feed

your disgusting fire!

We all die anyway.

Relax, Man, you've had your day.

Our brothers in jail

they are sentenced to death

one way or another.

But they are men.

A hater, a killer

(Yes! You! Don't stand in your palace

and disclaim guilt. If you don't know,

we do),

not a man, gave up

manhood for bloody history,

murderous "Cause," night dreams

in terror of castration

by those he "lowered"

to the animals.

The Indians knew long before you came.

The Africans knew thousands of years

before you

brought those (who didn't die in passage):

Animals are creatures of God.

Higher than you were, are, tonight

you proved it.

My country tis of thy people your dying,

the Indian sang.

"The Welfare and Security of the Majority . . ."

McNair, Man, stop talking!

You don't know anything.

Your actions speak for that fact.

Do our 17 and 18 year old men die

telling you something you don't understand?

You were a man once . . .

but you don't remember?

Then so be it!

"Their interests," is that what you are for?

We are not interested; not now.

Well, you said it. So be it.

If it is your wish . . .

WE WILL ALL DIE TOGETHER!

---

[1] The chapter title is taken from a poem of James Weldon Johnson. *Studies in the Literary Imagination*, Atlanta, Ga.: Georgia State University, 3:1, April, 1970: 65–72.

[2] Wilfred Cartey in introduction to Norman Shapiro, ed. and trans., *Négritude: Black Poetry from Africa and the Caribbean* (New York: October House, 1970), 23.

[3] Leon Damas, qtd. in Norman Shapiro, ed. and trans., *Négritude: Black Poetry from Africa and the Caribbean* (New York: October House, 1970), 46–47.

[4] Ibid., 50–51.

[5] Ibid.

[6] Ibid, 52–53.

[7] Ibid, 40–43.

[8] See note 1.

[9] Ulf Hannerz, *Soulside* (New York: Columbia University Press, 1969).

[10] Martin and Gabriel Prosser led a rebellion in Virginia in 1800.

[11] A revolt took place at Attica Prison (1971) in upstate New York under Governor Nelson Rockerfeller. A number of prisoners and guards were killed and wounded.

[12] Excerpt from *Gratitude from A Black Brother* by James Jenkins. The Orangeburg Massacre took place during the time that Robert McNair was governor of South Carolina. The author of "Orangeburg Massacre" indicated that a note should be added to the effect that he was grateful to Roger Phenix of New York City (who was living on Johns Island at the time) who helped with the writing down of the poems.

Joe Hunter, Johns Island, South Carolina, 1969.

"Let the Word of My Mouth"

Two Worker Bards Protest in Word and Song

T raditional songs have helped the African American people to survive from slavery times until now.[1] This function of the music continues, as conditions of near slavery such as sharecropping and the use of migrant workers persist. Remus Lee Prather lives in a situation close to peonage and has little freedom, personal or otherwise. Joe Hunter gets jobs when he can, driving trucks or going off with other men from the island as a migrant worker to other areas. His refusal to bind himself into the cycle which perpetuates the bondage, as well as his bachelorhood, leaves him freer than Remus but more precariously balanced economically.

Remus Lee Prather, thirty-three, came to the island some years ago as a migrant worker from Florida and settled on the island in the upper Bohicket Road area. He is married and has children. He lives and works on the land of the man who employs him. His life is poor, but he does not wish to upset the balance of things. His music gives him the outlet he needs and the illusion of control within his life. He rides the tractor and sings to himself, shaping his music if not his own life. His ability to do what he likes with his music lessens the feeling of helplessness that typifies his dependent life. He sings gospel material and likes to arrange both the music and the movement of the group. He has a sense of the dramatic approach needed to "put over" the songs and involve the audience, which is strongly based in the folk-religious traditions of his people. He plays many instruments including banjo and guitar and other items not normally classified as instruments, such as spoons, washboards, and jar tops. He also works over popular songs and likes to listen to them and sing them, making of them an expression of his own situation; "Big Boss Man" was one of these.

Joe Hunter, twenty-six, comes from a family that has been on the island for a long time. His grandfather, a fisherman, was an active tradition bearer and taught songs to his children. He also insisted on their doing the songs in the "right" style, that is, in the old tradition of the Islands. Joe's uncle, mother, and aunts, who are strong singers, mostly of church material now as they are living for God, used to sing "blues" but not now. Active in the church and the Moving Star Hall Society (one of many insurance societies for help during sickness and death), their outlet is there. Joe knows and makes up gospel songs, but he sees himself primarily as one of the last of the old time bluesmen, such as Son House, Lightnin' Hopkins, and Muddy Waters. He also responds to the jukebox material but reworks it as he reproduces it to suit his own needs at the moment.

Remus Lee composes his songs and then sings them, or arranges the song and then teaches the arrangement to the group. There are distinct internal and external stages in his composition. Joe, on the other hand, is more likely to feel, express, and compose simultaneously in response to events and people. He too sings in solitude, like Remus on the tractor, giving vent to his sublimated desires and ambitions. He hopes one day to make records and make something more of himself than seems possible in his present life.

The difference between the two singers is that they are involved in different aspects of the music and what goes with it. The communication aspect of their work is more important than the music or the words themselves. Remus Lee and his group sing gospel material like any of the modern groups— such as the Gospel Pearls, the Mighty Clouds of Joy, the Highway Q.C.'s. They do not rely so much, as the more professional groups do, on the tricks of amplification systems but more on their own voices and ability to move the congregation. The response they receive and the feeling they generate is the important aspect of it. They sing "Twelve Gates to the City," "Wade in the Water," and other well-known traditional songs.

Joe Hunter, on the other hand, works hard by himself to communicate with his audience. Occasionally, he sings gospel material when the "spirit" moves him. At one point, he broke into a shuffling dance, which was simply moving back and forth in a four- or five-foot space while singing:

My father and my mother are going over there,

My father and my mother are going over there,

My father and my mother are going over there,

Going cross the river at last.

He repeated it several times, substituting different members of his family and group of friends. His next numbers were reworkings of jukebox material, "It's My Own Fault, Baby," "Bright Lights, Big City," " I Need Your Loving So Bad."[2] This last song is sung in the traditional verse and chorus frame:

[e.g.]

I jumped in the river

and I started to drown

I thought about you

and I couldn't go down.

[Refrain]

Cuz I need your loving so bad, so bad, so bad.

Cuz I need your loving so bad, so bad, so bad.

Harry Jones of Morgan State College pointed out that consumed or elapsed time is of importance in these blues no matter whether it is old, traditional delta blues or the newer styles. The bluesman can make up words that fit the time slot without disturbing the audience or the meaning too much. The intonations, a part of the utterances of songs, and the movement and gestures, which go along with the singing and guitar playing, are of equal or more importance than the words taken by themselves.[3]

Textual examination or comparison is not a central consideration in this chapter. Samuel Charters, Paul Oliver, Leroi Jones, and others have done sensitive analyses of the words of the blues and the people who sing them.[4]

The main concern here is the evanescent complex of communication and entertainment that defies reduction to paper. The function of the musicians in this setting and their expression of the community's needs results in phenomena that could not be compared or reviewed properly except through videotape or sound movies.

Expressive culture of African people is something which must be approached holistically because to isolate the songs from the people leaves us in a very precarious position for making meaningful statements about the community and its members.

Both these men have traveled as migrant workers, usually in a contract situation where they are taken in buses or closed semitrucks to the site of the work to be done. Not only are they herded about for purposes of transportation, but also the camps are closed at night so they are thrown together in enforced community for the duration of the job. The camps provided are of the rudest sort, with few conveniences. Slowly but surely, the government is beginning to provide schooling and other needs for the otherwise neglected children and adults of this classless category.

One of the results of the formations of this community is the adjustment of its members to each other, because they are heavily interdependent for anything to make their lives bearable. Often illiterate and essentially unable to verbalize their plight, they love to hear Joe sing out their troubles, personal and otherwise. His songs are able to distill and express their longings and frustrations. Any material that he can use in this situation is pressed into service. This vent for their feelings serves two functions at least. One, the amount of disruptive behavior, fights and so on, is kept to a minimum, which benefits the people personally, perhaps, but chiefly benefits the "man." It is a self-regulatory form of social control. If the violence were not kept under control, that is, directed inwardly at members of the group, it would turn outwards and could be, and occasionally is, very destructive. Migrant workers are carried all over the country and have no stake in the communities into which they are brought, so the normal laws and sanctions and benefits of a permanent community have little or no meaning for them. Having so little education, they have no choice but to follow the crops as the season progresses.

Their folklore then is a potpourri of bits and pieces of popular culture and traditions from all over the country and beyond. Cubans, Puerto Ricans, Mexicans, Bahamians, and West Indians are all brought here as contract workers. Elements of popular culture from all of these areas, as well as the influences from African cultures, which affect them all, contribute to the stream of their folk culture. The mixture that results is highly suitable to the needs of the people involved. For obvious reasons, they are not tuned in to the standards of the dominant society; they both avoid its negative attitudes toward them and yearn for some of the things that Hollywood or TV images show them. On the whole, however, their standards of artistic experience of any kind are fluid and unfocused except toward their needs at the moment. The fact that the music may occasionally sound discordant and roughly executed to our ears is not important to them. The function of the music is much more important to them as fulfillment in their lives. The musicians are part of their group working alongside them every day, but when time off comes, they are specialists, singing and playing when they are moved or asked to do so. Their performance is uneven, often played with guitars lacking their full complement of strings[5] or on instruments made of ordinary items, which serve the function of instruments in this context as mentioned above in Remus Lee's repertoire. The organization of the music is loose and relatively unstructured in both composition and personnel. The resulting performance is just as likely to be transcendently beautiful as mediocre or awful to listen to. The people within this third world group are involved with the performance and enjoyment of the music, and for them, this experience is as good as the perfection of style and performance normally committed to instrumental and vocal development by the professional musicians in the dominant society.

The above situation applies to both men in terms of their function within the communities in which they find themselves. On the whole, they are mostly adaptable to the changing scene. In their own cultural milieu, however, they are quite resistant to change, to the point where they are almost unteachable. They have a firm sense of themselves and their identity and are quite satisfied with their culture and language. They see no need to acculturate to a society which has such different values. The participation of members of a society may fluctuate according to the amount of interference from the dominant culture. The degree of genetic integrity, the number of people who are Sea Islands Creole monolinguals, the proportion of literacy in English, and the numbers of school enrollments all offer a guide to the high retention of Africanisms in their culture, which was documented by Herskovits in *The New World Negro* and *The Myth of the Negro Past*.[6]

There is a relationship between such indicators of acculturation and the teachability of the people on the Islands, and it makes the middle-class, white-oriented education seem meaningless to the Islanders. Formal teaching gets low results partly because of the attitudes of the schoolteachers and administrators; the selection of useful elements from the surrounding culture brings together the material used by the artists in their creative process. They edit out the superfluous material and process what they need to use for their special purposes as well as the needs of their audience. Both of these men are hopeful of a new life less dependent on the factors that control them and their present existence now. On the other hand, Joe Hunter is also looking for a new life more radically different even than that envisaged by Remus Lee. An age gap of approximately ten years separates them and their hopes. Joe wants to succeed in the recording world in order to make money, not only for his own enrichment but also to help the people who are part of his life now.

Their ambitions, their feeling for their people, their personal frustrations, religious background and sentiments, and last but not least, their folklore influence and shape their creative impulses. The expression of it is partly influenced by their own personal need to pour out their feelings and the deep need of the community, both permanent and temporary, for its minstrels who express their feelings, entertain them, and give them some measure of structure and security in a world containing a disproportionate amount of unreason.

---

[1] This essay was originally published as "'One of These Days': The Function of Two Singers in the Sea Island Community," *Studies in the Literary Imagination* 3, no. 1 (April, 1970), 65–73; it was taken from my fieldwork on Johns Island, South Carolina.

[2] Songs popular in the late 1960s and the 1970s.

[3] Harry Jones, Personal Communication, 1969.

[4] Samuel Charters, *The Roots of the Blues* (Boston: M. Boyars, 1981); Samuel Charters, *The Country Blues* (New York: Da Capo Press, 1975); Paul Oliver, *The Story of the Blues* (Philadelphia: Chilton Book Co., 1969); LeRoi Jones (Amiri Baraka), *Blues People* (New York: W. Morrow, 1963).

[5] The instruments often get damaged in the rough travelling conditions or during fights in the trucks. I have spent time working in the migrant camps of New York State and have seen firsthand the risks and dangers in the lives of the workers.

[6] Melville Herskovits, *The Myth of the Negro Past* (New York: Harper and Bros., 1941); Melville Herskovits, *The New World Negro* (Bloomington: Indiana University Press, 1967).

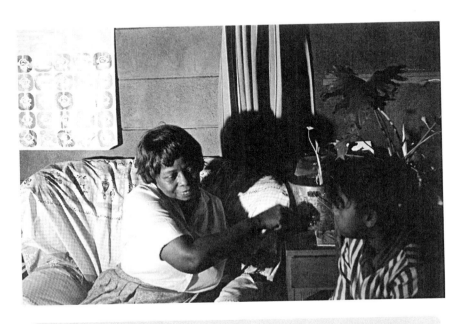

Ms. Bessie Burkes, St. Simons Island, Georgia, 1970s, telling "Tom Wasn't There."

Cootah and Rabby Compare Notes

Sea Islands and Yoruba Folklore

I n the introduction to *African Sculpture*, William Fagg states, "Art, in fact, like language, religion, social institutions, and customary law, is one of the ways in which a tribe (by its nature an 'in-group') distinguishes itself from its neighbors."[1] This particularity of African art forms (including verbal) may well serve a group's search for identity, even though its members have suffered anonymity and undergone vast changes. Tales on both sides of the Atlantic establish positive reaffirmations of cultural identity of a people who daily experience positive and negative reinforcements which "distinguish them from their neighbor."

North America, according to Melville Herskovits, has the lowest retention of "Africanisms" in the whole New World.[2] This statement does not mean there are none at all. It indicates two things mainly—first, the state of research at the time of Herskovits's compilation; and second, the inability of American society to acknowledge such phenomena, though research data were within its grasp.

Suffice it to say, Africanisms are there to be found. Masked figures, which appear in the ubiquitous animal stories, are present in the heritage of African people, which is perhaps best known through Joel Chandler Harris's bowdlerized versions of transplanted West African stories.[3] The human beings masked as animals appear in Richard M. Dorson's *American Negro Folktales* as well as in other collections of African American folklore.[4] Abigail Christensen's early (1892) collection of Sea Islands tales has animal *personae* representing frailties and weaknesses of human kind.[5] Charles Jones's collections from his grandfather's plantation on a Georgia island contain animal fables with morals attached at the end of each.[6] Stoney and Shelby's *Black Genesis*, also from the Sea Islands area, contains a group of aetiological stories told in Sea Islands Afrish with animal actors.[7]

Ananse, the Ashanti spider, occurs in the Americas as Anansi (Annancy) or Aunt Nancy. In the Caribbean, the animal characters appear often; in Jamaica, Anansi, the trickster, is made responsible for almost anything that goes wrong. Louise ("Miss Lou") Bennett fell into a deep pool of water in London after a 1992 performance and when she was fished out in front of her horrified husband and audience, she went to the microphone and triumphantly declared, "Anansi mek um" (Anansi did it). The audience howled.[8] Stories in Daniel J. Crowley's study of the Bahamas include the character "Boy Nasty," a transmutation of B'Anansi.[9] Elsie Clews Parsons has also published a group of animal stories, many of which she collected from schoolchildren on Lady's Island, South Carolina.[10] A few tales show up in Guy and Candie Carawan's *Ain't You Got a Right to the Tree of Life?*[11]

Clearly, in these stories the characters represent human beings acting out familiar situations that reflect many positive aspects of life as well as man's inhumanity to man. The people's vital cultural concerns tend to show up in these stories. Melville Jacobs, upon questioning his informants, found that they knew the animal *personae* were humans.[12] E. E. Evans-Pritchard found in researching the Tuve stories of the Azande (East Africa) that the use of animal characteristics and human personalities were intermixed, sometimes featuring the keen knowledge of animal (including human) behavior.[13]

The masks used in West African societies are often displayed in museums and books as isolated objects. Little notion of the artistic and behavioral context and significance is conveyed in such displays making the masks merely interesting and exotic objects. In reality, masks are expressions of areas of importance within the society. Emerging fully formed from the carving process, they are invested with significance by the cloth raffia, cowries, feathers, and other materials with which they are embellished; the body movements of the wearer endow them with dramatic liveliness and power. The mask bearer's human characteristics are hidden or individuality de-emphasized by the masks. The embodied masks operate as arms of justice and arbiters of socially unacceptable behavior; they are like the story characters because the humanity of the person is covered. It leaves the actors freer to tell the story, teach the morals, or mete out justice. The masks lend a certain anonymity to the person as he enacts the force of justice or the voice of a god. As the carving appears from the surrounding wood, the masks become visible with the support of the secret societies, musicians, and preparers. In the stories, the teaching and amusing aspects of masks find acceptance.

The animal stories are particularly "safe" in the moral, political, and social sense. Whatever the creatures do is acceptable because they are nonhuman, therefore outside the limits of societal constraints. The stories whose *personae* are the animals are didactic in purpose, in many instances, and entertain the children and adults as well. The issue of what brings joy to people in spite of the weight of life's vicissitudes is binding to all humans who can find something to amuse even in tales containing some cruelty. T. O. Beidelman's articles on Hyena and Rabbit among the Kaguru illustrate an interpretation of how such stories can both entertain and convey a deeper structural meaning.[14] Among Afro-Americans, of course, the masked figures acted out the rage, frustration, and hostility they felt and were experiencing within the confines of the dominant society, which though featuring Christianity as an ideal value, actually rewarded aggressive and hostile behavior.

The masked figures are not only amusing, entertaining, and pedagogical in function, but are also acceptable to humans as imitators and preceptors of their behavior. Although in Afro-American folk drama the masked actors seem not to have the wide usage and significance as they have in the West African societies, there are instances of (face) masked figures in North America in recent times. On Johns Island, South Carolina, the Wesley Methodist Church presented a revival of their traditional "Devil Play." The Devil, played by a woman, was a humorous character—homely rather than ugly. The other characters in the play (which was a series of morality sketches ostensibly) were costumed in ragged plantation-style work clothes of a bygone era. Most of the people played themselves—the drunkard was the drunkard and duly went to hell with the gamblers, the dancers, etc.—so that one might say they were very "thinly" masked.[15]

Masked figures appear chiefly in the folk stories. The folk drama was more common and widespread in the past. The individuals in the tales are people in full body animal masks, much like the African masked people whose anonymity enables them to put across certain ideas which might be offensive if personalized. The songs and stories are narratives with dramatic elements, which the narrators add according to their skill. The *cantefable* forms of them include songs and refrains, which often give the audience a chance to participate.

There arises the question in looking at a group of stories collected by persons from outside the culture, whether or not their collections are representative of the complete corpus of material extant within the society as a whole. Furthermore, we find in the older collections, such as Parsons's and Crowley's, use of terminology which is nowadays unacceptable unless we understand it within the context of the time and the group in which it occurs. With the more open channels of communication, we no longer put dots in place of risqué words, and the collections of tales feature more stories starring humans and their foibles unmasked. Some animals in Yoruba, Kaguru, Bahamian, and Sea Islands groups' representations and antics have helped to ease the burdens of people far from home whose struggles for survival have been much the same throughout the African World.

In Yoruba folklore, the chicken seems to be a most important creature. It occurs in the plastic arts in various forms and media.[16] Chickens are important also in the Ifa literature as sacrifices.[17] The chicken appears in the creation story, spreading the earth so there would be some place to inhabit and grow things.[18] Birds are generally featured in the iron bird wands and in the myth to which Ogunbowole gave the title "Trickster and Fate." Trickster steals a cock and Fate changes himself into a bird in order to pursue Trickster, who has climbed a silk cotton tree from which he may not be separated, according to Thompson's analysis of the myth.[19] Bird motifs appear in woven and appliqué cloth, especially the Dahomean cloth, which formerly contained the insignia of kings of the pre-French Colonial era. Nowadays, the cloth is produced in quantity, so it does not always have the proverbial significance of the old cloth. Buffalo, Bear, Fish, and Lion also appear in the lineup.[20]

Tortoise is a major Yoruba trickster/hero. Ayo Bamgbose posits three classes of Yoruba folktales: moral, why, and tortoise.[21] Many of the tales have a display of cleverness by the tortoise as a feature, which might suggest that such ability to maneuver is an admired trait. Tortoise appears in the plastic arts, too.[22] Jan Westcott theorizes that the trickster figure is a socially approved outlet for the tensions and difficulties of surviving within a group in which the social hierarchy is fairly rigidly structured.[23] The trickster is an embodiment of the agency of evil and disruptive behavior so that responsibility for such acts will not fall on persons in the society. The trickster Eshu-Elegba is strongly associated with sexuality, admittedly a difficult force which most human societies seek to control in various ways. The trickster, often an animal figure, has license in different societies to act outside the confines of the rules. Tortoise is admired, as are Hare, Brer Rabbit, Anansi, and others, for his ability to shift in and out of the law. The cruelty of his tricks are wish fulfillments for some of the listeners who may not dare to do such things, but love to hear of those who get away with it.

Tortoise, among other animal tricksters, appears in the Americas:

> Mr. Bullfrog and Mr. Terrapin was having a race. One went one road, the other went this one, and at the forks of the road they was going to meet up. The bullfrog jumped in a rut, and a truck come along over him, and busted both eyes. Along came Mr. Terrapin, crawling. "Well Mr. Bullfrog, you made it?" He said, "Yes, I made it, mighty hardest." Says, "What's the matter with your eyes?" Says, "Oh, just a little straining on them."
>
> (The terrapin didn't have sense enough to know the bullfrog hopped faster than he could crawl.)[24]

*

> Every day John had to tote water from the bayou, and every time he'd go to the bayou he would start fussin'. "I'm tired of toting water every day." The next day he went to the bayou and he repeated the same thing (you know just like you repeated the same thing). So last one day John went to the bayou, the turtle was sitting on a log. Turtle raised up and looked at him, and told John, "Black man, you talk too much."

So John didn't want to think the turtle was talking. He went back to the bayou, got another bucketful of water. The turtle told him the same thing. John throwed the buckets down, took and run to the house, and called Old Marster, and told him the turtle was down there talking. And so Old Marster didn't want to go because he didn't believe it. But John kept telling him the turtle was talking.

So finaly Old Boss 'cided he could go. But he told John if the turtle didn't talk he was going to give him a good beating. So they all went down to the bayou, and when they got down to the bayou the turtle was sitting on a log with his head back halfway in his shell.

And so John told the turtle, "Tell Old Marster what you told me." So John begged the turtle to talk. So the turtle still didn't say anything. So Old Marster taken him back to the house, and give him a good beating, and made him git his buckets, and keep totin' water.

When John got back down to the bayou, the turtle had his head sticking up. John dipped up his water, and the turtle raised up and told him, say, "Black man, didn't I tell you you talk too much?"[25]

*

All dem rich men dat countee day got up a race. De fas'es' racehorse was ter race wid Cootah. So day set a day fo' de race. An' dese big mans put de money up. Now, Cootah know what was de amoun' o' money, an' de fas' racehorse know what was de amoun' o' money. So Cootah ax fo' a day. Dey 'gree to gi' Cootah dat day ter decide what he goin' to do. De race was twenty mile wid dat racehorse. An' dat day he get his fam'ly o' cootah, an' set a cootah to ev'y mile. So de nex' day was de race. Well, de judge decide when the race mus' start. Dey start off. An' de man 'rive to was (one) mile, 'cause de cootah was dere. 'Rive to anoder mile-pos', dere was a cootah dere. Judge at bof' en'. When de racehorse 'rive up to de twenty mile, de cootah was dere. Dey had to decide in cootah an' racehorse favor, an' each get half. De en' of de story. When it rained, it rained on Cootah.[26]

*

De terripin an' de deer ha' a race. Mr. Terripin git all his kinspeople togeder an' place one at each mil'pos'. W'en Mr. Deer git to de fi's' mil'pos', Mr. Terripin say, "Ise Heah, Mr. Deer." Mr. Deer jum' to de nex' mil'pos', but Mr. Terripin was deh; and so 'twas at ebery mil'pos'. Mr. Terripin say, "Well, which one can run de fas'est, Mr Deer?"— "I can't fo' say, fo' I still t'ink Ise de fas'est runner in de worl'."—Maybe you air, but I kin head you off wid sense."[27]

*

Hare an' Cootah goin' to have a race. Man count, "One, two, three! Le's start off!" Hare look back, didn' see de cootah. Say "I goin' to sleep." When he woke, he hurry to de river. Cootah say, "Man, it's good down here."[28]

His animal characteristics of slowness and smallness are capitalized upon in the stories about races with other animals. The fact that he wins is due only to his craft and guile. Tortoise is an everyman trying to make it the best way he can. The Bahamian trickster animal heroes, chiefly B'Booky and B'Rabby, are openly acknowledged to be people doing their best to get away with sheer chicanery—one of the few avenues left open to Africans for any opportunity to get ahead.

Once upon a time, was a merry old time, the monkey chew tobacco and he spit white lime. Cockero jump from bank, and never touch he toes to water yet (rhythmically chanted). Now, this was B'Booky and B'Rabby again, two t'iefing Niggers. Man, this man had a shop. Couldn't find anyone to wait in the shop, so he had to hire B'Booky and B'Rabby. Now, this day, the man keep missing his butter, missing his butter. Say, "Wonder where the butter's going to I ain't see no money coming in for no butter, but there's missing it." B'Booky first swallow, "Son, I don't t'ief, Son, I's a good boy." B'Rabby tell him, "Be like me, Son, I don't t'ief." Man say, "Okay, you don't t'ief, eh! I can find out where all this butter going to." This day, now he miss some more butter. He say, "Okay now, I going put you all two boys in the sun, and who melt eat the butter." They ain't melt that day. The sun is a little too cold. The next day it wasn't too hot. This day now, the sun hot hot hot hot! Put them in sight of the sun, ain't see nothing but butter run out of them. Man say, "Okay, you going pay for all my butter." Two Niggers were working about three weeks, and they ain't get paid.[29]

Themes of prime importance to any given group will keep recurring in their folklore as noted above. This repetition is not always found, as some items are so much a part of the daily scene that they are taken for granted, and so do not appear in the lore although they are basic to the culture. In the introduction to *Folk Tales and Fables* by Gurrey and Itayemi, ". . . as expected; they are the natural mode of behaving, and so there is no need for the storyteller to point them out; for example, hospitality to strangers and politeness are never commented on."[30] They see three primary themes in oral lore:

1) the value of knowledge,

2) the importance of good social behavior, and

3) the upbringing of children.

The trickster's abilities to manipulate and maneuver may not be classified as knowledge, but cleverness, which can be coupled with common sense in some instances. In the matter of tale analyses, Bamgbose divides the stories into three categories: moral, why, and tortoise.[31] The first two are concerned with abstract quantities, but the third presupposes the knowledge of Tortoise's qualities on the reader's part. What this classification does show is the importance of Tortoise's (trickster/fate) character. This depiction also shows the supremacy of Tortoise as a mover and manipulator in Yoruba folklore. The story of the fox who talked the leopard right back into the cage out of which he (the leopard) had just talked himself is a fine illustration of the value of persuasive speech. One might say the tale concerns the value of knowledge and how to use and communicate it. Needless to say, the other two items involve communication as well. They bring up the point that the stories express the values of the people while entertaining them. The themes of hunger, the fear of it, and the consequent greed show up particularly in the tortoise stories. The story "The Greedy Tortoise and the Generous Porcupine" has an approximate parallel in Carawans's collection, "The Rabbit and the Partridge."[32]

Throughout Afro-American lore we find tremendous concern with food, its acquisition, and sources. The selling-the-grandmother story, which occurs among the Kaguru, appears in almost the same form in the Sea Islands collection.[33]

> Oncet upon a time Ber Rabbit an' Ber Wolf made a frien' an' dey agree to sell deir moder, an' buy some bread an' butter. So dey was goin' to do ahction, an' had deir moder tied on to de wagon. An' Ber Rabbit say, "Oh look at somet'in' good! I see somet'in' good!" An' Ber Wolf looked. An' Ber Rabbit loose his own moder an' t'n his own moder loose while Ber Wolf was drivin' de horse. An' when dey got to de ahction, poor Ber Wolf had to sell his mother alone. Anyhow, Ber Wolf bought de bread an' butter wid his own money.[34]

The Bahamian stories of the house filled with food are another example:

> Well, anyhow, Rabby sing the house up in the air, "Mary go up so high, Mary go up so high, Mary go up so high, till he touch the sky." The house going up so high. Any, John Brown, Rabby didn't stand, he sort he stuffs, he get he lard, he pork, he beef, he flour, he rice, he grits, and everything like that, and when he think he had a load, he sing the house down.[35]

"The Tortoise in the Animal Kingdom" story in Ayodele Ogundipe's collection seems to combine some of the elements of both these stories—the killing of the mother in the famine, the trickster's deception, and the food source in the sky.[36] In the story "How the Dog Became a Domestic Animal" by a Yoruba informant, the race between Tortoise and Hare appears.[37] The same story is in the Parsons Sea Islands collection in three versions.[38] "Too Great a Pride Can Lead to Disaster" includes monster people in a neighboring town who were only heads.[39] B'Head (contracted Brother Head) is a trickster in Crowley's collection:

> Damn, when he juke the knife in the hog, damn if a head
> jump out the hole [in the ground]. Was only a head, no
> body, A head jump out the hole, say, "Oh damn," he say,
> "you think you want to eat allee."[40]

Yoruba folk stories seem very concerned with social interrelationships and proper behavior. Though the animals trick, they are often caught by their own maliciousness. The humans are supposed to act in a moral manner, more in the sense of what is right within that society than any sort of Christian "morals." The interdependence of the members of the society and their interactions occur in the stories in the Ifa corpus of Yoruba Society as well as elsewhere. Social skills and verbal dexterity are of maximum importance. Association patterns are as intricate and complex as the hierarchy of gods.

The same values are found in the Sea Islands. The social network is complex and obligatory for all members of the group and involves reciprocal obligations in social, economic, and emotional categories. What shows up very strongly in the folklore in the Sea Islands, however, is the ever-present problem of survival and the violence visited upon them by the dominant society, expressed in their violent tricks on each other in the stories.

Closer examination of the tale collections published from Yorubaland and the Sea Islands area may establish the kind of evidence that may well help to pinpoint the movement of African peoples and learn more of their history. The last line in "The Moon and the Sun" in Ogundipe's collection— "And sometimes, they both meet and have an argument, that is when we have an eclipse"—tells a story which is found on Johns Island, South Carolina.[41] The story contains mythic elements saying that an eclipse is a battle for supremacy between the sun and moon to see whether it will always be night or day. When asked what had been decided, the narrator (W. C. Saunders) said they have not resolved the conflict yet, so we have half night and half day.[42]

Beier, in his article about dogs, opens up another interesting question.[43] Here one would find parallels between the attitudes of the Sea Islanders and the Yorubas toward dogs as working members of society. The Islanders hunted more in times past than they do now because of increasing restriction by the Euro-Americans on their movement. More investigation is needed on this topic. Shango appears with a dog in Babatunde Lawal's dissertation.[44] The dog wears beads and looks well fed, a bit bulky around the middle. Other animals occur in the representation of masks, such as chickens or birds, ram horns, snails, and horses.

In Yoruba mythology, Obatala steals a horse and gets put in jail instead of doing what he was supposed to in the beginning of the world.[45] Animals keep constantly appearing and reappearing; for was it not the chicken, coming down the chain with first man and palm nuts, that spread the earth? Even the creation force is clothed in animal guise for its vehicle in the complex Yoruba world view.

We have looked briefly at some artistic themes such as masking, poetics, folkloric and plastic arts, and folktales which exhibit similarities between Yoruba and Sea Islands cultures in spite of the passage of time and uprooting from home cultures. In both the material and nonmaterial culture traits, we find echoes, traces, and occasionally, imprints of continental African societies. Folklore is one of the ways that we can reestablish the continuity of African culture through time and space. Demonstrating the connection builds our catalog of proof of the durability of African culture and its people.

---

[1] William Fagg in introduction to *African Sculpture* (New York: Dutton, 1970), 6.

[2] Melville Herskovits, *The Myth of the Negro Past* (New York: Beacon Press, 1967), 66–123.

[3] Joel Chandler Harris, *Uncle Remus* (New York: Appleton, 1880).

[4] Richard M. Dorson, *American Negro Folktales* (Greenwich, CT: Fawcett, 1971).

[5] Abigail M. H. Christensen, *Afro-American Folklore Told round Cabin Fires on the Sea Islands of South Carolina* (Boston: J. G. Cupples Co., 1892).

[6] Charles Colcock Jones, *Negro Myths from the Georgia Coast* (Boston: Houghton, Mifflin, and Co., 1888).

[7] Samuel G. Stoney and Gertrude M. Shelby, *Black Genesis* (New York: Macmillan Co., 1930).

[8] Louise and Eric Bennett-Coverley, personal communication, 1993.

[9] Daniel J. Crowley, *I Could Talk Old-Story Good: Creativity in Bahamian Folklore* (Berkeley: University of California Press, 1966).

[10] Elsie Clews Parsons, *Folk-Tales of the Sea Islands, South Carolina* (New York: Stechert, 1923).

[11] Guy and Candie Carawan, *Ain't You Got a Right to the Tree of Life?* (New York: Simon and Schuster, 1968).

[12] Melville Jacobs, *Content and Styles in an Oral Literature* (Chicago: University of Chicago Press, 1959).

[13] E. E. Evans Pritchard, *The Zande Trickster* (Oxford: Oxford Library of African Literature, 1967), 10.

[14] T. O. Beidelman, "Hyena and Rabbit: A Kaguru Representation of Matrilineal Relations," *Africa* 31 (1961), 61–74; T. O. Beidelman, "Further Adventures of Hyena and Rabbit: The Folktale as a Sociological Model," *Africa* 33 (1963), 54–69.

[15] See "The Devil Made Me Do It: African American Folk Drama" in this volume.

[16] Dennis Duerden, *African Art* (Middlesex, UK: Hamlyn, 1968), 48; Robert Farris Thompson, *Black Gods and Kings: Yoruba Art at UCLA* (Los Angeles: University of California Museum and Laboratories of Ethnic Arts and Technology, 1971), chap. 2, facing p. 1; chap. 14, 8, fig. 3; chap. 19, 8, fig. 27.

[17] William R. Bascom, *Ifa Divination: Communication Between Gods and Men in West Africa* (Bloomington: Indiana University Press, 1969), plate no. 8; 181, nos. 4-1A and 4-1B; 185, no. 5-1.

[18] William R. Bascom, Personal Communication, 1969.

[19] Robert Farris Thompson, *Black Gods and Kings: Yoruba Art at UCLA* (Los Angeles: University of California Museum and Laboratories of Ethnic Arts and Technology, 1971), chap. 1 figs. 13–17; chap. 11, facing page 1.

[20] Kate P. Kent, *Introducing West African Cloth* (Denver: Denver Museum of Natural History, 1971), 73–78.

[21] Ayo Bamgbose, "Yoruba Folk Tales" (abstract) in *African Abstracts* 22, no. 4 (1971), 146.

[22] Thompson, *Black Gods and Kings: Yoruba Art at UCLA* (Los Angeles: University of California Museum and Laboratories of Ethnic Arts and Technology, 1971), chap 5: 12, fig 24; William R. Bascom, *Ifa Divination: Communication Between Gods and Men in West Africa* (Bloomington: Indiana University Press, 1969), 8, plate no. 11.

[23] Joan Westcott, "The Sculpture and Myths of Eshu-Elegba, the Yoruba Trickster," *Africa* 31 (1962), 336–354.

[24] Richard. M. Dorson, *American Negro Folktales* (Greenwich, CT: Fawcett, 1968), 106.

[25] Ibid, 148–149.

[26] Elsie Clews Parsons, *Folk-Tales of the Sea Islands, South Carolina* (New York: Stechert, 1923), 79.

[27] Ibid.

[28] Ibid.

[29] Daniel J. Crowley, *I Could Talk Old-Story Good: Creativity in Bahamian Folklore* (Berkeley: University of California Press, 1966), 91.

[30] Phebean Itayemi and P. Gurrey, comps., *Folk Tales and Fables* (New York: Penguin, 1953), 67–69.

[31] See note 21.

[32] Guy and Candie Carawan, *Ain't You Got a Right to the Tree of Life?* (New York: Simon and Schuster, 1968), 120.

[33] Beidelman, "Hyena and Rabbit: A Kaguru Representation of Matrilineal Relations" *Africa* 32, no. 1 (1961), 61–62.

[34] Elsie Clews Parsons, *Folk-Tales of the Sea Islands, South Carolina* (New York: Stechert, 1923), 11.

[35] Daniel J. Crowley, *I Could Talk Old-Story Good: Creativity in Bahamian Folklore* (Berkeley: University of California Press, 1966), 50.

[36] Ayodele Ogundipe, "An Annotated Collection of Folktales from African (Nigeria) Students in the United States" (master's thesis, Indiana University, 1966), 51–53.

[37] Ibid, 36–39.

[38] Elsie Clews Parsons, *Folk-Tales of the Sea Islands, South Carolina* (New York: Stechert, 1923), 79.

[39] Ayodele Ogundipe, "An Annotated Collection of Folktales from African (Nigeria) Students in the United States" (master's thesis, Indiana University, 1966), 41–43.

[40] Daniel J. Crowley, *I Could Talk Old-Story Good: Creativity in Bahamian Folklore* (Berkeley: University of California Press, 1966), 108.

[41] Ayodele Ogundipe, "An Annotated Collection of Folktales from African (Nigeria) Students in the United States" (master's thesis, Indiana University, 1966), 103.

[42] W. C. Saunders, Personal Communication, 1973.

[43] Ulli H. Beier, "The Yoruba Attitude to Dogs," *Odu* 7 (1959), 31–37.

[44] Babatunde Lawal, "Yoruba Sango Sculpture in Historical Retrospect" (PhD diss., Indiana University, 1970), 217.

[45] William R. Bascom, remarks made at Indiana University African Folklore Conference, Bloomington, 1970.

Three young ladies doing "Mama Lama" game.

The author learning how to knit net from Mr. Joe "Crip" Legree at the Penn Center Gullah Studies Institute, 2006.

"Old King Glory. The first one, the second one, the third follow me."

Young ladies on Johns Island, South Carolina, acting out the game "I know a girl from Baltimore, Lessee what she can do."

"Here Comes Uncle Jessie."

"Step, Uncle Jessie, Step Step."

The Devil harassing the Saving Angel.

The Moving Star Young Association Praise House, River Road, Johns Island, South Carolina.

Mr. and Mrs. Hunter with their daughter Tina on a visit to Ms. Louise Jones, basket maker, Mount Pleasant, South Carolina.

The late Mrs. Janie Hunter making a sedge broom on Johns Island, South Carolina.

Ms. Yacine Diop beginning a basket in Medina Fall, Senegal.

Pine straw and seagrass coaster.

Two rice fanners made of bulrush and pine straw by Ms. Mary Manigault, Mount Pleasant, South Carolina.

Storage basket by Ms. Yacine Diop, Medina Fall, Senegal.

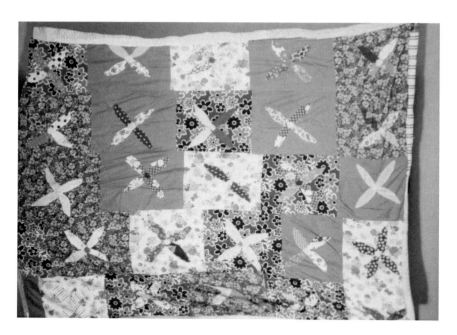

Above: Quilt showing the meeting of the Pennsylvania Mennonite and South Carolina Sea Islands cultures.

Left: Overtop handled basket made by Ms. Lousie Jones, Mount Pleasant, South Carolina.

Above: The author lecturing on the Africanity of African American—especially Sea Island—quilts. Institute for Gullah Studies, Penn Center, St. Helena Island, South Carolina, 2006.

Left: Dollbaby by Ms. Janie Hunter, Johns Island, South Carolina.

Above: Hat by Ms. Irene Foreman.

Left: Red Cross Quilt by Ms. Robert P. Johnson, River Road, Johns Island, South Carolina.

PART II

"Tryin' to Make It":
African Spiritual Endurance, Artistic
Strength, and Technology

Stewed Turkey Wings

Family of Althea Sumpter
Hilton Head Island, South Carolina

— Chop spring onions, sauté over low heat.
— Add pepper and salt to taste.
— Add turkey wings and water to cover.
— Add water as it simmers, cook slowly until meat is ready to fall off bones. Probably 1 hour.

Traditional Method: Make gravy by browning the flour, adding the pan juices. Add to pot with wings. Add seasonings.

Modern Method: Use Kitchen Bouquet. During the last half hour of cooking the wings, prepare the rice. Use Carolina Gold Rice 1 cup rinsed in cold water. Measure by placing your index finger just at the top of the rice. Add water up to the level of that first knuckle and add salt to taste.

Bring to a boil, then turn down to low heat. Cover and cook until water boils out, 20 to 30 minutes. Serve in the center of the plate with the wings on top.

"Tryin' to Make It"

Introduction to African Spiritual Endurance, Artistic Strength, and Technology

The Sea Islanders have endured many trials and difficulties through war, slavery, hard times, and discrimination, among others. The strength to stand firm in the face of all these tribulations is found in various modalities, which have several roots. Africanized Christianity is a source of sustenance within the web of family and their roles in life. The spiritual strength inherent in the bulwark of their culture was crucial to their survival. If asked how were they doing, the reply often came, "Jus' tryin' to make it." This statement encapsulates their determination to outlast the problems and a progress report on how it is going. The pulse of life is strong and ever present.

The performing of songs, movement, and dance is so interwoven with every aspect of life that its beat runs through such occasions as church services, informal get-togethers at home, a crab crack, hops at the club, or Saturday night at the juke joint (otherwise known as the "grab-all," as it grabs all your money). It spans the religious, spiritual, and secular spheres linking these social activities in a dynamic continuity of aesthetic expression. In addition to these nonmaterial manifestations of the culture are the material and technological features—such as their African heritage and modes of being (village banking methods and the practice of domestic arts of quilting, basketry, fishnet making, cooking, broom making, and healing).

Songs, like "The Grey Goose," celebrate the durability of African people. Games, like "I Come to See Miss Julianne John" (Bessie Jones), teach manners along with color values. The lively, inspiring shouts, such as "Walk Believer, Walk Daniel" (Bessie Jones), and the spirituals, like "Ain't You Got a Right to the Tree of Life?" (Carawans) are where models of courage and endurance are provided. On Johns Island, South Carolina, a great natural wonder known as "Angel Oak" might be symbolic of the steadfast nature of the Africans who were brought here when the tree was an acorn or very small. Its huge, spreading limbs recall the large trees in Africa under which their forebears and contemporaries sat in council meetings.

The usage of cultural methods of coping is woven into daily life. As the textiles are crafted together so too the web of ongoing life, so we understand the utility of savings society, the interrelationships of the dancing song games, and the buttress of religious and spiritual expressions. The underlying web of support in the society consists of the African technologies that helped provide the tools to feed their families.

As they did in West Africa, the Sea Islanders of Georgia and South Carolina fish, hunt, plow, and cultivate to feed themselves and their families and animals. Many of the Africans were brought over because of their skills in rice culture, as they originated in agricultural societies. Women and men are practiced fisher people with cast, drop, drag, and seining nets, which they have made themselves. With both fishing and agriculture, they cooperate to increase yield and lighten the load for the individual. They cook okra soup just as it is done in West Africa from food items they have raised, caught, or harvested themselves.

In the articles in Part II are details of how this supportive technology worked out in daily life and how the women sustained the societies in the African World, leading off with spiritual and healing practices.

Life Everlasting

A Note on African and Christian Elements in Sea Islands Healing Practices

My introduction to traditional healing beliefs and methods was in the store of "Miss Elvinna" who upon my inquiry told me she, among others, wore silver money, such as dimes, on her person to help relieve pains of arthritis. She was one of the first people I met on Johns Island and was most welcoming to a strange white lady appearing in her store in a fairly remote section on a rainy February day.

Folk healing processes have been a matter of necessity on the Sea Islands for years because of the factors which have kept the area isolated until recently. The Islands, which lie off the southeastern coasts of Georgia and South Carolina, are a region well known for the African retentions still found there. Culture traits in many fields are found there—such as language documented by Lorenzo Dow Turner; crafts by Mary A. Twining; folklore by Jones, Christensen, Twining, Carawan, and others; music by McKim, Ballanta-Taylor, Spaulding, Starks, et al.[1]

An area designated "magic, superstition, witchcraft" recorded in a mighty compendium by the Reverend Hyatt[2] is often associated and confused with the healing arts. Newbell Niles Puckett published an excellent source in *Magic and Folk Beliefs of the Southern Negro* in 1926.[3] The terms "magic," "superstition," and "witchcraft" have fallen into disrepute and have somewhat destructive connotations vis-à-vis a culture. It is preferable to think in terms of positive cultural phenomena such as belief systems, healing practices, and practitioners rather than exoticism and black magic. Puckett became so fascinated with this research that he became a "mojo" or "'conjur' man" himself in order to prove a point to his informants. It would appear that he may have sacrificed objectivity in the process.

The United States dominant society has been so involved with the creation of a medically iatrogenic culture that the folk healing processes of many ethnic subgroups have become lost or discredited. Due to the high cost of medical care, however, people are once again becoming aware of the healing capabilities of certain natural substances and the people who are knowledgeable of them. The culture can be seen in the light of a strong provider of information and healing rather than a victim of scientism and technology. Suffice it to say, Afro-Americans in rural situations have relied on these cultural resources more than other Americans, especially in the isolated circumstances of the Sea Islands.

Part of the reason for the use of traditional healing methods was the marginalization of the African population in both slavery and postcaptivity labor times. The social and geographic segregation figured into the unavailability of allopathic doctors and medicines. Portia Fulford indicates, ". . . the institution of folk medicine used by enslaved persons was invisible to persons outside of the enslaved community and remained a communal network until the present day."[4] Her contention is that what was a necessity from exclusion became a matter for voluntary inclusion in later years. The secrecy resulted from the isolation and exclusion as much as from intentional behavior. Fear of a lack of understanding of the African-based healing modalities led to creating a barrier of communication. In Fannie Kemble's *Journal*, she recounts the miserable conditions of the women in the so-called hospital on their plantation:

> . . . here lay some burning with fever, others chilled with
> cold and aching with rheumatism, upon the hard cold ground,
> the draughts and dampness of the atmosphere increasing
> their sufferings and dirt, noise, and stench, and every ag-
> gravation of which sickness is capable, combined with their
> condition . . . [5]

This description demonstrates one of the reasons why the people may have sought alternative means of alleviating their wretched situation. This eyewitness account does not communicate any idea that the midwife, who was also present, had utilized any traditional methods to lessen their pain and suffering. Either secrecy was well maintained or these described women were the ones who did not subscribe to traditional healing. It presents a bleak picture and underscores the need for alternate arrangements in their care.

Many other less well-documented aspects of the culture relate to the African background of the Afro-American Sea Islanders. These traits include association patterns, artistic behavior, institutions, foodways, and healing practices. All of these culture traits are so interrelated as to be inseparable and religion is ever present as a binding force.

The most well known in Afro-American Sea Islands' culture of folk healing practices is that called "roots," or "working roots." One goes to root men or women to get a "bag," "hand," or "root" to influence a life situation. One of the affective units (bag, hand) is made up of herbal substances—such as oak bark, life everlasting (a kind of sage also called rabbit tobacco), mint, and other organic items such as frog legs. The mixture can stop pregnancy, ensure safe delivery of babies, help people to win card games, win a lover, find lost things, or neutralize something that has been done to the patient whose illness may be thought to have been put on them by such means. The process of "doing something" is called "fixing," echoed in the spiritual lyrics "Fix me for my long white robe, fix me Jesus, fix me." Jesus is seen as the ultimate root doctor or healer, as in the song they sing, "Jesus is my doctor, give me all my medicine in the room." The bag can be recharged by remaking it; the root person tells the patient how to use the bag effectively. They may also instruct the patient to "feed the bag" (gin or other potent fluid) to give it renewed strength.

Root people can be men or women, though there seems to be a widespread belief that the most powerful ones are men. The best known of these root men is the famous "Doctor Buzzard" of the Beaufort, South Carolina, area. People come from all over to get an appointment with him. These shamans are thought to be sharp enough to understand the physical and mental problems of the patient. They might select the problem that they can deal with and send the patient on to another specialist. My informants indicate that belief must be strong in the powers of the root doctors or the bag will not be efficacious. There have been instances of bags with stronger roots in them overpowering opponents' weaker bags and causing them to come out of the owners' pockets.

One such specialist may work both good and evil spells; there are also specialists in each area, though my sources indicated that the evil root people were lesser known for obvious reasons. This parallels a situation in southeast Nigeria among the Anang Ibibio people who have people who practice "white" magic and "black" magic. The white magic society meets in the daytime and the black magic people meet in secrecy at night.[6]

There is another stream of belief in Sea Islands culture that relates illness to the will of God and all healing to the intervention of Christ. The function of the church is supposed to be to relieve tension, to keep people emotionally stable, and, therefore, physically healthy. Recovery from an illness is greeted with the attitude that everything happens for the best and that there is a purpose to every event, though we may not know what it is. Death is thought to come when an old person has to die to make room for a new baby coming along. Some believe that the old person who died is memorialized in the new life most recently arrived among the young babies. It has been known that an old person might hide him or herself or cease to eat in order to die in a timely fashion to have room for the new arrival.

Clearly, several aspects of the folk belief related to healings have African backgrounds—such as the last-named belief that the new baby reincarnates the older relative. The Yoruba names "Babatunde" (male) or "Yetunde" (female) are given in just such a case. The notion that illness is caused by supernatural forces and can be stabilized or cured through the intervention of these powers is certainly found in West Africa. Janie Gilliard of Yonges Island was amazed to find that cases of fixing, curing, and root workings that she had encountered in her home area, were corroborated by Africans as present in their societies also. She found that practices identified by anthropologists as "exuvial magic" were common among their own people and members of African groups as well. She documents the wearing of "protection" on the body to counteract evil influences.[7] Geoffrey Parrinder notes the use of amulets or talismans in *West African Religion*. He also makes a statement about the care exercised in disposing of personal items because of the risks associated with anything closely associated with body exuviae.[8] Such items, which may have sweat, urine, blood, hair, or nails embedded within, may be utilized as a basis for the building of a bag.

The root doctor, like his African counterpart, is treating the whole person in matters affecting social, emotional, and cultural pressures as well as physical ailments. Vennie Deas-Moore characterizes the practitioner of "good magic" as a "Christian" doctor who believes his skill to be a gift of God to be used responsibly and helpfully. He, of course, will be called in to help someone to neutralize the effects of a spell put on by a practitioner of "evil magic." The latter kind of root doctor specializes in fixing people who wish to get revenge or make trouble for an enemy.

There are ways to combat the root work that may have been done against you, including using salt, chewing garlic, and spitting in well-chosen spots. A package may be worn around the waist to keep off the evil others may wish you; silver money is worn to ward off arthritis, diseases, and evil intentions, which may in fact be thought to cause the ailments. Coins are given out of packets worn on the body to aid someone who may need it.

The custom of wearing amulets around the waist, in the hair, or in a bracelet on the arm for the protection it offers is widespread and well known in West Africa. The leather or cloth packets contain herbs and other substances thought to be helpful in the purpose of the wearer. The third wife in a polygynous marriage with a man in Senegal told me that she wore the amulets (of which there were many) in her hair so that her husband, who had taken an inordinate interest in wife number two, might favor her again. Men also wear the pouches to aid them in their concerns, and this may be reaffirmed by Afro-American men keeping something in their wallets.

Now there is a Sea Island Health Care Corporation located on Johns Island, South Carolina. It provides a number of jobs and fills a gaping need in the health care of the Islanders. Charleston is far enough away, twenty miles or so, that emergencies such as births and accidents can be life threatening in the absence of more available care. The Sea Islands clinic was ahead of the present (1993) impetus on a governmental level to insure decent health care to rural Americans due to the vision of some community organizers there. Bill Saunders, Esau Jenkins, and his son, Bill Jenkins, were among the persons instrumental in getting that mobilized. People still use roots, but they also rely upon the modern medical technology to help them when it is needed. It is to be hoped that Islanders and other Americans can do what the Chinese are doing: research the chemical and healing components utilized by the "barefoot" doctors and use them in conjunction with the modern technological advances.

Deas-Moore, in her article on the African contributions to Sea Islands health care, attributes her mother's excellent condition to the knowledge brought from Africa. The article gives information about Latin names of the herbs and plants used for healing.[9] Faith Mitchell's *Hoodoo Medicine* gives names and uses of Native, African, and Euro-American sources.[10] It would seem that people are looking to the traditional, natural healing properties of wild plants. Presently medical personnel are doing studies to convince themselves of the worthwhile nature of this research, such as Dr. Sabra Slaughter[11] in Charleston. Soon the Sea Islanders might be able to continue to use the riches of the earth for healing purposes as they have done in the past.

---

[1] Lorenzo Dow Turner, *Africanisms in the Gullah Dialect* (Chicago: University of Chicago Press, 1949); Mary A. Twining and Keith E. Baird, *Sea Island Roots* (Trenton, NJ: Africa World Press, 1991); Mary A. Twining, Fieldwork and various articles; Charles Colcock Jones, *Negro Myths from the Georgia Coast* (Boston: Houghton, Mifflin, and Co., 1888); Abigail M. H. Christensen, *Afro-American Folklore Told round Cabin Fires on the Sea Islands of South Carolina* (Boston: J. G. Cupples Co., 1892); See Chapter "Telling Lies" in this volume; Guy and Candie Carawan, *Ain't You Got a Right to the Tree of Life?* (New York: Simon and Schuster, 1967); Guy and Candie Carawan, "Living Folk Heritage of the Sea Islands," *Sing Out!* 14 (1969), 29–32; James Miller McKim, "Negro Songs," *Dwight's Journal of Music* 19 (1862), 148–149, repr., in Bruce Jackson, *The Negro and His Folk Music* (Austin: University of Texas Press, 1967); N. G. J. Ballanta-Taylor, *St. Helena Island Spirituals* (New York: Schirmer, 1925); H. G. Spaulding, "Under the Palmetto," *Continental Monthly* 4 (1863), 188–203; George Starks, "Singing 'Bout a Good Time," *Journal of Black Studies* 10, no. 4 (June 1980), 437–444.

[2] Harry Middleton Hyatt, *Hoodoo—Conjuration—Witchcraft—Rootwork,* vols. I and II (Hannibal, MO: Western Publishers, 1970).

[3] Newbell Niles Puckett, *Folk Beliefs of the Southern Negro* (Chapel Hill: University of North Carolina, 1926).

[4] Portia Fulford, "The Practice of Folk Healing Medicines by African American Women as Gynecological Resistance," Unpublished Dissertation, Clark Atlanta University (Spring 2010), 40.

[5] Fanny Kemble, *Journal of a Residence on a Georgian Plantation* (New York: Harper and Bros., 1864), 104–105.

[6] John Messenger, Personal Communication, 1970.

[7] Janie Gilliard Moore, "Africanisms Among Blacks of the Sea Islands," *Journal of Black Studies* 10, no. 4 (June 1980), 467–480.

[8] Edward Geoffrey Parrinder, *African Traditional Religion* (London: SPCK, 1954).

[9] Vennie Deas-Moore, "Home Remedies, Herb Doctors, and Granny Midwives," *The World and I* 2, no. 1 (January 1987), 474–485.

[10] Faith Mitchell, *Hoodoo Medicine* (San Francisco: Reed, Cannon and Johnson Co., 1978).

[11] Sabra Slaughter, Charleston, South Carolina, Personal Communication, 1990s.

Coffin Point Praise House at St. Helena Island, South Carolina.

Mr. Ben Mack explaining the collection basket to the author in interior of Coffin Point Praise House.

Hold Your Light!

Spiritual Presence and Practice on the Sea Islands

I n many African societies, the impetus toward spiritual religious thought is pervasive in the culture. The momentum of such philosophy has so penetrated throughout the activities of the lives of group members that it is taken for granted by its practitioners. The stance contrasts with Western or Euro-American positions where religion is an activity of a social and institutional nature in the main, not regarded as a worthwhile sensibility for the management of daily life.

There are at least three branches of African religious thought in the Americas, which parallel the "triple heritage" cited by Dr. Ali Mazrui in *The Africans*.[1] First, were the traditional religions that manifested themselves as Macumba and Candomblé among others in Brazil, Cuba, and other parts of the Caribbean and South America as well as private ritual observances and heavily syncretized theology and ceremony in the Sea Islands. Second, the Muslim presence in some parts of the United States personified by Bilali and others who are mentioned in *Drums and Shadows*. Third, the Africanized Christianity practiced by people who recognized the need for protective syncretization in ceremonial manifestations.

Unfortunately, the traditional religions of Africans were submerged because of the repressive atmosphere in the United States. There is all too little evidence of their presence except for some observed traits such as the

"Yangala" position of the man on Siras Bowens's gravestone and other carvings, which were known to be in the Sunbury Church (Georgia) graveyard.[2] Sun worship is noted in *Drums and Shadows* and *Musical Quarterly*. A woman known as Maum Hester who lived on Julia Peterkin's plantation would do a sunset ritual three times, chanting "Do Lawd Jesus I please you this day?" (in the manner of a muezzin). She did a circle walk (dance) similar to the "shout" with an increase in volume and intonation. She then said, "But de t'ird time, de sun he 'gin move, I see he shoutin'. Den I happy by I know den I done please de Lawd Jedus dat day!" This understanding of Jesus as dominant manifester of the natural world is similar to early Christian expressions—such as "Fairest Lord Jesus, ruler of all nature, robed in the blooming garb of spring," which was sung by the Carthusians in the fourth century. It seems to see him as permeating throughout the natural world, a different attitude from the later heavily personified figure. The "shouting" celebrants in the Methodist Church on River Road on Johns Island danced like that and knew the Lord as they did so. Deep in the trees of Johns Island, they could not see the sun, but they felt they had shared in the light of the spirit as they found an altered state of consciousness. The Ring Shout and shouting as practices in the churches and praise houses are still done on the Sea Islands. "Several men moved their feet alternately, in strange syncopation."[3] The "strange syncopation" could have been the shout step, the Knee Bone Bend or one of the other calls of the Shout Dance. The stick fighting in the graveyard, however, has passed along with the Siras Bowens's carvings, which were once an outpost of African aesthetic sensibility.[4] The use of glass jars, which contain water from time to time, embedded mica in stone markers, and other embellishments of surface interest, light reflectivity, and collections of items belonging to the deceased still can be seen in Sea Islands graveyards.[5] Funerary rites—including the use of drums and flutes, circling the grave, and touching the corpse to say good-bye—may also connect to African homelands from the outskirts. Harvest dances on the Sea Islands, which last most of the night until sun worship in the early morning, are recorded in *Drums and Shadows*. Present-day oyster roasts and crab cracks may be regarded as contemporary harvest dances and feasts.

The section in *Drums and Shadows* "Possum Point" records message drumming, offerings for the spirit of the dead, language traits, exuvial magic, and other cultural reinforcements for the Africanity of the cultural and religious behavior of Sea Islands people.[6]

Islam is a separate religion, which was brought into Africa by conquest. For some, the practice of Islam was traditional African religion. However, we can differentiate between older traditional religious observances in African societies and the later Muslim and Christian ones, which were profoundly altered by the African cultures into which they came.

Bilali

The Bilali manuscript is presently in the University of Georgia Library in Athens, Georgia. A small brown leather packet measuring approximately six inches in length and four inches in height, it contains one of the few known Arabic manuscripts written by an African in the United States.[7] Several instances of enslaved Africans literate in Arabic have been recorded in Afro-American history. One famous example is Omeroh or Umar Ibn Said, "the boredom of whose sojourn in a North Carolina jail was relieved by writing Arabic upon the wall."[8] It was regarded as something of a curiosity at the time, and people came to gape at the sight. In George Callcott's article about Umar Ibn Said, he includes some biographical information about him. It seems he lived in the Senegambian region of West Africa, a member of a Muslim family of Fula speakers. His father owned slaves, and he himself was taken by Hausa slave merchants and sold.[9]

Bilali, whose manuscript survives in Georgia, was also treated as an interesting phenomenon as reflected in the novelist's art. Both William Caruthers, in *The Kentuckian in New York* and Joel Chandler Harris, in *Aaron, Son of Ben Ali*, picture Bilali as an oddity.[10] He is shown off in *The Kentuckian*—a slave who is literate in Arabic as well. In *Aaron, Son of Ben Ali*, he is a central character of the book who is portrayed as a shaman with magical powers and recondite knowledge, which includes being able to talk to and understand animals. Actually, the latter of the two portraits may be closer to his historical truth. Charles Spalding Wylly, in *The Seed That Was Sown in the Colony of Georgia*, writes about Bu Allah, his grandfather's foreman. Wylly's description shows us an elder of a Muslim family complete with prayers, sheepskin, and other paraphernalia of authority. When the British were thought to be at hand during the War of 1812 (1813), Bu Allah was entrusted by his owner, Thomas Spalding, with the job of arming the other captive workers from the Spalding plantation.[11] The Spalding plantation was on Sapelo Island, Georgia, still one of the Islands accessible only by boat.

Wylly states that Bu Allah kept the plantation "Acts" in Arabic. If this manuscript is the body of written materials to which he refers, it is not plantation records. Who would have known Arabic so as to be able to check its contents? It is the considered opinion of Ahmed Saber, who has recently completed a translation, that the writer was reinforcing his religious knowledge by writing the prayers and rites of the Islamic faith, both to recall them and in order to teach them to a coreligionist, enslaved like himself far from their West African culture.

The manuscript has suffered discoloration, foxing, and bleeding from the passage of time and is very difficult to decipher. There is a well-filled file on it in the University of Georgia Library, as the manuscript attracted the attention of Lydia Parrish and Margaret Davis Cate, both of whom were very interested in the local history and culture. They persuaded Joseph Greenberg, an expert in African languages, to look at it, and he then arranged to take it to West Africa for translation and exegesis. When Greenberg did so, he reported (1940) that the wise men in West Africa declared it inhabited by "djinns" because they could make little sense of what they read (or did not care to). Greenberg's article claims to establish the manuscripts as extracts from the *Risala* of Ibn Abi Zayd al-Qayrawani, a North African law book.[12]

Some scholarly attention has been paid to the evidence of the historical Muslim presence in North America. E. M. Thornton wrote a short article in the *Law Library Journal* recounting what was known of the Bilali manuscript up to that time (1955).[13] B. G. Martin has written an article in the *Georgia Historical Journal* establishing the provenience of the paper used in the book.[14] J. A. Rogers has written of a family named Maxwell in Georgia who owned a slave named London reputed to be Arabic speaking.[15] Lydia Parrish writes, "Cornelia, whose lean fine frame, beaked nose, and keen eyes bespeak her Arab ancestry."[16] Several persons with Arab names and African language and culture traits are mentioned in *Drums and Shadows*.[17]

According to Lorenzo Dow Turner, the word "shout," denoting religious dances came from the Arabic word "saut" (from sawt meaning "voice").[18] The question arises that this definition seems to be an isolated instance of this particular linguistic provenience. One reason for its presence in this cultural context may be the similarity of religious experience between the Sufi brotherhoods in North and West Africa and the Afro-American Christian churches on the Sea Islands whose freedom and intensity of emotional expression is typical throughout its churches.

Both groups use rhythmic repetition in songs and dance to produce hyperventilation and, because of the change in the oxygen content in the brain, eventually convulsions. Physical prostration, gasping, and feelings of lightness in the body are typical of this state of possession, and the religious dance and the "shout" is used to produce it. Members of the Afro-American churches or praise houses call it "getting happy" while the dance or shout continues and "falling out" when the prostration begins.

"I went down to the valley to pray my soul got happy and I stayed all day." Religious participants on the Sea Islands have been heard to state in open testimonial, "I prayed to the Lord to get happy!" The women (in the group) seem particularly sensitive to the pressure created by the mounting tension of rhythm and sound. Often the first person to "fall out" will be someone in the group who has had a difficult time emotionally and who may seek the relief provided by the experience of possession.

On the Sea Islands, the Sunday services constitute an integral part of community life. The shout is still done during those services, but possibly found more frequently in the "praise" house services on Sunday evenings where no hireling ministry prevails, but the gatherings are conducted by the elders of the community. It is in these praise services that the community unity is reinforced as people release into the possession experience. The group outpouring of emotion is indeed "the tie that binds," and though they place it and themselves under the broad rubric of Christianity, it serves the same function in the society as the ceremonies of the Muslim Sufi brotherhood.

B. G. Martin, in his work *Muslim Brotherhoods in Nineteenth-Century Africa*, writes of this phenomenon of group possession.[19] He has also commented on the similarity of the emotional reactions to the ritual movement and song and chant typical of both groups. When the religious service reaches a certain point, the words to songs or chants become repetitive, more emotional, and the utterances increase in speed. The resultant convulsive reactions are part of a group experience in a social context, which tends to act as a binding force in the society.

It appears that similar manuscripts to that of Bu Allah in Georgia have been found in the Archive of the State of Bahia in Brazil. Some of these documents are similar in appearance to the Georgia manuscript and express many of the same sentiments. At first, the papers were suspected as subversive writings. Now that they have been translated for the first time, they seem to be little more than pious religiosity. Their hope for spiritual restitution in the next world echoes the feelings exhibited in the Christian spirituals of the Afro-Americans in North America; in neither of these situations did they have any faith in rewards, understanding, or justice in their present circumstances. Like the Christian dances of the shout and the Muslim Sufi cult members, the manuscript writers may have been far apart in space and religious convictions, but were actually very close in their political and social experiences.

The history in Brazil has recorded the Muslim presence more fully than North American sources. Arthur Ramos, Donald Piersen, and Nina Rodrigues all speak of the Haussas (a categorical name not necessarily entirely reflective of their ethnic origin) who were thought by some to be superior to the other captive workers, possibly by virtue of their literacy. Nina Rodrigues records that the so-called "Haussas" could read and write and taught each other, continuing the Muslim schooling they had begun in Africa though the circumstances were radically changed. In Joel Chandler Harris's *Aaron, Son of Ben Ali* the same attitude is shown in the author's description of Aaron, who is considered to be more intelligent because of his different ethnic origin, appearance, and knowledge.[20]

It would appear that the style of Arabic writing is very similar in the two instances, and as it seems most unlikely that the writers from the two areas could have had contact, we might assume a similar origin for the two. The *Risala* was written in a maghribi (West Africa) style of writing; we find that Ibn Abi Zayd al-Qayrawani was attached to a chain of Arabic-speaking law scholars whence the Maliki teachings emanated into North America, the Maghrib, and West Africa. In a more recent article, Martin discloses the sources of the paper on which the manuscript, now housed in Athens, Georgia, was written.[21] As this system of law and learning was fairly popular and widespread, it is not surprising it lasted until the mid-1880s and spread as far as Brazil and St. Simons Island, Georgia.

The establishment of this continuity in time and space makes clear the durability of human culture, a fact seemingly in question in the case of Africa. It furthermore puts to rest, for all time, the notion that only uneducated, poor culture bearers were brought in the slave trade. This historical evidence goes even further to show people making heroic efforts to maintain their culture, though distant in time and circumstance from their homes.

In considering the Bilali manuscript, we will briefly look at literary references, oral testimony, religious and linguistic evidence, personal reminiscence, and some historical reconstruction. This approach may seem diffused, but we must accept evidence from many disciplines in the quest for information and unravelling of a subject surrounded by a certain amount of mystery. Historical negligence, repression of facts, carelessness, and a relegation of actual evidence to an obscurity hardly to be credited to a benign neglect have all contributed to a lack of information. We, therefore, are faced with the task of piecing together the enigma of Benali, Bilali, or Bu Allah, as he is variously called.

If the historical memorabilia of young Spalding can be relied upon, clearly the relationship between Thomas Spalding and his foreman was one of cooperation in an isolated situation. Thomas Spalding, unlike other landowners of the Civil War period who broke and ran, martialed his forces to fight the British in the 1812 War. He trusted Bu Allah to arm and organize the available manpower. One does not wish to romanticize the Old South in any way, but one cannot help but sense a mutual respect between these two.

Bilali has learned some of the *Risala* of Ibn Abi Zayd al-Qayrawani, who had attached himself to a chain (*isnad*) of scholars which went right back to the Prophet himself. The evidence of Bilali's attempts to recreate and remember what he had learned might be construed as an effort to teach another coreligionist or cocaptive the proper way to do things. In one sense, it puts him at the tail end of the *isnad* to which Ibn Zayd had joined himself.

The inclusion and continuation of these religious practices attests to the importance of religion in African World life. From earliest times when the twenty-fifth dynasty of Taharka in Kush was bringing the foundations of religion and philosophical thought to Egypt, Africans have relied upon their religious culture to structure their lives; it is not substantially different in the Sea Islands in spite of the passage of time and the interference of distance. The hindrance of imposed laws, unfamiliar customs, and the intolerance of people of other cultures has not prevented the religious commitment from manifesting itself. The island dwellers have demonstrated the cultural imperative of religious expression and have Africanized Protestant Christianity in the process.

Africanisms in the religious observances of Sea Islanders express themselves in music, singing style, language, dance, shouting, and possession. The graveyards, some of which are in stands of trees, are clearly the relocation of such things as the sacred groves and evil forests of West Africa. Governance in the community has long been managed through the church and lodges, and Esusu, which parallels the religiously pervaded secret societies of West Africa that formed part of the governing nucleus in West African societies. Although the main Christian rites are Sunday services, the Islanders have expanded the round of institutionalized activities to include Seven Speakers, gospel concerts, prayer meetings, praise house gatherings, praying band visitations, lodge meetings, savings societies, and various church committee meetings. It is the interweaving of the generational family continuation and the membership across the society that forms the fabric of community life and the perpetuation of the African heritage.

Africanized Christianity clearly has been influenced by the input of Sufi Muslims and practitioners of traditional African religions. Each has contributed its cultural vitality to the Christian practice of religion to form a triple religious heritage that was forged in the early times when such religious observances were ridiculed, forbidden, or ruthlessly suppressed. Often the performance of the traditional and/or Muslim rites were carried on in secret in order to avoid unwelcome attention or lack of comprehension of their significance. They did leave their marks, however, which became subsumed into the Christian conduct of spirituality and ritual.

---

[1] Ali Mazrui, *The Africans,* TV Series, 1986.

[2] Harold Courlander, *A Treasury of Afro-American Folklore* (New York: Crown Publishers, 1976), photo 298–299.

[3] *Musical Quarterly* 16 (1930), 49.

[4] See note 2.

[5] See note 2.

[6] *Drums and Shadows: Survival Studies among the Georgia Coastal Negroes* (Spartanburg, SC: Reprint Co., 1974), 152, 154, 158.

[7] Bilali manuscript (Athens: University of Georgia Library); See note 2 photo between pages 298–299.

[8] George M. Callcott, "Omar Ibu Seid, A Slave Who Wrote an Autobiography In Arabic," *Journal of Negro History* XXIX, no. 1 (January, 1954), 58–63.

[9] William Caruthers, *The Kentuckian in New York* (New York: Harper and Bros., 1834).

[10] Joel Chandler Harris, *Aaron, Son of Ben Ali* (Boston: Houghton, Mifflin, and Co., 1896).

[11] Charles Spalding Wylly, *The Seed That Was Sown in the Colony of Georgia* (New York: Neale Publishing Co., 1910), 52.

[12] Joseph Greenberg, "The Decipherment of the Ben Ali Diary: A Preliminary Statement," *Journal of Negro History* XXV (1940), 372–375.

[13] E. M. Thornton, "Bilali, His Book," *Law Library Journal* 48 (1955), 228–229.

[14] B. G. Martin, "Sapelo Island's Arabic Document: The Bilali Diary in Context," *Georgia Historical Review* 78, no. 3 (1994), 589–601.

[15] J. A. Rogers, *World's Great Men of Color,* vol. 1 (New York: Macmillan, 1974).

[16] Lydia Parrish, *Slave Songs of the Georgia Sea Islands* (New York: Farrar Strauss, and Co., 1940), 145.

[17] *Drums and Shadows: Survival Studies among the Georgia Coastal Negroes* (Spartanburg, SC: Reprint Co., 1974).

[18] Lorenzo Dow Turner, *Africanisms in the Gullah Dialect* (Chicago: University of Chicago, 1949), 202.

[19] B. G. Martin, *Muslim Brotherhoods in Nineteenth-Century Africa* (Cambridge: Cambridge University Press, 1976).

[20] See note 10.

[21] W. S. Haas, "The Zikr of the Rah maniya Order in Algeria," *Moslem World* 33 (1943); Rolf Reichert, "Os Docmentos Árabes do Arguivo Estado Da Bahia," *Afro-Asia* (June–December, 1966), 169; (B. G. Martin, personal communication).

Two members of the Association escorting the banner at a "turnout," 1970s.

A Penny Saved Is a Penny Earned

African, Caribbean, and Sea Islands Savings Clubs

One Sunday on Johns Island, I saw some younger adults in a house a little distance from where I was standing. The sun shone brightly through the open door of the house where they had gathered. It was spring and they were seated, clustered near the door for the light and warmth of the sun. I inquired what they were doing and was told it was a periodic meeting of a savings club. The concept was explained to me, which seemed somewhat like Christmas Club at a savings and loan association in my hometown in Connecticut. It was not until later that I understood how those Sunday meetings connected them to the rest of the African World, both continental and diasporic.

I n West Africa, there are many so-called secret societies that are involved in the governance of the communities. They constitute the judicial arm of the group, the executioners, the decision makers, and the keepers of ceremonial and traditional knowledge. Participants dance the carved masks to demonstrate the presence of the societies' activities after they have had their meetings out of the sight of the general public. Kokahvah Zauditu-Selassie reports that the Susu groups in Liberia had monthly meetings, paid dues, had special projects such as at Christmas, and were based on cooperative work groups with both men and women cooking.[1] Michael Gomez makes a definitive statement as to why these groups should not be called secret societies.

The secret societies of Sierra Leone were, in fact, the functional equivalent of social, cultural, and governmental agencies, and the secrecy within which they operated was only a means to the realization of their purpose. When placed within this context, these societies are not very different from their Western analogues. To be sure, secrecy is important and was maintained, but it does not at all follow that these organizations should be reduced to one of their working principles.[2]

On the Sea Islands, there are several such societies that were instrumental in socialization, education, and government within the community, reestablishing the counterparts from African cultures. The groups are known to be there within the society, but persons outside of the ethnic group or area are not informed of the workings and meetings of the groups. It is possible that the societies could be termed private since their meetings are not open to nonmembers or nonqualifying personnel. The secrecy consisted of not advertising or publically notifying people not relevant to that community about their meetings and activities. The marginalized situations in which the Islanders found themselves made necessity of opportunity, and they began to use the modalities which had served their societies in Africa very well to structure their communities. Among them are lodges (Masonic and other), praying bands, and savings clubs.

Savings clubs, or rotating-credit associations, exist in many societies around the world. Shirley Ardener's article has amply demonstrated the universal quality of these institutions.[3] In folk societies, banking facilities—such as more formal financial businesses in urbanized societies—are not readily available and do not enjoy much credibility among ordinary people. This attitude was a reason for the seeking out of the credit clubs for rural development in Nigeria. These rotating-credit associations function in remote areas all over the world to provide a means of amassing funds for large purchases or important family occasions for people on low salary scales. The clubs are found also in major cities where the members are remote from their own natal cultures but in all other senses are urbanized, often making excellent salaries that enable them to contribute large sums each month.

In general, the principle of the savings club at this basic level is the same, though there may be a few cultural variations from place to place. Some people come together to form a group for the purpose of saving money. In its most elementary form, the society has positions in a hypothetical circle; each week the money is collected, and then the members take turns keeping the total amount. One member may ask to exchange places with another if a pressing need arises, then he, in turn, will yield his place to that member who exchanged with him. The person who receives the total then has more money than he might otherwise be able to assemble without the help of his neighbors. Ardener states that "there does not seem to be any documentation on rotating-credit associations among American Negroes."[4] Relying upon P. Hills's citation of Myrdal in a personal communication, she dismisses the subject in a couple of lines.[5] There are citations from West Africa and the Caribbean, so logically the trait may be found in a region known for its Africanisms in other aspects of life. In 1964, when Ardener was writing, not so much was known about Africanisms in Caribbean and other African-World cultures. In spite of their isolation from the United States mainland because of social and political pressures, and from the Caribbean due to geographic distance, the savings clubs continued to serve their social and economic functions.

While the Sea Islands have been notable in North America for the continuation of African customs or culture traits, it is usually in the areas of folklore, music, and religion that these continuities are considered. Political and economic behavior have been generally neglected, possibly following on Herskovits's and Puckett's analyses, which indicated little or no activity of an African nature in these fields.[6]

The Sea Islands are close to the continental land mass of the southeast coastal United States and one may reach them by means of roads, bridges, and boats. Most of the Islands are connected to the mainland by bridges and causeways, though a few are still remote enough to be reachable only by boat. Up until the 1930s, most of the Islands were served by ferries and private boats owned by the residents. Partly as a result of this isolation, the people were very remote indeed from the dominant society and its workings. Therefore, it is in this context that we see the African mechanisms handed down from one generation to the next for dealing with unavoidable problems. Much of the Islands' economic life centered around such instrumentalities as credit associations and barter of goods and services to satisfy daily needs.

Furthermore, in the context of African reaffirmations, one sees in the Island economy the mutual obligatory gift exchange common among West Africans, many of whom, like the Sea Islanders, live in an agricultural economy. On the Islands, one may receive—depending on the importance of the occasion, visit, exchange, or possible request involved—the gift of a cabbage, other garden produce, or animals. These may later be traded for preserved foods, eggs, or any other needed item.

Needless to say, some of the mutual gift exchange in some cases obviates the necessity for economic barter, as it fulfills a few of the quotidian needs in the normal course of social life. Barter suffices for the other goods and services, and what money is available could be dealt with by simple individual hoarding or the savings clubs.

The institution of the savings society is found among the Yoruba of Western Nigeria and is called "Esusu." It is a custom among the Igbo speakers of southeastern Nigeria as well and goes by the same name which, in fact, may be a loan word from the Yoruba "Isusu."[7] Victor Uchendu gives credit for accuracy to Ardener in her description of the Igbo contribution in the context of rotating-credit associations on a worldwide basis. In addition to the information contained in Uchendu's ethnographic study, it seems that these contribution clubs work in conjunction with a more modern banking system. The clubs take up their periodic contributions and put them into a bank account, which is subsequently divided among the membership at the designated time.

It appears the Isusu can consist of a group of females with seniority governing the selection of the chairwoman and vice-chairwoman. The location of the meetings rotates to the homes of the different members each week. The group may be composed only of women, or it may be a mixed assemblage. The determinant of group membership may be an economic rather than a sexual division. One person may belong to one group or several. The term used is the Igbo word for "meeting" which is "nzuko." If the number of lexical items in a language reflects the value placed on that trait within that culture, then it is clear that the society in question has an abiding interest in savings clubs. Uchendu lists six names without exhausting the total number by any means.[8]

Mark DeLancey indicates that the folk credit institutions have been instrumental in the development of the credit union movement in Cameroon.[9] He cites Emmi Meyer, who reported the existence of these credit clubs in Cameroon in the 1930s.[10] Meyer translates the Duala word "njangi" as "collection." Njikam Fomenky of the Cameroon opines, however, that the word is literally associated with the feasting reported at the "utu" clubs among the Igbo as well as others in the West African area.[11] The person who is the recipient of the money for that particular time period is responsible for feeding the others. Fomenky further indicates, as do Nwaohu, Dim, Nwiwu, and Igho-Osagie of Nigeria (1978), that the folk form is still much in use, particularly in the cities as mentioned by Delancey, where migrants from the rural areas go to find work. The clubs are based on kinship or regional ties and wield the mighty arm of social control among the young people, possibly away from home for the first time. Membership is more or less obligatory, and the share can be contributed in labor or money if the latter is short. Failure to attend the mandatory meetings may result in a fine or beating.[12]

Cooperative endeavors among African American groups have been an embedded pattern in the culture since slavery times, particularly in the South, where large labor groups were used on huge plantations. In West Africa, young people got together in labor groups in order to complete seasonally demanding work. They earned money, which then went into the group's central account to pay for a big party for the participants. In earlier times, in more remote areas, where money was less available, voluntary labor teams performed tasks too large for one person to accomplish for considerations of food and beer. Such jobs as harvesting, house construc- tions, wall building, and finishing were done in teams by many hands in the expectation that reciprocity was always the rule. This week the group raises this roof, and next week, someone else's in the group. Needless to say, the ideal culture in African continental and diasporic groups included the notion of full and willing participation in these economic patterns. In the real culture, however, lapses from cooperative duty occur, and preventive actions must be taken or restitution made in such instances.

In an article appropriately titled "Cooperation—Nothing New," Cornelius King points out that cooperative labor patterns, community organizations, etc., are an old, established customary pattern among African Americans.[13] Browning indicates that the credit union movement in Afro-American communities has its roots in the benevolent men and women's societies, which go back to before the Civil War.[14] Traditional voluntary African American institutions—such as the lodges, burial societies, praying bands, and saving clubs—have provided structure in those communities over time both through kinship and nonkinship affiliation patterns.

Such voluntary associations have been described by W. E. B. DuBois who states that these "beneficial" societies were many in number and very important in African American groups who lived in cities as far north as Canada. He cites lodges with biblical names, such as "Mount Olive" and "Samaritans," and some societies with names having significance in African American history, such as "Toussaint" and "Wilberforce." He mentions an "African Society" in New York, similar to ones in Philadelphia and Newport, which marched "with music and flying colors."[15]

This parading, often called a "turnout," is a custom followed by lodges during which they troop their colors in festive dress, with banners, music, and drumming. Accounts of such activity are found in a novel by Washington Irving about New York in the 1800s.[16] Hubert Aimes's article recounts similar occasions.[17] The parades and colorful behavior, sometimes called "Pinkster," which took place at the time of pfingsten (Pentecost), were the outward manifestations of the inward and serious purposes of these secret societies, which in Africa were the judicial and organizational units of governance within the communities.

On Johns Island, the lodges have turnouts that used to involve members riding horses in the parading part of it. Now they walk dressed up in their finest garb and then go into the church, where nonmembers are not permitted to enter at that time. Afterwards, they serve cake and ice cream, referred to as "cream," and everyone in the environs is invited to partake.

Communities in Afro-Caribbean cultures have such societies that provide similar structure for coping with life emergencies and daily problems. In Jamaica, the savings club is titled "Partners," in the Bahamas, "Esu."[18] Crowley reports that African Americans in Florida, coming in contact with Bahamian contract workers, have joined Esu with Bahamians as well as forming their own clubs. Raymond Smith asserts that it is called "throwing a box" in Guyana and that East Indians and Afro-Guyanese belong.[19] In Jamaica, the partners group had a "banker;" members contributed "hands," and once every so often it was their turn for the "draw." The last person to draw gets to be first and the second to last gets to be second the next time around.

Many of these groups had special concerns for which they utilized their funds, but most common were sickness and death benefits with dividends, which went back to the members in case there were any left over at the end of the fiscal year. Louis Lynch tells a humorous anecdote about members of one of the clubs called "Meeting" in Barbados who were duly lined up for their "bonus," armed with shopping baskets to carry home the items to be bought with the expected money. When told that the forthcoming "bonus" was not to be issued, the club members expressed their displeasure in such vigorous terms as to necessitate the rescue of the hapless messenger by a flying wedge of local police.[20]

DuBois says of these organizations:

> A few have changed to secret societies. Very few of them
> have been badly managed, although unincorporated and
> without any public oversight, and everybody seems to speak
> well of them and their work.[21]

Noel Gist, on the other hand, characterizes "Syetties" as fly-by-night, local organizations with meager resources and incompetent management.[22] As the custom of the savings club has persisted so long in the African World, to say nothing of the world at large, it seems that the truth about them must be somewhere between these two assessments.

The death-benefit societies, of course, operate in much the same manner as the rotating-credit associations, but your "turn" only comes with the grim reaper. These associations, operating for the members of the community, are the foundations of the later and more complex insurance companies, whose interests tend to be strictly commercial. James Browning talks about the role of some of these community-based organizations in the foundation of African American insurance companies.[23]

The Sea Islands have much in common with the Caribbean societies, not the least of which are similar patterns of culture, such as the savings clubs. They have social gatherings for birthdays of their members, provide a floral tribute at funerals of their members, and gifts for babies born to the members. An invitational free party is held at Christmas. The members wear matching dresses for dances, which they have made specially so they can show their allegiance to each other and the group. It is the mutual cooperative banking and social activities which bind them together in common purpose just as their African forbears did and contemporaries do and which the Caribbean societies also do.

It was a Caribbean person who helped the Johns Islanders to use this traditional community institution as the foundation for the Progressive Club to expand its activities beyond those of a simple rotating-credit association to include a food store and a motel unit. The management of the organization remained in the hands of the original members of the club.[24]

It would seem evident that the credit associations were already established in the society by the Africans, many of whom had been brought through the Caribbean on their way here. The Progressive Club was formed on the basis of a still viable African culture trait and expanded from that foundation. There are also savings clubs among different age groups on the Island, which approximate some of the features of age-grade societies in West Africa while fulfilling their economic functions as well.

The Sea Islands groups are similar to their Igbo counterparts in that membership may depend on one's socioeconomic status, sex, or age. Some ladies on the islands who wish to signify their rise in social and/or economic status do so by changing clubs. This change may also come about because of advancing age, though, if the group were strictly organized according to age-grade, they would all age at the same rate even though their socioeconomic status might change.

When the clubs meet, they rotate to the different members' houses and the lady in charge of the meeting puts on a spread for the other members in the manner of the Cameroonian clubs. Fomenky indicated that the traditional-level credit organizations still function along kinship and ethnic group associations, especially in urban situations. People who join are responsible for either services or money for shares, and if they cannot pay or attend meetings, they are fined and/or punished if they are slack. When the payout comes, then the receiver cooks for the group, which is how they do it on Johns Island. DeLancey and Fomenky (Cameroon) cite the *njangi* [Duala], a form of rotating cooperative agricultural labor, which was taken as a model for the economic husbanding of financial resources.[25]

In spite of the fact times are changing on the Sea Islands due to development of resorts on the shoreline, offshore drilling, and suburbanization, these time-honored patterns of folk institutions still function in African American communities. Simon Ottenberg mentions the existence of a savings club in the coastal Georgia community, which is an area that has been settled since Revolutionary times. From this evidence, it would appear that the credit associations go back in time and are widespread over the Sea Islands.[26]

Although it cannot be claimed that there is an exclusively African provenience for the savings clubs and their outgrowths, it seems that the African parallels, which have proven very durable, show us a probable influence in the direction of the transmission and establishment of these African American community institutions. In the Sea Islands, the custom of grassroots-based savings societies exists as elsewhere in the African diaspora. Their presence and continued vitality in the Sea Islands communities is more evidence that certain traditional customs, which are Africanisms with practical utility, still survive in the Sea Islands in modern times.

---

[1] Kokahvah Zauditu-Selassie, Personal Communication, 1993.

[2] Michael Gomez, *Exchanging Our Country Marks* (Chapel Hill: University of North Carolina, 1998), 95.

[3] Shirley Ardener, "The Comparative Study of Rotating Credit Associations," *Man* 94 (1964), 202–228.

[4] Shirley Ardener, "The Social and Economic Significance of the Contribution Club among a Section of the Southern Ibo," presented at Annual Conference Sociology Section, West African Institute of Social and Economic Research, Ibadan, Nigeria, University College (March 1953), 128–142; Keith Baird, Personal Communication, 1981.

[5] See note 3.

[6] Melville Herskovits, *The Negro in the New World* (Bloomington: Indiana University Press, 1967); Newbell Niles Puckett, *Folk Beliefs of the Southern Negro* (1926; repr., New York: Dover Publications, 1969).

[7] Francis A. Okorie and Leonard F. Miller, "Esusu Clubs and Their Performance in Mobilizing Rural Savings and Extending Credit in Chaozara Sub-Division, East Central State, Nigeria," Technical Report AETR/76.1, Department of Agricultural Economics, University of Ibadan, Nigeria (1976).

[8] Victor Uchendu, *The Igbo of Southeast Nigeria* (New York: Holt, Rinehart and Winston, 1965).

[9] Mark DeLancey, "Credit for the Common Man in Cameroon," *Journal of Modern African Studies* 15, no. 2 (1977), 316–322.

[10] Emmi Meyer, "Kreditringe in Kamerun: Ein Beitrag zum Eingeborenen-Bankwesen," referenced in Mark DeLancey, "Credit for the Common Man in Cameroon," *Journal of Modern African Studies* 15, no. 2 (June, 1977), 316–322.

[11] Njikam Fomenky, Personal Communication, 1978.

[12] Akasie Nwaohu, "Utu in Akirika Village," Unpublished Paper, 1978; Azubike Nwiwu, "Isusu: Revolving Credit in Africa," Unpublished Paper, 1978; Osa Igho-Osagie, "Savings Clubs(Esusu) in Benin City," Unpublished Paper, 1978; Uche Dim, "Indigenous Banking" and "Contribution-Isusu," Unpublished Papers, 1978.

[13] Cornelius King, "Cooperation—Nothing New," *Opportunity* 18 (1940), 328.

[14] James Browning, "The Beginnings of Insurance Enterprise among Negroes," *Journal of Negro History* 22 (1937): 417–432.

[15] W. E. B. DuBois, *Economic Institutions* (Atlanta: Atlanta University Press, 1907).

[16] William Piersen, *Black Legacy* (Amherst: University of Massachusetts Press, 1993).

[17] Hubert Aimes, "African Institutions in America," *Journal of American Folklore* 18 (1905), 15–32; "Pinkster" is a corruption of the German holiday, pfingsten.

[18] Raymond T. Smith, "American Credit Institutions of the Yoruba Type," *Man* 53 (May, 1953), 80; Daniel Crowley, *I Could Talk Old-Story Good* (Berkeley: University of California Press, 1966); Mark DeLancey, Personal Communication, 1975.

[19] Raymond T. Smith, "American Credit Institutions of the Yoruba Type." *Man* 53 (February 1953), 32; Raymond T. Smith, *The Negro Family in British Guiana* (London: Routledge and Kegan Paul, 1956).

[20] Louis Lynch, *The Barbados Book* (London: A. Deutsch, 1964).

[21] W. E. B. Dubois, ed., "Economic Co-Operation among Negro Americans," Atlanta University Publication 12 (1907), 12.

[22] Noel Gist, "Secret Societies: A Cultural Study of Fraternalism in the United States," *University of Misssouri Studies* 15 (1940), 1–184.

[23] James Browning, "The Beginnings of Insurance Enterprise among Negroes," *Journal of Negro History* 22 (1937); see note 13.

[24] Ms. Mary LaRoche, Personal Communication, 1972; William Saunders, Personal Communications, 1972.

[25] See note 10.

[26] Simon Ottenberg, "Leadership and Change in a Coastal Georgia Negro Community," *Phylon* 20, no. 1 (1959), 7–18.

Textiles of Remembrance

Africa and the Sea Islands

I lived on the Sea Islands in South Carolina and visited on the Georgia Sea Islands, both in African American communities, and so observed firsthand the customs and attitudes of the African American Sea Islanders. I did few formal interviews and no questionnaires. Discussions about quilting and other facets of life came up in conversations as I visited repeatedly many households on the Islands. Frequent visits allowed me to recheck subjects we had discussed on previous occasions. Since I visited island homes on a constant basis, I was privileged to participate in and observe the family core of the society. It was in that setting of Africanic traits and behaviors that I first saw the quilts in all their splendor. They were set in the context of okra soup, swept yards, layered clothing, hair tying, head loads, basketry, patterns of community and family governance, music, song, dance, and language usage, to mention a few of the Africanisms apparent in daily life.

The fabric of life is thought to be woven by the vertical threads of ancestry and descent crossing with the horizontal threads of contemporary life.[1] Similarly, the textiles of Sea Islands life and productivity are mirrored in the quilts, baskets, nets, and brooms used in everyday life. As they are pieced, sewn, knitted, and wrapped to bring them into being, they are utilized as tools and to solve problems with modalities from the African past.

Terminology

There are several concepts of folk art and what it constitutes, various schools of thought on what the term embraces, and what is true and pure in the field. Certain nations have nationalized folk arts, so to speak, by means of folk museums, folk schools, and the deliberate fostering of the traditional arts. The most commercially successful people concerned with folk art in the United States are certainly the antique enthusiasts and collectors. Because of the relatively high stakes involved, some people who deal with folk items use words like "primitive" to indicate the more domestic of the things in question. In fact, some of these things are just old, not antique, but nonetheless collectible, according to the taste of the collector. Copying has gone on so long as to render some of the copies antiques almost in their own right.

There is also a kind of folk art which manifests in individuals who are expressing the values and aesthetic judgment of their culture. Although such artists and artisans conceive and embellish from their own artistic imagination, the overall framework is from within their culture. Again, the word "primitive" is brandished especially in reference to paintings. Another term utilized is "naïve," which also insults the artist if all the implications are duly thought out. There is also heard the term "innocent," which is hardly a less-loaded term when used in reference to human beings and their art.

The usage of "folk" and/or "traditional arts and crafts" is appropriate to the intent and ambiance of a show in a museum. In this context, interest in art as one of humankind's enduring preoccupations and accomplishments is manifested. In that cultural frame, there is a concern with how folk art fits into the ongoing life of the community and what it expresses about the values of that community while it charms, amuses, entertains, and enhances peoples' lives.

It is necessary to look at the terminology applied to artists or people of African heritage. In speaking of traditional arts and artists, scholars are talking about expressive behavior within a cultural context. In that case, ethnic identification is appropriate and suitable. Euro-American groups are designated by Greek American, Italian American, and other appellations, which reflect their ethnicity and their new alliance with the United States. African Americans, however, are often subjected to divisive terminology, which sets them apart from other immigrant populations. The use of the term "black" is inappropriate and used as a technique to divide ethnically diverse populations. The use of the term "slave" in conjunction with cultural artifacts is also incongruous because it is a term of economic and political misfortune which has nothing to do with culture aside from being disruptive to its continuance. In slavery days on the plantation, the quilts were made by enslaved Africans; the operative word here is "Africans;" they were not slaves from the Near East or Europe. They had been brought from Africa complete with cultural templates and memories, as we can see from the Powers quilts, for instance, with their connections to Abomey cloths and the strip quilts so evidently related to the Ewe and Ashanti kente cloths.[2] In the quilts, either in their patterns or the complex of behavior which produces them, scholars are looking at cultural reaffirmation among African peoples who were carried far from home under duress. It is time to encourage the most ethnically precise terms when speaking about one of the world's great art traditions, of which these quilt artists are a part.

In earlier times up to the 1930s or so, people had to travel to and from the Islands by boat. Social, cultural, and economic isolation was fairly complete and insured the preservation of lifeways brought from Africa. Because of the swamps and mosquitos, enslaved African people lived on islands while the Euro-American owners and administrators lived elsewhere to escape the mosquitos and the diseases they brought. In more recent times, bridges have been built, easing travel between island and mainland, and even more recently, bringing uprooting and serious change to the African American peoples of the Islands.

Because of the extreme isolation in which the Islanders lived, as captive workers and beyond, various traits and patterns survived in forms close to those of their African background. Suffering less acculturation than their mainland fellow Africans, they were free to reenact their own cultures as they remembered them. Examples of congruent Africanisms are the coiled baskets now centered around Mount Pleasant, South Carolina.[3]

Basketry

Basketry, which is domestic and rural in nature originally, has been a part of the culture. It is an integral ingredient of the folklife of the Sea Islands, a comprehensive study of which might include folk architecture, crafts, foodways, artistic, and useful household objects. Other such crafts include quilting, broom making, and fishnet knitting, and all of them are being produced and utilized now on the Islands. The basketry display stands from which they are sold constitute a kind of folk architecture, and the basketry a workman-like craft that yields both decorative and useful domestic objects.

Today, the basketmakers are seen in a hundred or so roughly built stands along Route 17. Some of these craftsmen live right by their stands while others commute a short distance to tend them. The stands themselves are worthy of study, as they vary in construction from little hollow houses with roofs to easel-like stands with no roofs and little more than a rack on which to hang their wares.

Some of them are little sheds in which the products are stored for those women who commute to their stands. The returns from the basketmaking are hardly sufficient to support the manufacturers of them; mostly the makers have small incomes from other sources, which they augment by the sale of the baskets. Most of the stands are built by the men in the families and manned by older ladies who learned the trade from their aunts, grand-mothers, or mothers a long time ago. They are often accompanied by members of their family who sit alongside making baskets and enjoying traditional jokes and stories while they work. They sing and tell tales on each other as they produce the baskets. As they work, the baskets are arrayed for display and sale on the stands, some more modern and Euro-American in their styling and some still echoing and reaffirming their archetypal Africanity.

History

In the past, oak-split basketry was practiced in this area by Allan Green of Sapelo Island, Georgia. The main basketry style, however, is coiled basketry made by the craftswomen of Mount Pleasant and other islands of South Carolina.

Mount Pleasant, through which Route 17 (a main route between New York and Florida) runs, is a coastal community somewhat east of Charleston, South Carolina, bounded by the Cooper River and the Atlantic Ocean. There is a high retention among the townspeople of genetic association with their West African ancestors. Social institutions, such as burial and insurance societies and lodges, and culture traits, such as music and dance styles, clearly define this area as one of conservative attitudes within the whole realm of African American culture. The factors which caused other culture traits to survive in Mount Pleasant, as well as elsewhere in the Sea Islands, have operated to preserve the basketry.

In Mount Pleasant, the baskets are handmade by one of the oldest groups of African American craftsmen who hand down the art of basketmaking from one person to another. The transmission, which has been going on since they were brought here from Africa, is often from an older woman to a younger person or from one woman to her children. In the past, Sea Islands men were basketmakers as they often are in West African societies where there were men making mats and woven (as opposed to sewed) baskets in Senegal. The women in the Senegambian region of westernmost Africa manufactured the sewn coiled baskets. In modern times, Sea Islands men still make baskets, though usually out of sight of people from outside their community. The children all join in the family industry of basketmaking once they are old enough to hold and manipulate the materials; the boys relinquish the practice at about the age of ten or so when they declare it women's work.

Revival of the Craft

In the 1930s, a Works Project Administration worker came down to the Islands to effect a revival of this craft, which was not as widely practiced as in former times. One older woman in the community claimed that she was the only one making baskets at that time and the rest of her Mount Pleasant neighbors learned the skills of basketmaking again from her. The service that the WPA worker provided was to help the women to understand that their baskets would sell and it would be worth their while to set themselves up in stands at the roadside. Persons in the culture find it hard to believe that outsiders value culture traits that they themselves take for granted. The Depression years (1930–1939) hit this already marginal population extremely hard. The reestablishment of this traditional craft worked so well as a method to increase their meager cash flow that the basket sewers are still doing it. Unfortunately, the need to augment their insufficient means remains as inflation widens the gap between their monies and the price of necessities many years after the Depression.

Historic Uses

In days past, baskets served useful functions in the plantation economy. The rice fanners were used for harvesting nuts and winnowing grain. Corn or rice rations were distributed in them on the plantation. Sewing baskets and other types, including special little toy baskets, were made for the "big house." Some of these items manufactured by enslaved Africans can be seen in the Old Slave Mart Museum in Charleston, South Carolina.

Today, as in the past, basketry is a distinctive feature of the Sea Islands culture. Though it may have enjoyed a wider spread throughout the Southeastern United States in the past, it probably had its strongest manifestation here at the area of first contact. The geographic conditions would encourage people to continue their African practices. The riverine marshes of South Carolina are similar to those of the Senegambian region in West Africa. It is not, however, the geographic/climatic conditions alone which determine the production of these items. They are also produced in the arid western section of Senegal where the climate is extraordinarily dry and different sorts of grasses are used to create the same coiled style basketry.

Technique

The foundation of the basket made by the artisans of Mount Pleasant, South Carolina, turns upon itself to form the nucleus of the basket. The knot, which can also be used as a foundation and is not as simple as a coil, would be a spiral or a helix doubled or reinforced. After

Drawing by John Vlach

the foundation is secured with either the knot or the coil, the basketmakers use the bundle of grass or pine straw for each increment secured to the whole structure with the palmetto.

The stitching is formed by an awl being pushed through the bundle, withdrawn, and then palmetto is inserted into the resultant hole and pulled through. The palmetto has been made into narrow strips about 1/8 to 1/4 inch wide with a pointed end, cut with scissors. To obtain a tightly sewn basket, the sewer must catch a little section in the preceding roll of grass.

Actually, this method of stitching plus strong tension exerted by the basketmaker's hand creates the hard, tight baskets that last. The materials from which the baskets are made have more tensile strength when first harvested, treated, and used than they do after a period of time, as they tend to dry out and become brittle, especially in the centrally heated houses for which this basketry was never designed.

Conversation with Mary Manigault, National Heritage Foundation Winner (1984), revealed that she worked hard during her more physically active life and turned to full-time basketmaking only when she was not strong enough to do the heavy agricultural labor anymore. Also, basketmaking provided an opportunity to put her skill to profitable economic use. Mrs. Manigault's fine craftsmanship is reflected in the handiwork of her cousin, Louise Jones, who hurriedly makes baskets, whereas Mrs. Manigault sews with a tight stitch and the resultant baskets are tough and hard. The sea grass, palmetto, and pine straw (needles) tend to dry out and fade to a yellow and brown color pattern from their original green color and cause baskets not sewn tightly enough to loosen and weaken eventually.

The sewing is done with two tools, one of which is called the "bone." This implement was originally made of animal bone and shaped flat with rounded edges. Now, however, it is made from a stainless steel spoon from which the bowl end has been removed. The handle is then smoothed down to make an effective prying tool. The basketmakers stick it into the roll of straw to make a place for the strip of palmetto to enter, sometimes between the rolls and sometimes into the roll itself.

Drawing by John Vlach

Another tool is a pair of scissors used to evenly cut off not only the ends of the sea grass but also the rough ends of the pine straw. The scissors and "bone" rest in the basket being made, if it is shallow enough, or in the lap of the sewer. These two tools are primary ones because they are used directly and often in the making of the basket. Technically, the lap cover or apron the women use is a secondary tool—an associated tool of the trade. They spread an old shirt or apron over the lap, whatever the condition of the clothing underneath, in order to protect themselves from the litter of straw and the pricking of the newly cut ends. The cover is well spread out and shields the whole lap area, forming a surface on which the women work.

The palmetto, sea grass, and pine straw are used for different purposes in the making of the baskets. The sea grass forms the base for the basket, the palmetto is the binding thread, and the pine straw gives color variation. Mrs. Manigault had indicated the importance of color. On the mats, one can plainly distinguish which is the right or wrong side because the color alternation appears only on the side where the coil turns clockwise. Many of the baskets in the Mount Pleasant area do indeed coil clockwise. The stitches slant somewhat to the left as one looks into the basket. Both of these factors might be thought to be a function of which hand the maker favors. One basketmaker was left-handed and she made one particularly large basket in which the stitches of the section completed by the right-handed basketmaker had the stitches slanting as usual while those of the left-handed basketmaker had the stitches slanting the other way, somewhat in the manner of handwriting. The community aspect of the craft does not usually show up quite so plainly because the people, sewing on one or a group of baskets, follow along on one another's work smoothly.

Raw Materials

The materials for the baskets are usually harvested by the makers themselves, but there is no proscription against having others do it for them. Often, they ask members of any age in the family to go to the areas known to be good for harvesting by the presence of all three necessary materials. There doesn't appear to be ownership of trees or areas, but people will keep a good harvesting spot secret for as long as they can. The palmetto fronds come from a short tree for which the state of South Carolina is named the Palmetto State; it is the cabbage palm (*Sabal palmetto*). The sea grass is a single-strand grass that grows in marshy areas; it is called sweet grass (*Mulenbergia filipes* m. a. curtis), which can be found all over the Sea Islands area. The people from Mount Pleasant often go as far away as Johns and James Islands (about twenty miles) or even as far as Florida, where there are some good harvesting spots. The long-needle pine trees that characteristically grow in sandy soil provide the third ingredient in this type of basketmaking. The pine straw comes from the *Pinus pilustris*, which grows in the so-called Lowcountry area of South Carolina—i.e., below Columbia, South Carolina—and is found increasingly toward the coast. The palmetto is hung up to dry in the sun and air before it is slit into ribbons and used. The pine straw dries out or is harvested from the ground. At that point, it is already brown and is then soaked in water, ideally rainwater collected in a tub is used. The sea grass is spread out indoors out of the sun to dry for a varying amount of time according to the weather.

The baskets are built in many different shapes and sizes. The rice fanner is an old type of basket not made any more except by special order. One of the ingredients of the fanner was oak splits. The oak bark was peeled, soaked, and used to make the baskets. Oak-split basketmakers used to reside in the Sea Islands area, but this type of basketry seems to have fallen into disuse in the Charleston area in recent years. The oak splits are difficult to obtain because their harvest required complex knowledge and precise timing according to the seasons of the year. Added to that is the fact that the island area is building up and there is less wooded acreage to utilize for this type of wild harvesting. The big fanners Ms. Manigault makes today are made of a rush called *Juncus roemerianus scheele,* which is larger and stiffer than the sea grass and grows in the salt marshes (which just about reach their northern limit in South Carolina). They are dried on the roof of a shed after harvesting so they get both sun and air. The harvesting is seasonal, mostly during the summer and fall months, and is dependent on weather. July, sometimes June, is extremely rainy and it slows down the drying process. The modern fanners are sewn with palmetto, which means they are not as strong or durable as the oak-split styles of former times. Interestingly, the color alteration, a kind of checkerboard effect, more closely resembles that of an oak-split basket than the three coils in a row of pine straw ideal of the coiled baskets.

Tourist Trade

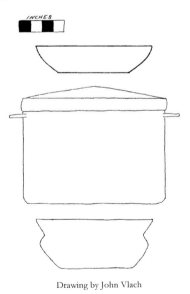

During the plantation time and post-Civil War era, the basketry was mainly manufactured for local uses. Now, however, the baskets are geared mainly to what the tourists will buy, for the makers rely upon the travelers on Route 17, the occasional shop owner, and special orders for their sales. Their prices vary according to the amount of time put into the products. Mrs. Manigault and others report a day or so to make a small basket. The basketsewers try to keep a good selection on their stands at all times, but variety fluctuates with sales and the women's ability to produce at a fairly consistent

Drawing by John Vlach

rate. Other members of the family help out by either making baskets or minding the stand. Family responsibilities also occasionally impinge on their ability to concentrate on making and/or selling the baskets.

In the past, the baskets were used for many practical items—such as fanning rice, winnowing corn or other grains, measuring food allotment, traveling and harvesting, sewing, and collecting money in the churches. The church offering basket is still an integral part of the culture; it looks like a small fanner and is used for gathering a different kind of harvest. As stated above, the patterns are now more suited to what sells. Knotted and sewed, the wall vessels, purses, bread trays, mats, glass coaster trays, waste baskets, and flower baskets are among the shapes which reappear with fair consistency.[4]

African Connection

Peter Weil reports from his work with the Bambara-Djula ethnic community in Mali (West Africa) that the coiling techniques as used by the Mount Pleasant people are found in this area of Africa as well. In Mali, they use coiling to make bowl covers that will fit down inside the bowl on top of food given to the men working in the fields. The covers keep the food hot and the bugs out. The coiling technique is also seen in the flat face masks worn by the newly circumcised boys when they run through the village whipping their sisters and other women in a show of their changed status. Thinly disguised in their straw masks, they symbolically wreak their vengeance for the physical humiliations of their childhood years.[5] The masks are very similar to the mats from South Carolina, but they have holes for eyes and a loop or handle at the side, executed in exactly the same way as on the South Carolina baskets, either for use as handles or for decoration. Among the Bambara-Djula speakers, the basket containers are associated with females and their roles in the society, specifically the holding capacity of the baskets is equated with the women's carrying children. It seems interesting that there is an obvious connection among the Mount Pleasant people, as well, between women and basketmaking.

From my research conducted in West Africa, it would appear that the model for the coiled basketry found in the Sea Islands came over often but not exclusively with enslaved Africans from the Senegambian region of West Africa. Coiled basketry, one of man's oldest patterns, is easy to find in many societies. In the Sea Islands and the Senegambian area, however, we are dealing with groups whose genetic, historic, and linguistic links are known, so the basketry merely adds one more piece of evidence that the same routes that carried the people and their language also transmitted the basketry patterns.

Ruth Finnegan reports the tremendous importance of rice in the Limba culture, a prominence once enjoyed in Sea Islands life.[6] Peter Weil also reports that rice is important in the group he studied, as are the keeping and holding capacities of women and baskets. In the past, rice was an important crop in the Sea Islands, and its production and technology were associated with the baskets; it was, no doubt, part of the culture in a much more integral way than it is now, though it is still a staple food eaten three meals a day in some families.

Fanning and Farming

One of the tools used in rice production and technology was the rice fanner, which is actually a winnowing tool whose motion is reminiscent of a fan. It is held with both hands grasping the basket edge one hundred and eighty degrees apart, directly in front of the person "fanning" the rice; the wrists move up and down, causing the basket to flap and jostle the grain around, up into the air, and back into the basket or down into another basket placed on the ground. The heavier grains are winnowed by holding one fanner facing outwards from the worker and shaking the grain out so it drops into the basket directly beneath and the wind blows the chaff away meanwhile. Before the actual fanning is done, the farmers "ray" the rice, which consists of a sliding action around inside the basket so that the husks will catch on the rough material of the basket and be loosened from the kernel. In Edith M. Dabbs's book, there are fine pictures of fanners in action and baskets being made within the context of Sea Islands life in 1909.[7]

Ms. Florence Mahoney from Banjul, the Gambia, reports that the Djulas in her area also make coiled basketry of the type made on the Sea Islands today, citing the example of the bowl cover. The creole word for fanner in the Gambia among the liberated Africans is "fanna." She also said that in Senegal, the Djula build beehives in the shape used by Mrs. Manigault for a mail basket.[8] The fanna is manipulated in the same manner as among the Sea Islanders. Here we have an interesting case not only in reaffirmation but double transferal, once over here and once back to Africa.

In the *Man in Africa* installation at the Museum of Natural History in New York City, organized by Colin Turnbull, there is a section entitled "The New World Experience." In it are four coiled baskets, two from the modern period and two winnowing baskets from an earlier period. The two large winnowing baskets were dated before 1860 from South Carolina and circa 1900 from Angola. The two modern baskets were marked as having come from Senegal and South Carolina. Each of the two sets of baskets is similar in materials of manufacture and style of execution. They are a silent demonstration of the continuity of material traditional culture between West Coast Africa and the United States.

By determining the range of types of these baskets, perhaps the characteristics which separate them from those of other culture groups who also make coiled basketry can be delineated more clearly. Most of what has been done is concerned with Native American baskets, which seem generally to be classified by the technique of manufacture, such as coiling, twilling, or weaving. Studies of this type are useful in considering coiled basketry. Clara Lee Turner in *Southwest Indian Craft Arts* talks about coiled basketry:

> . . . coiled weave is the most productive of design, it is simply sewing wefts about warps. The foundation in this weave can be varied; over the bundle, two rods or a bundle of one, two, or three rods is sewed, the weft which may be wider or narrower and the color of which can be changed at any point. Rims vary in basketry; they may be simply wrapped, or sewed in the regular coiled stitch, or finished off in a more elaborate herringbone stitch.[9]

The Sea Islands baskets basically fall into Mason's category of coiled work without foundation.

As coiled basketry is such an old, widespread method of basket construction, we must define our particular coiled basket in order to see what is peculiar to it. Turner's paragraph above states some of the variables involved fairly succinctly. The rods are analogous to the grass strands in Sea Islands basketry, as they are bundled to form a stronger construction element. The Sea Islands baskets are made entirely of natural materials, which are not treated or dyed. The wetting of the pine straw and drying of the sweet grass in air and sun, cutting with scissors, and splitting of the palmetto are the only modifications the materials undergo before being used to make the basket.

Once the coils are made, they are not covered with any other material. Alan Merriam's article, "Art and Economics in Basongye Raffia Basketry," shows a style of coiled basketry whose coils are completely masked by the dyed material, which is wound over the basic coiling work.[10] Among the Basongye of Zaire, it is considered poor esthetic practice to have coils show. It is an example of coiled basketry, which is completely different from the work we are considering and the production of which is governed by different standards and which illustrates some of the variety of styles within the classification of coiled basketry.

It has been noted that techniques of manufacture make a difference as an awl can be manipulated in, at least, two different ways. This point about the awl is only one of a number of those possible concerns with techniques of handling tools and materials. Perhaps this is a small issue and possibly useless to the archaeologist; however, research from one point of view is as interested in process as product. The Mount Pleasant basketmakers use an underhand stroke as they thrust the awl ("bone") into a bundle of straw whereas the Wolof basketmakers of Senegal use an overhand thrust. Moving a bit further along the transatlantic continuum to Jamaica, we find the coiled basket makers there use a hand position similar to that of a grip on a pencil, which puts it midway between the under- and overhand thrusts of the African and African American basketmakers. The end result is the same— a hole has been opened up for the binding material to go through. The technique for this style of manufacture is adequately described and classified as "sewed coiling."

Classification by techniques of manufacture is probably the most useful line of inquiry because West African societies have wide ranges of fiber textile and basketry styles and techniques, many of which were present in the Sea Islands in times past, as can be seen in historically oriented displays— such as the one at the Old Slave Mart Museum in Charleston, South Carolina. Use, size, shape, and function would also help us to ascertain where these baskets were used, for now they are sold to tourists almost exclusively.

It would appear that the approach from the gross morphological features may be one method of grouping the baskets in combination with a classification scheme based on techniques of manufacture. Establishing gross morphology could be the key to function in the life of the community once the manufacturing techniques had been described. Possibly, there is a typical profile which might emerge after measuring several hundred baskets at predetermined points. I have measured fifty baskets and find they range from simple types, such as fanners and church collection baskets, to complex types, such as footed curvilinear vases with high overtop handles. The results of this preliminary study show two basic basket outlines: a low, flat profile found in the fanners, which would correspond to Shepard's restricted-type vessel. The fanner style and the round basket with lid and handles are older, traditional utilitarian containers, while the purses, vases, and glass-holding coaster

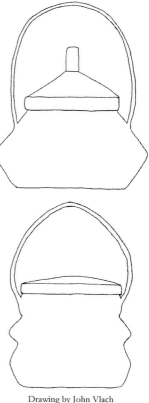

Drawing by John Vlach

trays are European-influenced decorative items. Although the techniques of manufacture and early useful shapes clearly point to African analogs, European influence is evident in the shapes of the more modern baskets.

It seems reasonable to conjecture that the shapes of the baskets relate to the values of the societies producing them. The communitarian lifestyle of West African agricultural economies gives rise to the open-flared or straight-sided basketry profile. However, the more individualistically oriented societies of Europe and America tend to produce the more protectively closed outline observable in the more modern baskets.[11]

While it is risky to propose broad conclusions of this type without reservation on cultural matters, it is not unsafe to suppose that the climate and culture which surround the manufacture of the baskets predispose their design and use just as the ecology of the producing area determines the materials from which the products are actually made.

Alan Merriam's analysis of the cognitive process regarding the arts in anthropology neatly encapsulates the influence of the cultural-ecological framework of the final artistic product. The *concept*, fed by cultural values and input, develops into the *process*, which utilizes available materials in such a way as to result in the final *product*. This resultant artistic trait then feeds back into the conceptual stage by providing a model for the expressive behavior within the culture.[12]

The film *African Carving: Kaguru Masks of the Dogon of Mali* shows such a process graphically and impressively as the audience follows the artist in the culture from the ritual prayer to the tree, yielding up the wood for the masks, through to the ceremonial occasion during which the product functions in a religious context. The ceremonial appearance of the masks is the apotheosis of the process, which began at the base of the living tree.[13]

This pattern of artistic behavior in human societies applies to the Sea Islands baskets as well. The basketmakers conceive of ideas for new baskets within the framework of their traditional culture as well as through stimulus from the outside world. With the materials found in their new environment, they fashioned implements using the templates of their home cultures. The products of this cultural reaffirmation, in turn, reinforced the remembrance of their parents' homes and carried forward the crafts learned in a similar agricultural setting. Only time and distance from the home culture decreased the chances of survival of the whole culture complexes, but certain unmistakably African stylistic traits remain in the traditional lifestyle of the Sea Islanders in spite of undeniable culture change.

Of late, there have been economic developments which cannot help but impact this culture even more. Hilton Head, with its golf courses and condominiums, doubtless provided the model for the development on Daufuskie Island, Georgia. Kiawah Island, South Carolina, was a place for harvesting for the basketmakers, but it too has been developed into controlled, high-priced wilderness recreation, so the basketmakers must go farther afield to obtain their essentials.

A member of a more recent generation of basketmakers says they have to go as far as Florida now. She has been experimenting with more modern forms of basketry as well as recreating the traditional shapes. Like many of the other artisans in the Charleston area, she learned from older female relatives and is transmitting her knowledge, both as an artist and a tradition bearer, to her daughter. She thereby perpetuates a long, truly African tradition in the Americas which has evolved from making useful vessels for the plantation to making items attractive to tourists in the Charleston area. She has also developed her own aesthetic stylistic contribution to the art of African American basketry as a whole. It might, therefore, be said that it is precisely because of the culture's flexibility to change, through such innovation of its practitioners, that arts like the basketry continue to adapt and survive.

Quiltworks

The quilt patterns in the tops of the quilts are pieced reconstructions of the weaving of the Ewe and Ashanti people of West Africa.[14] Needless to say, that patterning looked quite different from the quilts made by the traditional Euro-American quiltmakers. Persons outside the Sea Islands culture and men within the culture tended to dismiss the quilts as not having a discernable pattern but simply being the result of throwing together whatever pieces of cloth are available and making up a quilt.

During the 1970s, there were Mennonites from Pennsylvania doing alternate service (to the military draft) who came to Johns Island, South Carolina, to help with building safe, dry housing for the Islanders. The young women started a quilting group and carefully instructed the Island women in the "proper" method of doing quilts, as they regarded the strip patterns as nondesign. It was a clear case of ethnocentrism with the best intentions! The Mennonites cut cardboard templates, just as they would at home, for the Island ladies to use as patterns to make the evenly balanced, centrally organized quilts with which they were familiar in their Pennsylvania homes. The Islanders, being among the most gracious people in the world, went ahead to make the quilts in the required designs. The results were significant. The home culture of the African Americans surfaced through their interpretations of the Euro-American patterns. It was also clear that appliqué,[15] epitomized in the Harriet Powers quilts, was not part of their lexicon of techniques. It became apparent that the Islanders were reaffirming their African heritage and that those culture bearers doubtless came from areas of West Africa where they do the strip weaving of rectangular/block patterns. In a review of all the slides submitted for Roy Sieber's show of African Household and Domestic items (there were hundreds, some in the show and some not), I found the typical offset patterns which resulted from the woven belts being edge sewn to each other to be reasonably widespread in West Africa. Often the staggered pattern effect was planned to come out that way, as the border always lined up at the end. Rectilinear emphasis, partially due to the belt-weaving setup of the weaving looms, prevailed in most of the patterns.[16] Not all of the weaving was done on the narrow belt looms; for example, the Senufo wove on wider looms twelve to fourteen inches.[17] These narrow belt dimensions are the patterns that came to the Sea Islands with the African culture bearers. Appliqué work may have been there at one time; however, it may be speculated that the prevailing patterns are indicative of the ethnic and cultural origins of Harriet Powers in rural Georgia (Dahomean) and the Sea Islanders (Ashanti and Ewe from Ghana).

The Mennonites came from a religious group that constitutes the nucleus of their society in closely associated settlements, which also form the basis of their culture, including folkways, aesthetic judgments, and pattern formation. Their eyes were trained to the balanced centrality that was traditional in their group. Like the Sea Islanders at that time (1970s), the Mennonites had been a somewhat isolated societal group of limited exposure to other cultural influences. Different influences operated and prevailed within each of these ethnic groups, so when they came together under the extraordinary circumstances of the 1960s—the civil rights movement, Great Society, Vietnam War, etc.—it took a while for there to be comprehension on both sides.

Creativity in African American quilting consists in the vision of each artist, the motivation or reason for creating an artifact, reinforcement between attitudes and patterns within the culture, means of production, materials and time available to do such work, and their own selectivity. The resultant patterns depend partly on the clothing and other materials utilized for the quilts, which might occasionally be yard goods. On the whole on the Sea Islands, quiltmaking was mainly a salvage craft using clothes and other household textiles otherwise discarded, putting them through the cultural mill and giving them a new lease on life as quilts or pillows.

Within a culture, *concept* feeds into *process*, which in turn creates a *product*; that *product* then recirculates back to inform the *concept*, and the cycle begins again. Whatever changes during the process and in the product by way of innovation feed into the concept, thereby producing culture change.[18] Creativity in African American groups features innovation as a valued characteristic; jazz, dance, speech, visual arts, broom making, net knitting, and quilting all emphasize the introduction of change by the manufacturing or performing artist. Sometimes the modification incorporates a novelty from the popular culture, from another culture, or may be expressive of an illuminating emotional, intellectual, or religious experience the creative artist may have had.

Many folk artists, including the quilters, will have a vision or dream which gives them the pattern for the item they will make. Since Sea Islanders are deeply religious, "the Lord" is often thought to be the source of this inspiration, and the experience of creativity a spiritual one. The term "soul" is an encapsulation of the secular adaptation of the spirituality of the Africanized Christianity the Sea Islanders practice. Art, as well as religion, is a route into the feeling of inspiration sometimes characterized as "like being in church." The final material product, with its practical utility, is most often secondary to the inspiration or concept which moves the artist to create. It is also secondary to the process which brings it into being—the creating of the piece. The Sea Islanders coming from a "spirit meeting" in the praise house (not a church, but a separate structure and institution) would sigh and say, "That was good experience meeting!" The creation of "folk" (which means to say art specific to the people) art, including the quilts, has a function as in African art, and that purpose, often spiritual, enriches the artist and the viewers' lives through the connection to that feeling of having participated in a "good experience meeting."

It is this quality of artistic and creative inspiration that in the West is called genius, and it is known that some people have it and some do not. It comes as the breath of life from another power.

Women as Conservators of Culture

An important function of the society is to guard the culture, so to speak. The women are conservative of the culture, as they are the generators of food, are responsible for the care of children and their upbringing, and they are the producers of quilts and quilt tops and other things significant of comfort and family. One of the reasons these African patterns present in the quilts of African American women were not known before they were is that the quilts and their use are part of the intimate core of the culture. This heart of the group's life is the source of the "basket" or nicknames, the manufacture of fishnets, basketry, and other domestic material culture, including the quilts. Although the notion of exclusively matriarchal families causes debate, it is true that there is strong matrifocality in Sea Islands families, and one of the symbols of the nurturing control women may exercise is the stockpile of quilts and quilt tops, which may be stored against the special occasion. These special events can include the annual onset of cold weather, a child going to live in a different household, or a youth departing for the mainland to attend school. Weddings and births are prime special times when quilts will be part of the trousseau or layette. The quilts are also given to male children, not only to young women, when they marry. Quilt tops will be hauled out to refurbish older quilts which have seen heavy use. Newer covers may be grafted onto the old quilts to preserve the warmth of the old one, on the point of becoming rags, thus fulfilling an ongoing need of the family for covers through matrifocal nucleation. Some older women within the community will make quilts for others for a small fee and a blanket given to the quilter for the armature or stuffing of the quilt. The quilt may be put together with two tops or backed with rice bags or yard goods. The pieced lengths of material can be tops or go on to become pieced yard goods or lengths of cloth themselves.

It is often assumed by outsiders or men in the culture that a "patchy" quilt, as they call it, is the result of a random bunching of handy materials to serve the purpose of keeping warm. It is evident in looking at the quilts that a process of aesthetic selection is involved in "setting together" the tops, which is done on tables, beds, or in chairs. The material, from whatever source, is cut into rectangles or strips and spread out to determine what is the best layout to conform to the vision they might have had. This selectivity is the heart of the creative process, since the aesthetic judgment of color, shape, and position is manifested by the quilter who is working securely within her cultural framework, but who exercises total control over the arrangement.

Euro-American traditional quilters work within their culturally prescribed catalogue of patterns for which they choose colors, but for whom the triumph is in the exquisite reproduction of the time-honored, prescripted exemplars. One can hear, in such an ambiance, nearly endless conversations about log cabins, bow ties, Dresden plates, double wedding rings, drunkard's paths, etc., whereas quilt scholars are the only ones who discuss African American patterns as each woman makes her own strip patterns. Because of the salvage nature of the craft and the importance of innovation in the culture, the raw materials available provide the opportunity for a new and varied creative undertaking each time.

The use of old clothing and other domestic cloths contributes to a textile of familiarity and meaning to those who can read the cryptic message. As a rule, only the members of the intimate family core can "read" these documents, which have personal historical significance. It is that group who knows and uses the "basket" name to whom these quilted documents are an open book.[19]

An example of the memorialization of family members through the use of textile documents is found in the "Smith" family of Alabama; the mother was cooking dinner in the kitchen, according to the family story, and realizes that her sixteenth child was about to be born. She repaired to the birthing room adjacent to the kitchen, bore the child, Carrie, and bled to death before anyone knew what was happening. The crying baby alerted the family that something had happened and they discovered the tragic situation. The mattress "tick" (ticking) was soaked in blood. Aunt Lula, her sister-in-law, gathered up the tick in spite of the urgings of the rest of the family to throw it out. Lula was a quiltmaker for a family and neighborhood. She did not fit the usual image of a sedate quilter stitching a fine seam. Lula chewed tobacco and sat where she could spit outside while working on the quilts. She integrated the bloodstained tick into quilts and pillows for each of the sisters as a memorial to her sister-in-law. To the uninitiated, the stain looks like rust or a persistent chocolate ice cream mark, but those who know the family history understand and appreciate the significance of the seemingly random stain. The quilt is now owned by a member of the fourth generation, holding it in trust for her children. One of the Harriet Powers quilts from Athens, Georgia (now housed in the Boston Museum of Fine Arts), has similar stains on a bordering material, which may be a textile memorial to a lost family member.

An African parallel to this family group of women is the "yafunu" among the Ashanti, a matrilineage kinship unit consisting of five generations tracing their relationship back to a common ancestress and typified by the expression "we are of one blood." Quite literally, the "Smith" family has perpetuated the memory of the sacrifice of the original mother, and the quiet heroism of the oldest daughter who raised Carrie is the message of the bloodstained quilts. All of it was transmitted through the women in the family and quilts handed down through them to the fifth generation.

What makes the Sea Islands quilts different from other quilts or other African American quilts? Clearly, the need for blankets, bedcovers, and aesthetic decoration are unifying factors with other groups. The same is true of the role of women as conservators of culture in African American groups and their centrality in the preservation of cultural practices and traits. Factors which might contribute to a sense of distinction could include the physical and social—hence cultural—isolation they have endured. These isolative factors—which are geographic, linguistic, and economic—have been instrumental in the continuation of African-influenced habits and attitudes. That unwitting reaffirmation of the African past is not a deliberate effort on their part, but simply doing things the way they knew how and had been taught to do them. The quilts on the Sea Islands have mainly been the "strip" quilts, and it may be that the Islanders do the appliqué style, which may be seen against a backdrop of suffusion of African traits in the rest of the culture.

The quilts of the Sea Islands clearly relate to the men's capes of Suriname,[20] the Haitian voodoo flags,[21] the checkered cloths of emblems of the Kongo culture spoken of by Robert Farris Thompson,[22] the patched sails of the boats in Benin,[23] West Africa, as well as the cotton kente cloth of Ewe manufacture and the glowing silk kente of the Ashanti.

The cotton kente of the Ewe is illustrated in the shirts worn by Ewe-speaking farmers with the offset linear and rectilinear patterns with the green/blue and other muted colors typical of the Ewe palette.[24] The Ashanti kente cloth tends to use a brighter palette—bright red, kelly green, yellow, sapphire, reflecting colors at a certain intensity obtainable with dyed silk. A Ga-Adangme student from Ghana seated in a class at Atlanta University, which was examining a quilt made by Ms. Janie Hunter of Johns Island, South Carolina, looked over and casually remarked, "Oh, that's Ewe." The quilt is replete with the muted greens, blues, and violets of the Ewe color palette and set in the staggered patterns of the edge-sewn strips.

The difference between the cloths—such as the capes, flags, kente cloths, etc.—found in other parts of the African World and the Sea Islands quilts is that the former all have their significance in public spheres and the quilts are found in close domestic circles. The flags, etc., are associated with heroic images and declaration of identity in societies where public display was permissible and appropriate. The emblems of identity among the African American households of the Sea Islands had to be more private because of the repressive situation in which they found themselves. And private they remained until researchers came along and began to talk about them, exhibit them, and put them in books. One other difference between the African cloths and the African American quilts is in the event of their manufacture. In Africa weavers are men who do the belt weaving,[25] which eventually results in the kente cloths, while the quiltmakers in the Sea Islands are women. Their aesthetic decoration and preservation of the typical designs of their people had to be banners that were displayed on the beds of their families, spreading out with them wherever they went, taking their family histories and cultural markers with them. The high display of the patched sails in Benin shows the aesthetic boldly displayed as the boats sail along in the lacustrine marshes of West Africa. They are clearly another proof of the durability of this staggered, offset pattern, which informs the Ewe cloth, the South American capes, Béninois sails, and the Sea Islands quilts.

Nets

The Islanders make fishnets to be used in setting, seining, drop, or cast-net fishing. In the winter, when there is less agricultural work to do and fishing is not so comfortable, people knit nets. There are a number of different kinds: a mullet net, with large holes; a shrimp net, with small holes; a "poor man" net, which will catch almost anything; and drop and seine nets, each of which have large holes. Cast nets are knit with cotton string (Gold Medal No. 6). The foot line, which runs around the lower edge of the net and up through the middle, ends in a loop called the handline, which slips over the wrist of the thrower and tightens up to fit the wrist. Round animal bones were usually used as rope guides; forty spent bullets are used to weigh down the foot line, so that when the net is cast, it will swing out into a curved, domelike shape in the air before it falls into the water.[26]

The nets are knit with a needle traditionally carved from palmetto wood, measuring twelve inches long, five-eighths of an inch wide, and a quarter inch thick.[27] The local hardware stores carry a plastic variety, which is regarded as a poor substitute by the net knitters. Another tool utilized in the making of the nets is the gauge, which can be a five- to seven-inch length of doweling, or other evenly rounded wood, whose size varies according to what size net is being made. One can use a piece of wood about the size of an ordinary pencil for a shrimp net; the gauge for a "poor man" net is seven by one-half inches and is slightly pointed. The gauge holds the stitches, while the needle functions as a shuttle and moves in and out forming the knots.

Ms. Janie Hunter had knit nets since she was very young. Her father was a fisherman and taught her and her six brothers and sisters to knit nets when they were children. Now the Bligen brothers and sisters are all up in years, but they still cooperated in making the nets until recently. Benjamin Bligen started the net, Ms. Hunter knitted the main body of the net, and then Benjamin put the lead weights on the foot line. Benjamin often went fishing in the early morning and cast nets in the same style as the present-day Nigerians do.[28]

Mr. Joe Engles knit nets in the winter when it rained. During spring, summer, and fall, there was plenty of agricultural work to be done, both for himself and other people. When the rains come, however, and the weather is cold, it is a good time to sit to the long task of net knitting. The net remains hanging on a peg or nail and can be worked by one or two family members, off and on as the opportunity arises. While they work together, they tell stories, jokes, gossip, or sing, depending on who is doing the knitting.

The nets are set, cast, dropped, and dragged. The Island men cast nets from rowboats and dories by holding them in both arms, although some hold the net at one point with the teeth. They twist the body away from the direction of the cast and then turn themselves around and fling out the net at the same time (the people who use teeth to hold must remember to let go at the crucial moment). The fisherman may then pull on the handline around his wrist and harvest his catch in the net. Some of these cast nets are mullet size to catch bigger fish; others are shrimp size to catch smaller creatures. Crabs, however, are caught with lines and drop nets, often using chicken necks for bait, when the tide is running in the brackish marshes.

The fishermen go around the Islands or into Charleston to sell their catch on the street. Things have not changed much in that respect since DuBose Heyward wrote *Porgy*.[29]

The nets are cast in the same way that the West Africans cast fish nets. The problem of origin, however, is complicated by the fact that explorers and travelers have been journeying from Europe to West Africa since the 1400s. It would appear that the Asturian fishermen in the Northern Iberian peninsula make and cast the nets in essentially the same fashion as the West Africans and the Sea Islanders.[30] Since there were Africans occupying Spain for seven hundred years, a cultural transmission may well have taken place at that time.

Brooms

Brooms have been a tool of domestic use, a focus of beliefs, and an object of fantasy and speculation. Whisks and brooms have integral uses in West African societies. Whisks are an indicator of elevated status in certain West African groups (Tshi, Ghana), flourished and manipulated just as the wavers of fans do in Ethiopian upper-class society. Whisks, fans, and brooms all move something—air, trash, sand/earth, insects, people—which implies issues of control consistent with the status of the people engaged in their use. Whisks help to keep other people and flies at a suitable distance from Ghanaian rulers, fans serve in much the same role for those who use them as well as indicating that their wielders do not have to do manual labor. Brooms are of use in more homely functions, contributing both to the decoration of an area, its cleanliness, and other domestic operations associated with the belief system.

Beliefs are often referred to as superstitions, a word which tends to devalue the worth of the subject under discussion. Beliefs held by persons in the culture are part of a demonstrable system sometimes because of the practical sense of it—such as not walking under a ladder. Less apparently, logical beliefs are just as much a part of a cultural belief system, in spite of a more wishful emphasis. The practice dictated by the logical or nonlogical belief gives the person a feeling of being able to take action about a situation possibly otherwise beyond their control.

In the South of the United States, African Americans have preserved some of their African heritage through various cultural practices. One of the least known or understood is the use of brooms. At the artistic level, brooms have been used to sweep yards and leave them with decorative patterns on the surface. Alice Walker's story "Everyday Use" begins:

> I will wait for her in the yard that Maggie and I made so
> clean and wavy yesterday afternoon. A yard like this is more

comfortable than most people know. It is not just a yard. It is like an extended living room. When the hard clay is swept clean as a floor and the fine sand around the edges lined with tiny, irregular grooves, anyone can come and sit and look up into the elm tree and wait for the breezes that never come inside the house.[31]

The practical use of the brooms in cleaning the house is hedged around with many beliefs governing their manipulation and use. I recently heard a mother lamenting the fact that she had not "fixed" the space in which her son was living with the result that bad things came about. The cleansing function of the sweeping done with brooms or hands is crucial to the making of an habitable place. In the Caribbean and the Sea Islands, it is believed that upending the broom in the corner, the lingering or unwelcome guest will leave. If you sweep out after dark, you will sweep out the luck of the household. One will also sweep out the bad luck, which may come in on the feet of an evilly intentioned person by sweeping the footsteps of that person after he has departed.

Short brooms are made of broom sedge, which grows all around the Southeast at roadside and otherwise unused arable land. The sedge is bundled and tied with grocery or net-knitting string or natural fibers. Everyone in the rural areas knows how to make them as they are in constant use sweeping hearth, house, and yard.

The broom in slavery times was used for one of the only kind of marriage ceremonies the owners would allow between enslaved Africans. The ceremony was called "jumping the broom."

Drawing by John Vlach

The brooms and sweeping make demarcations between one state and another: dirty/clean, visited/unvisited, or structured or patterned/formless. They are instruments of making order out of chaos, and therefore, have special or mystic characteristics. They relate to the thresholds between life/death, safety/risk or danger, and structured/patternless. They provide us with the tools to control our environment hence endowing us with certain godlike qualities. The song "Fare Ye Well" states, "Jesus gib me a little broom for to sweep my heart clean; sweep 'em clean by the grace of God, an' glory in my soul."[32]

Chinese and West Africans have path- and grave-sweeping ceremonies, which are annual important remembrances of the dead ancestors. Furthermore, these sweepings and cleanings open up the paths of the living to continue to honor the ancestors whose goodwill and aid is solicited from time to time. The sweeping ceremonies clear the environments for another year or ceremonially determined period of time while providing opportunity for festivities for the general populace, rather like our Memorial Day. Decoration Day, as it is sometimes called, has its serious aspects in the memorializing of the dead, but also in providing holiday opportunities for the public as the analogous occasion does in West Africa.

The magic attached to brooms includes the association with witches. In Louisiana, it was believed that anyone refusing to step over a broom was a witch. The broom was therefore an effective divining rod of sorts to help identify the witchly person and a barrier to keep a witch or hag from riding you. The sedge brooms formerly so common in the South were especially helpful as the theory went. The hag or witch had to count all the straws in it before she could come in the door. The broom-blocked door is also supposed to immobilize the witch once she was actually in the room.

It was once believed in Alabama that a crying child may be silenced by sweeping all the dirt in the house past him in the doorway. Near Savannah, African Americans held the belief that you could discourage an enemy from returning to your house by sweeping out after him, following that up by putting salt on his foot tracks and sweeping all that out the door as a kind of purification ceremony. The significance of brooms in the Sea Islands is the amount of sway over forces, natural and supernatural, one may control with brooms and sweeping.

The Africanity of the crafts is a mixed phenomenon as it is with the oral lore. There is an easily recognizable congruence between the baskets from the Senegambian region of West Africa and the Afro-Carolinian baskets from the Sea Islands of the Southeastern United States. The quilts, however, are synthesized combinations of African-style design on the tops, or occasional backing, and Euro-American technology for the filling and backing. The nets are manufactured, handled, and deployed in the manner of West African fishermen. Although the style of casting nets is not exclusive to African World peoples, the route of transmission in this case is clear. The brooms have African affiliations and meanings as well as traits peculiar to their American setting.

---

[1] The descriptive ethnography in this chapter is taken from my fieldwork and doctoral dissertation.

[2] Harriet Powers, quilter, Clark County, GA. See Regenia Perry, *Harriet Powers's Bible Quilts* (New York: Rizzoli Art Series, 1994).

[3] William Pollitzer, *The Gullah People and Their African Heritage* (Athens: University of Georgia Press, 1999).

[4] Mary Arnold Twining, "Sea Island Basketry: Reaffirmation of West Africa," in *The First National African-American Crafts Conference: Selected Writings*, ed. David C. Driskell (Memphis: Shelby State Community College, 1980), 35–39.

[5] Peter Weil, Personal Communication, 1979; Mary Arnold Twining, "Sea Island Quilts," in *The First National African-American Crafts Conference: Selected Writings*, ed. David C. Driskell (Memphis: Shelby State Community College, 1980).

[6] Ruth Finnegan, *Limba Stories and Story Telling* (Oxford, UK: Oxford Library of African Literature, 1967).

[7] Edith M. Dabbs, *Face of an Island* (New York: Grossman, 1971).

[8] Ms. Florence Mahoney, Personal Communication, 1979.

[9] Clara Turner, *Southwest Indian Craft Arts* (Tuscon: University of Arizona Press, 1968).

[10] Alan Merriam, "Art and Economics in Basongye Raffia Basketry," *African Arts* 2, no. 1(1968), 14–17, 73; See Julie Dash, "Praise House," film, 1991; Michael C. Wolfe, *The Abundant Life Prevails* (Waco, TX: Baylor University Press, 2000), 5–6.

[11] I am indebted to Henry Glassie for this observation.

[12] See note 10.

[13] Film available at Indiana University, Audio/Visual Department, Bloomington, Indiana, 47401.

[14] Kate P. Kent, *West African Cloth* (Denver: Denver Museum Pictorial No. 21, 1971).

[15] Appliqué technique involves sewing precut cloth figures onto a background cloth; it is used in Abomey cloths of Benin, West Africa.

[16] William Fagg, ed., *The Living Arts of Nigeria* (New York: Macmillan, 1971); Maude Southwell Wahlman, *Signs and Symbols: African Images in African-American Quilts* (New York: Museum of American Folk Art, 1993).

[17] Mary Arnold Twining, fieldwork, 1970s; Roy Sieber and Roslyn Adele Walker, *African Art in the Cycle of Life* (Washington, DC: Smithsonian Institution Press, 1987).

[18] See note 10.

[19] See L. D. Turner, *Africanisms in the Gullah Dialect* (Chicago: University of Chicago, 1949).

[20] Richard and Sally Price, *Afro-American Arts of the Suriname Rainforest* (Berkeley: University of California Press, 1980), chapter 3.

[21] Haitian Flags, Craig Centrie, Personal Communication, Buffalo, New York, 1980.

[22] R. F. Thompson, "Kongo Influences on African-American Artistic Culture," in *Africanisms in American Culture*, ed. Joseph Holloway (Bloomington: Indiana University Press, 1990), 148–184.

[23] Mary Arnold Twining, research in Benin, West Africa.

[24] See note 16.

[25] See note 16.

[26] See frontispiece in Guy and Candie Carawan, *Ain't You Got a Right to the Tree of Life?* (New York: Simon and Schuster, 1966).

[27] The identical tool called a "shuttle" is used among riverine groups in Nigeria; Patrick Akponwei, Ijaw speaker, Personal Communication, 1971.

[28] Twining, fieldwork with Nigerian and Sea Islands fishermen, 1972.

[29] DuBose Heyward, *Porgy* (New York: Grosset and Dunlap, 1925).

[30] Jeff Espina, Personal Communication, 1969.

[31] Alice Walker, "Everyday Use," ed. Melody Graulich, (New Brunswick, NJ: Rutgers University Press, 1980).

[32] William Francis Allen, Charles Pickard Ware, and Lucy McKim Garrison, *Slave Songs of the United States* (1867; repr., Freeport, NY: Books for Libraries Press, 1971), 93.

Cut a Step

Movement and Dance on the Sea Islands

One spring vacation from graduate school, I came to Johns Island to visit with the young girls and learn more about their games. I had worked with Bessie Jones when she had come onto the island on a Newport Revival of Folk Music grant. I had been introduced to a whole world of games, "plays," and songs that was eye opening. The children sang the songs and played the games, and I sang and danced right along with them. Afterwards, we all went inside the little store in the Progressive Club, and they got to pick out which candy bar they would like to have. When it rained, we went into the multipurpose room where the young men played basketball and the Islanders held "hops," human rights meetings, and seminars. Sound reverberated in that hall and the young singers enjoyed the echoing of their voices as we sang and stomped our way through the games.

A ll dancers utilize their own bodies as instruments manipulated in the surrounding space, alone or among accompanying people to create their artistic or expressive statement. As with language, music, and religion in the Americas where Africanisms have survived, dance belongs to the people, so performance has a cultural manifestation as well as an artistic component.

In many African communities, dance and movement are an integral part of the expressive behavior. Some movement is simple response to a beat or pulse set in motion, while on the other hand some dances are highly complex, ritualized movement done only by those whose knowledge or status qualifies them to participate.

Age range, sex, training, and status all influence who may take part in any given dance or ceremony. The people take seriously their dance responsibilities in the community and take lightly their own expertise in the execution of steps or maneuvers. Although the individual may dance in accordance with traditional patterns handed down in the culture, each one is traditionally encouraged to express his own artistry within that framework.

This model of dance as an individual expression within the dictates of the culture has carried over from the African societies, contributory to the Afro-American population, and is found in both sacred and secular contexts. People of all ages on the Sea Islands dance for varieties of reasons, rarely professional, and there are variations in excellence of execution, but these simply reflect the differences in human experience and accomplishment.

Sea Islanders do not dance solely for other people to watch except when they are courting or wishing to share their feelings. Dance is an expression of life and an important part of life for the people of the Islands. Rhythmic movement is a daily experience, and response to music is immediate. Jukeboxes and radios are everywhere and are used a great deal, so dancing is not saved for a special occasion. Young girls dance as part of their games and "plays" (the word "play" means a dramatic interaction within a game, not a dramatic representation on a stage). They can also do current popular dances that their older brothers and sisters do, and incorporate the steps into their games. They do the steps, though with entirely different motivations, theirs being a kind of "jump for joy" delight in life.

Bow and let me see how you jump for joy

Hey, Miss Sally, won't you bow![1]

For the older people, movement is more usually found within the religious framework of church or praise house. If all age groups are together having a party, however, the young people may stomp on with their rendition of the Popcorn dance, Funky Broadway (popular dances in the 1970s), etc., but as quickly, they will turn to a gospel song in which the elders will join, and the group makes as much noise with the religious songs as with the popular ones.

Generally, however, the older people confine their terpsichorean energies to "shouting" in church or at the praise house. All through these services, singing, rhythmic movement, and speech have been woven together into a unique pattern of religious behavior, which results in a strongly Africanized Christianity.

Each of the hymns starts with everyone seated. One voice "raises" the song. In each group, there are certain recognized leaders who are specially noted for their abilities, but sooner or later everyone gets a chance. Usually a strong second voice will come in with everyone else easing into the action as the spirit begins to move. Further involvement with the music, which is unaccompanied by any but human instruments, brings people to their feet one by one and rhythmic swaying from side to side begins, along with hand clapping, which can be done several ways.

The songs are almost always duple meter (the Islanders characterize them as "common" or "long" meter, referring to fast or slow) and the initial clap pattern is on the beat with an accompanying shift in weight in the feet. The feet take up a stamp in the foot not bearing the weight and the hands shift to a dotted rhythm. The weight shift develops further into a shuffling progression as the feet lift alternately off the floor.

During the shout, as this series of movements is known, the body is inclined forward, although the dancers may wave their arms or gesture with a handkerchief, during which action they may straighten up momentarily.[2] The use of a white handkerchief is an Africanism, as it is found in Yoruba practice.[3] The earlier swaying part of the movement sequence is done with the very erect posture characteristic of the Islander's normal or walking position. The offbeat clap lasts during the rhythmic movement and alternates with the swaying and stamping done to the straight beat-clap pattern.

The choir and ushers' anniversaries are characterized by a great deal of lock-step marching in single file in a step/hold pattern (also used by the deacons). One member of the participating choir or ushers' union delegation begins a song seated. He/she rises to begin the march, collecting people as the line forms in motion. A second song will be started by another member of the delegation once the procession has reached the front of the church. A loose grouping of individuals from the march joins in a general shout, which is a unique combination of moving and singing, not a loud cry.

In some cases, older people hit the ground as they move, with each foot striking a double bounce beat, following which they whirl around quite suddenly and violently. Although they move as the "spirit" moves them, at this point they appear to be in complete control of themselves unless they "fall out" or experience possession, which seems to happen more with women than with men. Their facial expression is one of intent and serious concentration, as though their gaze was focused inward rather than outward. The dance lasts as long as the "spirit" moves them, and then they stop; the reason for stopping is never apparently obvious, yet they all know when the time has come. Sometimes one person or more will not be satisfied that the time to stop has arrived and will start up again and continue until they feel at last that it is the moment to cease. Then they throw up their hands, utter phrases such as "awright" or "yes," and retire to their seats in the body of the church and sigh, out of breath, evidently feeling calm and tranquil.

The activity associated with the term "shouting" is, as described above, a movement/sound complex which includes singing, moving, clapping, and is best classified as a prayer executed with the whole self. Then there was David dancing before the Lord. This series of actions is different from the ring shout, which is a patterned group dance. Shouting can be done by one or many. Ring shout is historically represented in such songs as "Walk, Believer, Walk, Daniel," in which Daniel is exhorted to move, walk, rock, fly, and shout. The song is an escape song in either a prayerful or real sense. Escape from slavery may have indeed historically been the end purpose of all the movement. "Talk about John and you will see John, Hey John" is another Sea Islands ring shout. The Ring Shout is also a combination of all the constituents which are necessary to make a meaningful whole. Artistic experience in many African societies is a holistic complex of many arts and crafts of which dance is only one. The arts of the Sea Islands partake of the African heritage in that dance and movement are not singled out but integrated with song, instrumentation, and dramatic action.[4]

In days past, the ring shout was a major socioreligious phenomenon.[5] The late John Davis of St. Simons Island, Georgia, said the shout was done chiefly at Christmas on St. Simons Island and still is done at that time at Sapelo Island. There are also descriptions in the letters of the teachers who came down to the Sea Islands region to educate the so-called "contrabands of war," as the captured slaves were called toward the end of the Civil War.[6] Abigail Christensen describes it.[7] The late Mrs. Janie Hunter, an older resident of Johns Island, described that it was done to what she called a two-step, with people in the ring as a chorus and orchestra consisting of singers and clappers. This group of musicians might also have stood to one side to fulfill this function.

The shout was done on St. Simons Island by an older group of residents known as the Sea Island Singers. The Ring Shout itself was kept from sliding into oblivion completely by Lydia Parrish, an off-island woman whose love of the music and people impelled her to try to create an atmosphere in which the people would feel comfortable in reconstructing their own heritage. She had a praise house built for the Islanders so they could have a place to foregather. She succeeded in this endeavor; in fact, the Islanders appreciated it, and the results are seen in her classic book *Slave Songs of the Georgia Sea Islands*.[8] The pictures and song texts are invaluable to the researcher now. The descendants of the people researched in that book are still on St. Simons, and the Sea Island Singers have had many participants since those days. Formalized as a group by Alan Lomax, they used to tour the United States and attend folk festivals sharing their heart-stirring music.

When the Ring Shout was to be done, first came the prayer meeting; when it was over, the benches were moved to positions along the walls clearing the floor for action. Educator and activist Septima Clark claims that members of the congregation then chose partners and formed the ring. (They also participated in the ring singly.) All commenced to sing, the participants to keep on around the ring until they were exhausted, when their places would be taken by others. The opening phase of it was a rhythmic walk, the dancers proceeding around the ring, clapping. The rhythm shifted to a syncopated beat as with the general shout, "the jerking hitching motion" described in *The New York Nation* (1867) began, and they wove through a grand right and left according to Septima Clark.[9] The "ring shout" is no longer done now on Johns Island, but fragments of it still remain in the loose formations of "shouting" that go on during prayer meetings, usher's reunions, etc., as described above. It is still done at special times such as Christmas in other parts of the Sea Islands and in performance by the McIntosh County Shouters and the Sea Island Shouters, who recently performed at the World's Largest Ring Shout held on the grounds of the Anacostia Museum of the Smithsonian Institution.[10]

An indication of African continuity is to be noted in the fact that in Jamaica, the Cumina groups dance in a ring similar to the Afro-American ring shouts. Cumina is a Jamaican form of Africanized Christianity. Partners are chosen and dance facing each other their hands on one another's shoulders. They do a kind of two-step—slide, together, slide—without crossing the feet (considered a sign of diabolism or a lack of seriousness regarding one's spiritual state). The Cumina ring and the ring shout both proceed counterclockwise in response to a compelling beat, which is supplied by body percussion in the Sea Islands, and drums in Jamaica. The movement intensifies as it continues from the impetus of the drumming and the emotional involvement of the dancers. As in the Afro-American church shout, the ultimate result may be possession. The male Cumina dancers literally fly upside down out of the circle when the spirit takes them. This manifestation seems to correspond with Haitian voodoo practice and experience and that of the Sea Islanders who also executed that maneuver in times past.[11]

The community spirit and group solidarity shown in these moving experiences are evidently necessary to the survival of the individuals and the group. The dancing is a spiritual, emotional, and physical expression of their own personal difficulties as well as of their suffering as a group. These functions of living within an enclave amongst an alien dominant society have ramified the original culture traits brought by them from Africa. The phenomena of possession in the religious experience as well as rhythmic group movement and call-and-response song patterns were part of their lives before they came here to the Americas. These traits have been incorporated into the Afro-Christian religious complex here in varying degrees, depending on the group and the style of expression. Although none of the dancers is professional, outstanding talent or ability in dancing, however, is highly valued and much admired. Rhythmic movement and dance are integrated into the whole life pattern of the people, which makes it part and parcel of their communications with each other. The paralinguistic gestures, expressive movement, and dance steps all fit into the total pattern of communication, which is broad across the available range of human cultural expression. Although the Afro-American population is particularly active in verbal skills, communication flourishes in other channels. Rhythm is found in speech, song, and movement—a vital characteristic of Afro-American expressive culture.

The pervasiveness of dance and rhythm lead to the idea that movement is of maximum importance in the Afro-American community. If this is so, then the expressive language, not only body language, should manifest this concern. Here is some material as it occurs in the folklore.

Among the Student Nonviolent Coordinating Committee (SNCC) field secretaries, the verb "to move" was most common. The concept of "moving" or "being free to move" or "enabled to move" was a positive goal toward which all their manipulations directed themselves. They meant this in a social revolutionary sense as well as the practical, personally active sense. The movement itself, the organization to which they devoted their time and energy, was also the framework for their activity and expression of their self-image. One of the songs that was sung in Alabama at the time of the formation of the Black Panther Party was "Move on Over or We'll Move on Over You," to the tune of the "Battle Hymn of the Republic."

Ms. Janie Hunter of Johns Island sang a song, "You Got to Move," in which she sang, "You may be rich, you may be poor, but when the Lord get ready, you got to move." The song is expressive of the pervasive phenomenon of movement as a unifying thread within the Afro-American population.

The words obviously relating to movement are step, fly, move, walk, shout, rock, carry, rise, coming and going, motion, wiggle, etc. These words are in many of the songs, sacred and secular, and are often accompanied by specific pantomime or dance movements. For instance:

> Head and shoulders, baby 1-2-3
>
> Head and shoulders, baby 1-2-3
>
> Head and shoulders,
>
> Head and shoulders,
>
> Head and shoulders, baby 1-2-3
>
> I ain't been to Frisco and I ain't been to school.
>
> I ain't been to college, but I ain't no fool.
>
> To the front, to the back, to the front, to the back,

To the side, side, side.[12]

The girls pantomime—touching the head, shoulder, knee, or ankle, throwing the ball in the air, milking the cow—and then mutual clapping to the emphatically repeated 1-2-3 with each successive verse (as in "Pease Porridge Hot"). The last recitation is done jumping forward and back on both feet, then accelerated to the sides alternating.

Another song, called "Down in the Valley," from Johns Island overtly calls for motion:

> Let me see you make a motion 2 by 2, my baby, 2 by 2,
>
> my baby, 2 by 2
>
> Let me see you make a motion, 2 by 2.
>
> Now rise, Sally, rise.

The proving of oneself in these games is accomplished by showing how well you can move, or how inventively. Inability to dance is not considered as a possibility, and lameness, unless very extreme, is not a deterrent. People dance in their seats if unable to take the floor. When the text calls for motion, the players who wag their hips from side to side the most rhythmically and vigorously are given much approval by the surrounding onlookers. In "Miss Sue," the child dancing is encouraged, "Now let me see your hustle, Miss Sue, Miss Sue, now let me see your hustle, Miss Susiana Sue." Everyone is then clapping in a syncopated pattern and singing while "Miss Sue" dances.

The games have many functions, among them exercise, education, introduction to island literature, social behavior, and preparation for the future. "Little Johnny Brown" contains a section "Lope like a buzzard, Johnny Brown," which constitutes a child-size rendition of "The Buzzard Lope." The Buzzard Lope[13] is a serious funerary dance and mimics the motions and attitudes of a buzzard coming after a dead body represented by a piece of cloth.[14] It is performed on St. Simons to "Throw Me Anywhere Lord in That Old Field."[15] The Johnny Brown game begins:

> Little Johnny Brown spread your comfort down
>
> Little Johnny Brown spread your comfort down

During which a handkerchief, bandanna, or other square piece of cloth is placed in the middle of the ring of players. The song continues:

>Fold one corner, Johnny Brown

>Fold another corner, Johnny Brown [in each succeeding verse]

And so on around the square of cloth. The Johnny Brown figure is instructed to:

>Take it to your lover, Johnny Brown

As he dances to a new person in the ring. Then he is instructed:

>Show her your motion, Johnny Brown

Then he is instructed:

>Lope like a buzzard, Johnny Brown

Then:

>Give it to your lover, Johnny Brown.

The new person advances to the center and recommences the game.

The enactment of a solemn ritual, which portrays the continuity of life, lies within the song "Throw Me Anywhere Lord in That Old Field." The game ensures practice for adult times when such a responsibility will fall on them. These "plays" are dramatic vignettes of Sea Islands life and are part of the traditional education process. The players move through the rituals and enactments of life and so begin to learn their appropriate roles.

In "I Come to See Miss Julianne John," a line or group of players advance toward the Julianne John figure singing:

>I come to see Miss Julianne John, Miss Julianne John, Miss Julianne John

>I come to see Miss Julianne John, and how she is today.

The reply is:

>She is ironing.

225

The group falls back saying:

OO OO OO OO

And sings:

I'm very glad to hear that, hear that, hear that, and how she is today

They approach again singing, asking after Ms. Julianne John, only to hear of her deteriorating health:

She is lying down sick.

The reply comes:

OO OO OO OO

I'm very sorry to hear that, hear that, hear that [repeat]

And how she is today.

And the answer:

She is

In the hospital.

Taking an operation

The doctor don't expect her to live

And she died.

The reply:

OO OO OO OO

I'm very sorry to hear that, hear that, hear that

So what you goin' to bury her in?

Yellow

[Chorus] Yellow is for babies, babies, babies

Yellow is for babies, so what you goin' to bury her in?

Blue

[Chorus] Blue is for sailors, etc.

Green

[Chorus] Green is for grasses, etc.

Red

[Chorus] Red is for fire, etc.

Pink

Pink is for babies, etc.

Black

Black is for darkness, etc.

Purple

Purple is for collars, etc.

Brown

Brown is for soldiers, etc.

Les see, White!

The Julianne John figure chases them since she is now a ghost (duppy in the Caribbean versions). They run screaming away.

The song tells a great deal about color values within the community. The long catalogue and their meanings or uses, as well as accompanying debates, open a window into such values. "Red is for fire" is substantiated by older members of the community who say red represents conflict, danger, fire, and anger. The consistent value and symbolism of red would point to this game having been around a long time. It occurs in much the same form in the Jamaican scene as recorded by Jekyll.[16]

Social behavior and manners are imparted in the polite exchanges and inquiries throughout the game. The African women who were the nurses and surrogate mothers in the South transmitted the African values, which had come to them in the course of such informal family and community-based teaching. Furthermore, the process of ordinary life declining into sickness and death is a theme of dimensions of the life cycle.

This song-game is done on Barbados and the Sea Islands:

> Draw me a bucket of water
>
> For my oldest daughter
>
> It's none in the bunch
>
> And all out the bunch
>
> Go under Sister Sally.

The players form up into squares. One on each side and continue:

> Draw me a bucket of water
>
> For my oldest daughter
>
> There's one in the bunch and three out the bunch
>
> Go under Sister Sally.

This continues until all four are united, hands linked, in the "bunch." The linked bunch jumps, propelling themselves around the circle chanting:

> Froggie in the bucket and I can't get him out. [Four times]

Since this game involves gestures, cooperation, and coordination of the players, discussions inevitably break out, and leadership patterns evolve. Thus, the game teaches the value of cooperation and coordination so that no one gets hit or left out of the game. I was teaching this game to a class of graduate students, one of whom was pregnant. When it came to the Froggie in the bucket chant, she expressed some anxiety about her physical state. The young men in the group on either side of her just picked her up and she was propelled around with minimum stress.

Games can be used to sort out bad feelings which may arise in a community. "Na Na Tread Needle" is one such game, which uses cooperative movement and dance to solve a knotty problem which emerges after the loan of a tool. The "Shake down this bunkum, bunkum" section is like the "Froggie in the Bucket" in that everyone jumps up and down as a group. By the time they "Unwind this bunkum," everyone is restored to good humor.

Neighbor, neighbor lend me your hatchet

Neighbor, neighbor step and get it.

Na na, thread the needle

I want my needle

Na na thread the needle

That Mama needle

I lost my needle

Thread the needle [Girls skip in and out]

That gold eye needle

Thread the needle

Na na thread the needle.

Neighbor, neighbor send me my hatchet

Neighbor, neighbor I ain't got it

Wind up this bunkum, bunkum

Wind up this bunkum [They wind up into a knot]

Shake down this bunkum bunkum

Shake down this bunkum [The whole knot jumps up and down]

Unwind this bunkum, bunkum

Unwind this bunkum [They proceed to unwind the knot][17]

"Shout, Josephine" is a game which is antiphonal and something of a physical test. The dancing continues throughout. It ends with a little Charleston-like dance to "Aunt Jennie's cornbread sweet, sweet, sweet, take some and leave some, sweet, sweet!" I saw "Shout Josephine" performed on MTV one day in the manner of the Electric Slide. It was a testimonial to the endurance of these games.[18]

This game is an older game judging by the markers of garlic, salt and pepper, and onion utilized as charms to bring about a desired effect. In spite of his difficulties and how he may feel about them, Uncle Jessie needs to keep moving along.

> Here comes Uncle Jessie
>
> A-running cross the field
>
> With his horse and blanket [sometimes horse and buggy]
>
> And I know just how he feels,
>
> Now step, Uncle Jessie, step, step,
>
> Step, Uncle Jessie, step, step.
>
> Here comes Uncle Jessie,
>
> He's looking very sad.
>
> He's lost his cotton and corn
>
> And everything he had.

Chorus

> Now, if you want a fella
>
> I'll tell you what to do
>
> Just take some salt and pepper
>
> An' sprinkle it in your shoe.

Chorus

The young girls loved to sing this song and do a little stylin' while they moved along.

> We are the little Miss Walk-um, Walk-um,
>
> We are the little Miss Walk-um, Walk-um,
>
> And we all go walk, walk, walk,
>
> And we all go walk, walk, walk.[19]

They "switchum," "stamp-um," "jump-um," "shake-um," and at the last verse "end-um" by crossing their feet and singing "end, end, end." It is this crossing of feet which is thought to differentiate between sacred and secular dance. While they are children, it is permissible for them to cross their legs, but when they are "living for God" as they get older, that practice stops. The older sisters exhibit leadership in teaching the dancers to line up and synchronize their movement, which gets complicated in the subsequent verses.

Movement in the Sacred Fold

In the sacred songs, we see motion and movement, not just up and down and side to side, but between earth and heaven. The concept of the journey, the road, and the river are found again and again. Bessie Jones sang no less than three versions of "Swing Low, Sweet Chariot." Another favorite tune is "I believe I'll run on an' see what the end gonna be." The following verses enumerate pray on, shout on, sing on, etc.

"I'm Pressing On" is another song that includes the dynamic concept of movement in time and space from the known to the unknown. The shout songs are marked by strong rhythmic utterance, backed by rhythmic clapping, foot stomping, and a percussion stick (often a cane). The lyrics of the songs express exhortations by the song leader to move on the physical plane as well as moving between the ordinary and an altered state.

> Walk until you shout, Daniel[20]

The shouters hope to be fit for the "Judgment Bar" as they urge the archangel:

> Blow Gabriel[21]

They take leave of each other in:

> Goodbye, everybody
>
> Goodbye and sing hallelujah!

Signaling the end of this particular session as well as a possible departure for other realms. Each verse recognizes different groups and individuals, which may emerge spontaneously as the singers file out the door. The song proclaims that Jesus himself is sitting on the altar handing out the bread and wine "to the members," reinforcing their belonging and unity as a group. It makes possible the ultimate leave taking and the easing of present difficulties. The shout songs embody movement, and they begin the singing as they enter the ring.

The religious experience context attempts to lessen the distance between here and beyond. Hymns, spirituals, sermons, and prayers all conspire to soften the blow of transition from earth to heaven or whatever the future may hold.

> When I get to heaven going to sing and shout
>
> Ain't gonna be nobody turn me out.

Sermons, designed to move the listeners, are the reflections of African storytelling sessions. Take, for example, the session described by Laura Bohannan in *Return to Laughter*.[22] We can see reflection of this in the Afro-American sermon. The preachers, sometimes called "stump knockers" or "jacklegs," tell a story with responses from the audience/congregation, with singing and movement, and may or may not be ordained ministers. They tell Bible stories or the story of their own conversion, but they also exhort the congregation to "live for God," "keep fighting," "keep moving up," or "to keep on keeping on," which may seem an obvious tautology to outsiders but is a very encouraging phrase when the going is rough. Their sermons develop from normal speech into a sing-song pattern, which then changes very subtly into a rhythmic chant and finally to song itself. It is very difficult to know what motivates the changes from one stage to another, but the changes themselves are fairly apparent. The interaction between the people and the preacher shows the dynamics of the occasion. A preacher who moves the people emotionally and spiritually will receive a good deal of vocal response and money when the collection is taken up, just as someone who moves well or a skilled storyteller will get money in Africa as recognition of his excellence or will be fined if he is forgetful of his story. Typical oral responses will range from an emphatic "yes," through "Yes, Jesus" softly intoned, to "Well, well, well" sung outright in a descending melody line. The responses become thicker and faster as the preacher's work begins to take effect. The preacher tells his story with appropriate gestures, moving up and down the space allotted to him—often a platform. A song begins after the sermon, started by either the preacher himself or a strong singer in the congregation.[23]

The singing builds up gradually. First one singer starts, then the next few join in, and finally, the whole congregation joins in. Feet begin rocking back and forth so that it sounds like an army marching—immortalized by Arna Bontemps in "Rock Church Rock;"[24] hand clapping is added, and one or two stand up and sway back and forth, emphatically thumping the foot that does not bear the weight. The torso turns from side to side. By this time, someone is getting ready to "shout." He/she may move out into the aisle or up to the front where there is room to feel freer to move, sometimes waving a white handkerchief, which in West Africa is done to keep off the evil spirits.[25] The shout is mainly pounding of the feet up and down like pistons, arms hanging loose, and gaze reflective. The women sometimes "fall out" as a result of the repeated rhythm, because the (holy) "sperrit" is moving them. After the "shout" has quieted down, then everyone returns to his or her seat. If the person who "fell out" continues to stay in a fainting condition, efforts are made to revive her/him, or he/she is carried outside for air. If he/she is making convulsive movements and yelling out, he/she is aided by members of his family or the congregation to prevent his hurting himself. A new off-island preacher, concerned by the intense quality of the possession experience, inquired what he could do for a fallen sister. She replied, "It's jus' Jedus." This lengthy description is to show the subtle progression of the sound and movement that accompanies the social interaction of the Islanders as they deal with the emotional buildup and release of tensions.

There are some culture traits and experiences that separate the Sea Islands area from the rest of the Afro-American population, but one of the factors that is common to the whole subgroup is this cultural imperative of movement, which is clearly one of the carry-overs from Africa. The

Ring Shout and Buzzard Lope from the Sea Islands are dances which survived the Middle Passage, but there are more subtle currents of movement eddying and flowing throughout the community more or less continuously. If we assume the existence of culture areas in Africa, then some communication among different members of such areas would be possible in spite of the language barriers through dance, gesture, and other culturally conditioned movement responses. West African culture is such a group of touching-moving cultures, and the proxemic dynamics of the situation came to the Americas with the culture bearers themselves.

The song verse, "I went down to the valley to pray, my soul got happy and I stayed all day," may seem incomprehensible to people outside the religious tradition, which includes "getting happy," but the process of reaching a state of possession is quite occupying and time consuming. It is also considered a worthwhile activity partially because of the escapist possibilities. A group prayer meeting, which includes a lot of "shouting" and possession, is considered part of "a good experience meeting."

On Johns Island, the people sing, "Time is like a river and time is winding up [or moving on]." As they name in their song the members of their family, the message conveyed is that we human beings move with it. There is movement in a diachronic sense. There is also synchronic movement experience, which in its evanescent existence, fills the void created by fear, oppression, or poverty. The children's ring plays show that their joy is derived not from material goods but from each other and the feelings they can create themselves, plus a brief magic which both amuses and comforts. The "motion" is a rehearsal for later years, when it will have a more specific purpose; for now, they are practicing. The "gospel" sense of motion impels the Ring Shout and shouting dances during which people are carried out of themselves and do certain things that no one thought they could do. In the dance, they reach deeper into the layers of spiritual and cultural experience, a moment suspended in time and space, theirs alone, and touch the heart of their Africanity where outsiders can neither corrupt nor steal. The people are left with a good feeling to face the next week of labor and domination with an intimation, however fleeting, that there is relief somewhere toward which they may move when so inclined.

[1] Bess Lomax Hawes and Bessie Jones, *Step It Down* (New York: Harper Row, 1972).

[2] Mary Arnold Twining, "An Examination of African Retentions in the Folk Culture of the South Carolina and Georgia Sea Islands," PhD Dissertation, Indiana University, 1977.

[3] Babatunde Lawal, "Reclaiming the Past: Yoruba Elements in African American Arts," in *The Yoruba Diaspora in the Atlantic World,* eds. Toyin Falola and Matt D. Childs (Bloomington: Indiana University Press, 2004), 291–324.

[4] Bess Lomax Hawes and Bessie Jones, *Step It Down* (New York: Harper Row, 1972).

[5] Sterling Stuckey, *Slave Culture* (New York: Oxford University Press, 1987).

[6] Charlotte Forten, *The Journal of Charlotte Forten,* ed. Ray Allen Billington (1854; New York: Collier, 1953).

[7] Abigail M. H. Christensen, *Afro-American Folklore Told round Cabin Fires on the Sea Islands of South Carolina* (Boston: J. G. Cupples Co., 1892).

[8] Linda Parrish, *Slave Songs from the Georgia Sea Islands* (New York: Farrar Straus, 1940).

[9] Charles Lyell, *A Second Visit to the United States* (London: J. Murray, 1849); Septima Clark, Personal Communications, 1968.

[10] Anacostia Museum, Smithsonian Institution, Anacostia, MD, July 23, 2011; Patricia Jones-Jackson, *When Roots Die: Endangered Traditions on the Sea Islands* (Athens: University of Georgia Press, 1987).

[11] William Saunders. Personal Communications, 1975; M. A. Twining, Fieldwork in Jamaica, West Indies.

[12] Bess Lomax Hawes and Bessie Jones, *Step It Down* (New York: Harper Row, 1972), 31–33; Mary Arnold Twining. "An Examination of African Retentions in the Folk Culture of the South Carolina and Georgia Sea Islands." PhD Dissertation., Indiana University, 1977.

[13] Lydia Parrish, *Slave Songs from the Georgia Sea Islands* (New York: Farrar Straus, 1940), 108.

[14] Ibid., 160.

[15] Ibid., 109, 175.

[16] W. Jekyll, *Jamaican Song and Story* (London: David Nutt, 1907).

[17] Bess Lomax Hawes and Bessie Jones, *Step It Down* (New York: Harper Row, 1972), 81–83; Twining, dissertation: 57–60.

[18] See note 10; Bess Lomax Hawes and Bessie Jones, *Step It Down* (New York: Harper Row, 1972), 58–60; Twining, dissertation: 67.

[19] Twining, Dissertation, 69.

[20] Twining, Dissertation: 72–3.

21 Lydia Parrish, *Slave Songs from the Georgia Sea Islands* (New York: Farrar Straus, 1940).

22 Laura Bohannan, *Return to Laughter* (New York: Harper, 1954), chapter 10.

23 John Messenger, Personal Communication, 1968.

24 Arna Bontemps, "Rock, Church, Rock!" *Common Ground* (September 1942), 75–80.

25 John Messenger, Personal Communication, 1968.

Mothers of the Earth

Women in the African World

I interacted with the women and young girls on Johns Island, South Carolina, and St. Simons Island, Georgia. They welcomed me into their midst and homes as I circulated around to take the youngsters to Head Start or the games sessions with Bessie Jones. Vehicles on the island during the day, when their riders were at jobs and school, were few and far between, so my station wagon and I served as transportation.

Women are a strong presence on the Islands. They function as decision makers in the families, churches, and workplace, be they secretaries, household assistants, or farm laborers. Many families are matrilocal (on the woman's property or with her family), matrilineal through inheritance patterns, and matriarchal (governed by elder women). What may appear to be matrifocal may actually be one part of a polygynous (more than one wife) marriage— residents on their own but tied by invisible strings to a marriage situation. Women are represented in the church as members of the choir, usher's union, and various other church committees. They lead singing in church and community and are instrumental in organizing Seven Speakers, visiting groups, turnouts, and other occasions. They are fully equal in the society except in instances where the man in the case has assumed the attitudes of the dominant society. Men and women wade in the streams seining together. The women also fish with drop nets, lines, and hooks. They farm doing everything the men do except possibly for the heaviest work. They work with the animals, plow, plant, and harvest. Some go to do domestic work locally or into the nearest city. Their lives are filled with hard work, the necessity to keep going after loss and tragedy. Without babysitters readily available, they must sometimes leave the children at home while they go to make a living; accidents and fires can take the children as quickly as they came. Through all, they meet life with courage and dignity and encounter people with graciousness.

Their life cycle is rich with accomplishment, children, and what comfort their strong sense of self provides. It shows evidences of their African background. In these examples, you will come to know women whose choices of life path may have been limited in some ways, but who persevered to make lives for themselves and their families in spite of hazards and setbacks.

> When a baby is born we supposively [sic] mourn and when
> a person dies, we rejoice but sometimes we get mixed up
> and cry when people die and become happy when a baby
> is born.[1]

Ms. Hunter expressed the feelings of the real culture as opposed to the teachings of the ideal culture. Babies are, in fact, welcome and plenteous. They are born often in the context of their mother's own family of orientation even before she has set up her own family. In a bid for recognition that goes with motherhood, a step closer to independent adulthood, they have the babies, who often are absorbed by their grandparents and raised alongside their mother, uncles, and aunts. They are also born into homes of young couples who may be living with their parents and in-laws or on their own.

Many beliefs surround the birthing of a child, and the midwives, who were the main personnel to bring them into the world, were storehouses of such information. There were folk beliefs about the birth order, presentation of the baby, and control of pain and bleeding as well as other events encompassing the baby's entrance into the world. One belief was that a piece of iron (plow blade, knife, etc.) placed under the bed would keep out (or literally, "cut") the pain. Tansy tea could be used to hasten the birth.[2] The caul should be disposed of in an orderly fashion; it has been believed that it should be buried under a tree, dried, or placed in safe storage. Once buried or otherwise deposited, it can be unearthed to make an infusion for the child to drink in case of being haunted or bothered by spirits.[3] This belief is held in West Africa, and dire consequences can ensue should someone disturb the tree-base burial of the placental tissue.[4]

The female baby's ears are pierced, and tiny gold earrings or posts are put through the holes made with sewing needles and thread. Short bits of straw are used to keep the holes open until the coveted gold is affordable. The cultural pressure towards femininity begins early and continues as their lives progress.[5]

When the children are young, they are not only cared for by their mothers but also by their older siblings. The young girls carry the babies on their hips just as their African cousins do. They are quite accomplished at taking care of little ones as they approach puberty. They are learning the skills of their future lives and helping their families. Cultural values define a broader focus beyond the learning of family roles.

Having mastered some of the family functions and traditional societal values, they work in the fields at remarkably young ages and begin the adult business of having children as well. One definition of maturation to adulthood says that as soon as one can handle a day's work, one is an adult. Furthermore, the proof of fertility with the onset of menses in rural agricultural communities often defines their readiness for marriage. These young girls fulfill both of these criteria at early ages and so think themselves ready to take on the world very soon in their lives.

The women on the Sea Islands constitute the heart of the culture. It is they who are the conservators of the sustaining folklife that has functioned to preserve their families and culture over the years. Their holding and keeping capacities are symbolized in the basketry and their love and warmth in the quilts. They are part of a long tradition, which transcends even the unities of their present situation, the ethnicities of Africa, and the national divisions of the modern world.

From the beginning of humanity until now, women have continued bringing forth food and progeny. They are the embodiment of Ceres (goddess of the earth) and Venus (goddess of love), both of whom incorporate the fertility principle so necessary to human survival. The Paleolithic representations, such as the so-called Venus of Willendorf (who appears to have African features) show rounded women filled with life and sexuality, an overt attempt to represent and penetrate the mystery of women and the origins and continuations of human life. African statues also present the productive and nurturing activities of women in their partnership with men and the natural world. "Mother" is the most respectful term of address in an African society. Women in the Afro-American church are often addressed as "sister," but when they get up in age and service in the church, they are raised to "mother" in the church. Recognition of the motherly capacities of a woman can be the finest salute to her; it is reflected in the folklore when a young man happens along in the course of the story's action and meets an older woman who helps him only because he addresses her as "mother." She indicates to him that it would have been the worse for him had he addressed her in any other manner. In calling her mother, he invoked a kinship obligation and thereby insured his preservation. In many West African societies, the kinship terms at one's parents' level for all women—such as sisters of the mother and father—are subsumed under the term "mother." This custom keeps in reserve a supply of nurture for the children and old-age support for the parents. Many such societies "gift" children to childless people[6] so that their motherly and parental capacities might be exercised, as that relationship is considered to be the crown of a woman's life. From a practical standpoint, though, it insures the survival of members of societies, such as widows and childless women who have had to function without social security or Medicare.

The figure of a matronly woman is valued and reflected in the language as well as the folklore. In West Africa, there are "mammy wagons," the market women flapping their breasts to show approval of young couples, and the symbolic "Mammy Watta." The "Mammy Watta" is based on the figure of the manatees who ply up and down the waterways. They are mammals, and nurse their young and carry their babies along as they forage for food. They are large and bulky and mild-mannered. The folk belief is that if you sing to the "Mammy Watta" she will come to you (in that manifestation, she appears as lovely female with long hair).[7] If she gives herself to a young man, he will enjoy great worldly success, but he must never marry an earthly woman or he will forfeit all that. Clearly, the notion of motherly support and nurturing is on all sides in such cultures.

The revering of mothers has carried over into Afro-American society and shows nowhere more clearly than in the Sea Islands. Women are called "Mauma," "Mammy," and "Big Ma," among other affectionate and respectful titles. The women bringing the food into the marketplace share in these attributes of bounty, as seen in the images of women called "vegetubble mauma."[8] Patently, she is in charge of the fruits of the earth; the women are invested with the fertile capacities of the land as they themselves are productive of life. It is toward that creative end that the establishment of the adult working and child-producing capacities are invoked as the young women strive toward woman- and adulthood.

In 1920, Harriet Leiding recorded street cries of vendors in Charleston, South Carolina. The African American ladies with their baskets on their heads would come into Charleston from James or Johns Islands, west of the city, on ferry boats to sell their fresh produce. Basically, we see the pattern of women arising early before the heat of the day and getting a good place at the market stall or roving the streets hoping for sales.[9]

In certain traditional African societies, the crops are divided between the men and the women. Among the Anang Ibibio, the men plant the yams (large African yams) and the women intercrop with cocoyams and other root crops and smaller vegetables. The men clear the fields, slashing and burning before planting the yams, and then the women hoe and keep the garden clear of weeds. When the crop has matured, the women may take their share and sell at market. They then can obtain money. The Ibo women, of southeastern Nigeria, have this freedom and take titles of respect as a result of their increased earnings. These powerful women may even take wives of their own as they amass the money to do it. In some groups, the women must turn over their earnings to their husbands to be used for the family as a whole, thus maintaining a certain bonding to the unity of the group.[10]

It has been reasonably predicated that women were the initiators of agriculture in the history of human technology, as they were physically less mobile than the hunting men. This early franchise on food sources has been thought to give them control over the agricultural products, hence control of the profit from sales of such products. Boserup found that where women farm, they dominate market trade.[11] Even in some Muslim areas, as in Senegal and Sudan, the women farmers do not wear the veil, signifying a certain freedom. The veiled Muslim women do not enter as freely into the market economy or the bazaar life as they do in some areas of Africa south of the Sahara.[12]

The women sell a variety of products, some of which are of their own manufacture, farm products and sewn garments for instance. On a more entrepreneurial level, they trade for or buy goods to sell in the periodic markets or simply at roadside stands. At an uncomplicated level, they put the bundles, tailor's table, and whatever equipment they may be carrying on top of their heads and walk to the marketplace. They also come to the urban regional markets on the group transport available in the converted trucks or buses, such as the "tro-tro" in Ghana, sometimes riding most of the night to reach the market early enough to obtain an advantageous spot. Some of the richer and more powerful traders fly from one market region to another, not trusting their bundles to the baggage areas. They take their stock-in-trade with them onto the planes, trains, or whatever conveyance, like the Sea Islands women on the ferries from the Islands in the past, keeping a firm eye on the goods. Really rich and powerful women—such as Madame Mercedes Benz of the Ivory Coast—have fleets of cars and more privately controlled methods of transportation so that they may move among their many interests at their own convenience.

Marvin Harris offers the notion that the freedom to market goods and services does not necessarily correlate with matrilineal kinship, though evidently it does in some situations.[13] The relationship may, in fact, have to do with polygynous marriage situations, which would allow one of the wives to leave home to attend market days, leaving children in the care of the other wives. It does, however, seem to correlate with the prolonged absence of men from the homestead or village for economic reasons. This periodic absence of the males in the population is precisely why, in the first instance, women started agricultural practices, as they were the stabilizers of the home-steads in Neolithic times when men went hunting. In Nubian communities, it seems that women had never gone to the Daraw market until the men left the village more and more to seek work elsewhere. Their going to the market has caused certain amount of opposition, but social and cultural customs gave way to practicality. Discussions were initiated on the idea of setting up a village market to obviate the need for travel on the part of the women when the men were away.[14]

In the Caribbean, the men absent themselves from the village to work in the cities, fishing, or economic enterprises such as the bauxite mines, the tourist industry, etc. The women grow food or make baskets and other items, which they bring down to market on the busses, traveling long hours like their sisters in Africa. In Haiti, the women ride the "tap-taps," a Haitian version of the "tro-tros" of Ghana, but often as not, they form caravans of human trucks (bundles atop their heads) and walk to the market. They will go on to one or another of the periodic markets if the sales at the first have not gone well enough to insure their not having to walk home bearing unsold merchandise.

The folk belief is that the women are better merchandisers than men, and so, the division of labor involves the men at the agriculture post and the women selling at the markets. They have a price list worked out which classifies people in their situations as perspective marks. Color, socioeconomic status, native to the area or tourist, and language capabilities all play a part in determining who pays what sum. Clearly, an English speaker pays more than the French speaker who in turn pays more than the Creole speaker. Lighter-skinned people pay more than dark and obviously middle- or upper-class people (should they happen to be shopping at all) pay more than evident strugglers. If you are known as somebody's domestic servant, you are classed near the upper end of the scale also.

In Jamaica, the higglers buy and resell farm produce and other goods. They also come into the cities to the markets such as Papeen. They ride the Jamaican omnibus service in minivans or country busses in which the drivers play music and otherwise try to make the journey appealing. The women have inherited spots at the markets, which they may share with family members who will cooperate to prepare the food and sleep over to make the best of the time there. The farmer women consider themselves as belong-ing to a higher calling than the higglers in their ethics in dealing with the public.[15] They like to sell out early on Saturday in order to do their own shopping for the preparations for Sunday. Sunday is the big day for dinner and visiting in the yard or residential compound. The higglers like to stay late to get every last sale and make as much money by as many sharp deals as possible. Like the traders in Haiti, they judge people by their color as to whether they'll be an easy mark or not. The farmer women standardize their prices and pride themselves on their honesty.

The women in Barbados years ago used to walk in to town to sell their produce; a group of mothers and daughters would walk with the baskets on their heads as the women do in Haiti. They had donkey carts loaded with root vegetables and smaller garden crops like okra and would deliver to the houses if people wished it. Nowadays people go to the supermarket like any modern community, but there is still an outdoor, centralized market to which people come on the busses. There are also women who sell from carts or barrows in town.[16]

Francis Bebey's novel *The Ashanti Doll* tells about a matrifocal, matriarchal family unit of three generations of market women who work out their destinies against the backdrop of a fictionalized version of an uprising of the market women in the political sphere when the British levied an unwelcome tax in colonial Nigeria (1929–1930).[17] Similarly in Jamaica, two sisters or mother and daughter will team up, one selling food they've grown and the other cooking and selling the food, thereby eliminating middlemen. Some of the African women and the Jamaicans inherit their spots at the market, and they pay a small fee, so no one else is supposed to occupy it if they are not there.

From an economic standpoint, the market women are many times in a matrifocal situation, where the economic focus is on the women in the family. In the strict patrilocal and patriarchal Muslim society in Nubian communities, it was only the leaving of the men for outside opportunity that opened the situation up enough for the women to negotiate being able to go to market.[18]

In the Sea Islands, the people who grew livestock and vegetables went to the market if they lived near enough to an urban center. Chickens were considered too valuable for the family to eat except on rare and festive occasions. They could get money by the sale of the fowls to buy items they had to purchase.[19]

Not only have the women taken charge of the marketplace in many parts of the African World, but they have also reigned over the kitchen, creating an impressive array of tasty foods which have put the stamp of cultural authenticity on southern cooking in general and soul food in particular. In West Africa, the so-called soups are closer to what we call stews; savory mixtures of meat, fish, vegetables, and pepper are served over rice (Senegambian region) or a cereal-like substance called "fufu," often made of pounded yams (Nigeria) or mashed plantains (Nigeria and Cameroons). African yams, (not like American sweet potatoes) which are long and brown like fireplace logs and white inside like an Idaho potato, are boiled and mashed as well as cooked in chunks in soup (stew) with meat and vegetables. Okra soup is one recipe which has travelled intact across the Atlantic and has been served by Sea Islands women from their earliest times on those islands. The syncretism of Irish stew and Nigerian "porridge" has produced a dish, the Africanity of which might not be immediately evident. These are secondary Africanisms but, in their cultural influence, just as African as the more obvious concoctions like okra soup.

Vertamae Grosvenor writes in *The Kitchen Crisis* that people don't want to take trouble over food anymore (witness instant coffee and TV dinners), and her contention is that taking pains to prepare nice food is the essence of life itself, as she herself illustrates in her role in Julie Dash's film master-piece *Daughters of the Dust*.[20] This role in the distribution of food is exactly the function of the market women now and through recorded and unrecorded times in African and other worlds.

Anthropologists have spent time on the notion of psychic unity as one of the binders of human cultures. In fact, few more basic and necessary economic factors are unifying to African World populations as the women fertility goddesses in trucks and busses ride down out of the hills or off the Islands to bring life-giving food to people.

The African American women of the Sea Islands are the providers of food as fishers and farmers and cooks; they are also healers when the occasion demands. In the isolated circumstances of the Island life, they had to make shift to take care of themselves and the family in time of childbirth or illness. They often belong to praying bands, burial, and insurance societies, which are institutions in the community for healing and financial welfare. They had a strong working knowledge of plants and herbs and methods to help a cold, a cough, or to bring a baby or hold one back. "Roots," as they were called, could also be used for putting spells or lifting them. Working roots is not done by every person; it is a specialized skill and regarded with a certain amount of awe amongst the general population.

The women work alongside their fathers, brothers, and husbands tilling the fields and fishing. They also undertake these jobs by themselves, if necessity dictates. They labor, planting or harvesting in the fields, hanging over from the hips. They also stoop and crawl to harvest cotton or other crops. The work is difficult, laborious, and exhausting, but the pride and independence with which they do it endures their whole lives. Until the 1960s, the women carried headloads just as they do in Africa. This custom requires a certain alignment of the back, neck, and head that guarantees an erect posture that characterizes their graceful silhouette.

Among other economic activities, the women make nets, brooms, quilts, and baskets. The crafts are passed on in the families along kinship lines. The transmission of them binds the family together in the diachronic (generation to generation) dimension, so the practice of the crafts and use of the products by the women foster a cohesive unity on the synchronic (contemporary) level.

One of the four craft objects, the baskets, have become part of the public realm in the sale to tourists in the market in the city and outside of Charleston, South Carolina, in Mount Pleasant, South Carolina. The other three—brooms, nets, and quilts—however, remain mostly a part of the more intimate sphere of the domestic scene.[21]

The women who make the crafts form a nucleus in the society and function to conserve their culture. They are artists in the culture and deserve attention as individual practitioners rather than indication as a group.

Mary Jane Manigault lives in a traditional family compound in a remote area of Mount Pleasant. She is the eldest female and reigns over her family in true African style. The houses are arranged around a common area, which doubtless functioned as a gathering and dancing ground in times past. She herself is a master craftsperson and makes baskets to supply her stand on Route 17.[22] She teaches her daughter and granddaughter the craft she learned from her female relatives. She received a National Heritage Fellowship in recognition of a lifetime of significant contribution to American folk art in general and African American folk art in particular. The Heritage Fellowships also recognize the historic import of the teaching activities of the fellows who pass on their art to others which will guarantee its survival. Ms. Manigault was accompanied by her daughter and granddaughter, who also practice the craft. These awards also acknowledge in a tacit way the nameless women who carried on the African tradition represented by these baskets.

The baskets are the truest Africanism to be found in the United States; there is a direct congruence between the baskets from the Senegambian area of West Africa, Central Africa, and other regions as well as those of the Sea Islands of South Carolina. The coiled baskets are made by women in Senegal and the Gambia just as they are in South Carolina.[23]

Women in the Sea Islands have many of the characteristics of their African cousins. The Afro-American Sea Islands population of South Carolina and Georgia retains many African culture traits in spite of modernization, suburbanization, and resort building. The women play a binding role in the families, moving easily along both synchronic and diachronic dimensions. They interact with assurance on any level within their own society. Their roles as mothers are paramount in their network of kinship relationships; motherhood or the capability thereof fills an important role in the functioning of the group. The notion of parenting within the Afro-American culture is a more diffuse one than in the Euro-American groups. The extended families provide more motherly and fatherly personnel than the nuclear family, and there is the concept of gift children, which occasions lateral movement from one family or parent/child dyad to another household or family group. If somebody feels they cannot raise a child for one reason or another they "gift" the child to another relative who could help with the raising of the child. This transfer of the child involves no traumatic adoption proceedings and there is no confusion on the part of the child as to who its parents are. A child may also be given to a childless person to comfort and help in the household in the absence of a child of their own.[24]

Janie Hunter, who was a fine storyteller, quilter, cook, and dollmaker, was quiet but nevertheless very much a matriarch in a matrifocal family unit. Her children and their families live near her in a kind of family neighborhood among the fields. The children moved easily among the households, feeling very much at home in all of them. Ms. Hunter was an excellent craftswoman, making brooms, "knitting" fishnets, and making quilts with consummate skill. She was also a master singer in the community, evidenced by her role in her family singing group and her performance as the Saving Angel in "The Devil Play." The family cultivated fields under her guidance and all its members shared in the work and the harvest. She taught games and stories to the young people inculcating a capacity for entertaining themselves as well as socially acceptable patterns of interaction, such as cooperative work patterns, synchronized and sympathetic movement, and lively conversational abilities.[25]

Courting behavior, dance, song, and the care of young children are part of the material imparted by the games. Elder sisters care for younger siblings in a childhood activity which is interwoven with the games while they sing hilariously, "Rockabye, Baby" to a jazzy beat. The young girls participating in the play behavior are rehearsing for later life, but they are also expected to accomplish some serious tasks with little quarter given for their being children. The young girls go into the fields as young as six or seven (or even earlier), usually accompanied by their older sisters or cousins. The older girls care for the younger ones, instructing them how to behave just as they do less seriously in the game situation. No one is left at home in harvest season except the very old ladies minding the very young babies. The division of labor involving women runs along age lines, and almost every woman in the traditional society has gone through the various stages of age-graded contributory labor from the time of about five years of age to eighty-five years. Everyone feels useful and integrated into the society and, although life is hard and poverty common, a mentally healthy atmosphere prevails.

It is in this setting that Ms. Hunter operated for most of her life. One of seven brothers and sisters, she was taught to make fishnets with them by her father who was a fisherman. He was also a man who knew about herbs and how to make decoctions with them. He taught her some of that knowledge, useful in a remote area where it was not easy to get a doctor. The rural extended household was a nearly self-contained unit with gardening; gathering of wild plants and herbs; the manufacture of domestically useful items such as baskets, quilts, brooms, and nets; the keeping of livestock; and cultivated ability to provide their own entertainment with stories, song, games, and plays. On the whole, the men provided fish, though they can be helped in seining by the women; they do some of the gardening, wood chopping, mechanical jobs, net knitting and finishing off of nets knitted by women, farming (here women and men work side by side), keeping of church and cemetery grounds, grave digging, truck driving, and the one hundred and one myriad of jobs that keep a rural community going.

In addition to doing rural farm-wives' tasks, Ms. Hunter was a skilled quilter, broommaker, storyteller, and singer. She was discovered by Guy Carawan in the 1960s. He subsequently took her and others in a group called the Moving Star Hall Singers to festivals and concert dates, where they found, to their surprise, that people in the outside world were interested in their music and their lives. Up to that point, Ms. Hunter's life had been more or less typical of the rural Sea Islands life, although she also went out to work as a household assistant.[26]

She toured with the group whenever the Carawans found work for them, and in her seventies, she arranged some jobs for them herself. She had also begun to maximize her abilities as a fine craftswoman, making excellent quilts and "dollbabies." Though handicapped by arthritis in her ankles, she was still as strong and devoted a singer as ever and toured with two of her daughters and her sister-in-law. She was honored for her lifetime of contributions to traditional lore by receiving a National Heritage Fellowship Award.

Ms. Mary LaRoche is a housewife on the island, where she has lived all her life. She is a fine cook, excellent fisherperson, talented singer, and good dancer. She has been an active churchgoer all her life, singing in the choir and taking an active interest in all phases of the church. She was made a leader in the church a few years ago, a recognition of her devotion to that institution. She and her friends all belong to a women's savings club. They gather once a month, rotating around to their different houses. They collect money to be used when a member has a baby or gets married. They sponsor dances and parties for which occasions they might have matching dresses made so that their allegiance to their club and their feeling of unity with each other will be obvious to everyone there. The club has both social and service functions, such as a savings society, in the Island community as well as providing a network for the women. Ms. LaRoche is a mother of four, or was before she suffered the loss of her eldest son who suddenly died of a heart attack. She has grandchildren and is very proud of them. Although she and her family are hardworking and upwardly mobile, she is cognizant of and active in the traditional culture of the Islands.

It is often the women in a culture who are the preservers of the intimate core of family life and therefore the culture. They are placed at the heart of the survival of the group as child bearers, cooks, jobholders, agricultural workers, singers, artists, and artisans. It is their unifying activities that insure the continuance of the family, particularly when the families are matrilineal and/or matriarchal. The family's inheritance through the female line welds together the descendants by means of cooperative activity among the females.

It is, therefore, the women who are strongly affected by the impact of destruction perpetuated by the society at large. The ecological disaster of polluted waterways affects fishing, oyster picking, and other water-related activities and provides the model in miniature for the pillage from the outside world of the food-gathering occupation so vital to the survival of the group. By threatening and destroying modes of subsistence, the people who control the corporations initiate an irreversible trend. The women are less able to continue the delicate balancing act; their world literally falls apart. The real estate expansion in the form of condominia and commercial developments to encourage tourism, horse farms, and vacationers locks up land formerly used for agricultural purposes. It furthermore takes the other land which may have appeared to be waste land but was, in actuality, a harvesting ground for basket materials, broom sedge for brooms, fishing, and oystering. When the waters are polluted by both industry and leisure settlements, the waterborne life and swamp-spawned future evolution is poisoned and rendered effete.

It is against this background of change over the past half century that Ms. Bessie Jones lived on St. Simons Island, Georgia, where she worked as an agricultural laborer, had a family, and continued a strong heritage of games, songs, and plays, teaching them to her children and grandchildren. When she and the other singers on the island got together with Alan Lomax, they formed a group called the Sea Island Singers and toured around to clubs and festivals. It was they who persuaded the Moving Star Hall Singers of Johns Island, South Carolina, that people would be interested in their music.[27]

Ms. Jones was a spectacular storyteller volubly telling her stories complete with gestures, facial grimaces, and flowing language. The audience was always rapt whether in a formal concert situation or a casual assemblage of children. She related to people with enthusiasm and joy. She taught the songs in the *cantefable* stories to the audience so they could sing at appropriate moments in the narrative.[28] She also taught games to anyone who would ask her to do it. On one occasion, some people were at Atlanta University for a seminar in folklore and community organization. A lapse occurred between sessions which were late starting, and Bessie moved into the hiatus without hesitation and began teaching games to this mixed group of Euro- and Afro-Americans, getting the adults skipping all over the place. She instructed race relations through games and an irrepressible sense of humor. She came to Morris Brown to do a games workshop with the young people attending that college. They had a Euro-American instructor who was feeling uneasy and as though he were not getting through to the students. She put him and the class through "Here comes one Johnny Cuckoo."[29] The game, as with many of the Afro-American games, subsumes an ease of movement and dance. This young man good-naturedly galumphed through the game, reducing the class to hysterics in the process. Once they knew there was something they could do better than he and that he was ready to be a regular fellow, they all got along much better. Ms. Jones was a keen observer of human behavior and understood that one could teach interpersonal dynamics through folk culture, because that is what its function in the community had been for centuries. She just expanded her sense of community to include more people and then taught some others to do the same.

If an occasion arose for which there did not seem to be a suitable song or game, undaunted, Ms. Jones would compose something, tambourine in hand. I took her to an Azanian family's house when on a visit and they were celebrating a child's birthday. Bessie promptly composed "Mary Had a Party."

> Mary had a party, a party, a party
>
> Oh what a party Mary had!
>
> They were drinking at the party, the party, the party
>
> Oh what a party Mary had!
>
> They were dancing at the party, the party, the party
>
> What a dance at the party Mary had!

It went on for several more verses with the children happily dancing and miming the activities described in the song.

The Newport Revival of Community Folk Music sent her on a grant to Johns Island. I had the privilege of driving Ms. Jones around the island, gathering up children and circuit riding to various community institutions where she taught me and the children to "*Step It Down*"! She also taught us to "truck," do the Charleston, and to "put our hand on our hip and let the backbone slip!" along with other constituent elements of the dance and game vocabulary. Before she was through, she had taught all over the United States and had performed everywhere from New York City to California. She was singlehandedly responsible for educating more Afro-Americans and Euro-Americans about folksong, dance, games, and stories from the Sea Islands than anyone else.

Some of the Island families, such as that of Ms. Jones, show clear patterns of matrilocality where the mother's residence is surrounded by the married children in households on her family land. The families also exhibit matrilineal characteristics, as the land is inherited through the mother's line. The extended residential units are also governed for the most part by the senior female of the main household, making them matriarchal and matrifocal in nature. The senior female functions governmentally in the family.[30]

The Sea Islands region and its people tend to make a deep and lasting impression on anyone who comes there. There are some women who were not native to the Islands but who wrote about them in a way that tells us of their abiding affection for the people there. Among these women who introduced the Sea Islands to a wider world were Fanny Kemble, a well-known English actress, Charlotte Forten and Septima Clark, Lucy McKim Garrison, Abigail Christensen, Lydia Parrish, and Elsie Clews Parsons, who were all interested in recording the folk culture. All except Charlotte Forten and Septima Clark were of European descent but nonetheless sympathetic to the life of the Africans in bondage and freedom.[31]

Fanny Kemble, daughter of the great English actor, Charles Kemble, came to the Georgia Sea Islands as the bride of a rich slave owner, Pierce Butler. Her life on the English stage and their whirlwind courtship did little to prepare her for the life on the Islands among enslaved people. It is clear from her writing that she came to care very passionately about the people who were in her sphere of daily life and who could do so little to control the circumstances of their lives. Eventually, she and Butler divorced, chiefly because of his philandering and careless treatment of the enslaved Africans. In one particular edition of *Uncle Tom's Cabin*, two special essays were added in answer to the disbelievers who said slavery could not have been that bad. The essays, one by Frederick Douglass and one by Fanny Kemble, simply stated that it was, in fact, as bad as it had been portrayed or worse. Their perspectives of formerly enslaved person and former slave owner had to be respected.[32]

Charlotte Forten was a member of a prominent, free African American family from Philadelphia, and her grandfather, James Forten, born in 1766, was a well-known abolitionist and wealthy, self-made man. Through his unrelenting absorption in the cause of truly liberating African Americans, he influenced the thinking of such people as William Lloyd Garrison, John Greenleaf Whittier, and other people who became interested in abolition.[33] Whittier, in fact, wrote a poem extolling the virtues and activities of Forten's daughters. Charlotte was remarkable, but she was a member of an extraordinary family. Her aunt, Margaretta, was also a teacher, and all of her sisters were ardent abolitionists. Her father enlisted in the Forty-Third United States Colored Regiment but died before he could really fight in the war. Other members of her family also contributed to her knowledge of the abolitionist cause. Robert Purvis, who was married to her Aunt Harriet, was a foremost figure in the Underground Railway and the Pennsylvania Anti-Slavery Society.

Charlotte made a niche for herself with her talented writings and fulfilled a lifelong ambition to provide a living example of the inherent gifts of African Americans. Her sentiments in favor of proving the abilities of African Americans led her to join the newly formed Port Royal Experiment in 1862, where she encouraged the young African American Sea Islanders to learn all they could about their own heritage. She used to tell them stories about Toussaint L'Ouverture, the great Haitian liberator.

The teachers in the Port Royal Experiment came from three states, Massachusetts, New York, and Pennsylvania.[34] Many of them were idealistic, like Charlotte, about helping the "contrabands of war" as the ex-enslaved Africans were then called.[35] This educational program was designed to set up schools and to commence teaching the three Rs. When Miss Forten became acquainted with Thomas Wentworth Higginson, who was the Colonel of the First South Carolina (African American) Volunteers stationed nearby, he was so impressed with her enthusiasm for African American subjects that he invited her to come with the all-African-American regiment to Florida to teach the men to read. Charlotte Forten was an inveterate diarist and wrote about her travels and experiences. She sent essays she wrote about the Sea Islands and her love for the people there back to Boston, which was her home, where they were published in *Atlantic Monthly,* a popular magazine of the day. These publications had the result of bringing the Sea Islanders to a wider audience.[36]

Lucy McKim (later Garrison) arrived on the Sea Islands in the Port Royal Area as her father, James McKim's, amanuensis. They were there to make arrangements for the missionary teachers to come down and start work teaching the newly emancipated enslaved Africans. Miss McKim was impressed by the music she heard. As a trained musician herself, she instigated a project to collect the folk music, mostly spirituals, with Reverend William Allen and his cousin, Charles Ware, they gathered up a collection of songs and wrote an introduction about the Islanders and their culture.[37]

Abigail Christensen came to the Sea Islands in the post-Civil War period and found fascination in the folktales. As a member of the newly formed American Folklore Society (1888), she adhered to their express purpose of preserving the folklore by collecting and publishing it. Her volume, *Afro-American Folk Lore Told Round Cabin Fires on the Sea Islands of South Carolina* (1892), was one of the first published collections of folktales in the United States. Other women who interested themselves in the culture of African American Sea Islanders were Elsie Clews Parsons, who also collected folklore in South Carolina, but on a broader scale and in a more systematic manner, and Lydia Parrish, whose collection of songs from the Georgia Sea Islands both echoed and continued the earlier collection by Lucy McKim Garrison and her associates.[38]

Septima Clark was a teacher from North Carolina who came to the Islands when she was sixteen years old to teach the young African Americans. She taught in schools that were not only rural and segregated, but also painted with creosote to demark them as African American schools. She also taught in the civil rights movement workshops until her late age. She was one of Martin Luther King's right-hand people in South Carolina. She died in Charleston in her nineties. She wrote *Echo in My Soul*, which told of her earlier years. Her essay, "Voting Does Count," taken from a larger work entitled *A Fabulous Decade*, appeared in *Journal of Black Studies* (June 1980). She was a warrior in the human rights struggle and spent most of her productive life fighting for education and justice in Charleston and on the Sea Islands.[39]

Lydia Parrish was the wife of then prominent artist Maxfield Parrish and became interested in the culture of the Islanders. She put a small house at the St. Simons Islanders' disposal to use as a praise house where they could do the "shout" and have meetings. Her book, *Slave Songs of the Georgia Sea*

Islands, is a testimonial to her interest in and commitment to the songs, both secular and religious of the Island people.[40]

Elsie Clews Parsons was a folklorist and member of the American Folklore Society. In concurrence with the stated aims of that society, she undertook fieldwork among Native and African Americans. Her book, *Folklore of the Sea Islands*, was one of her major works in a career filled with accomplishments. It made a major contribution to our knowledge of Sea Islands folklore. She was a colorful character, and stories are told of her wearing unconventional clothing, smoking cigars, and wearing large hats to protect her from the sun.[41]

Perhaps because of the lively sense of identity of the Sea Islands women and the atmosphere they create in living their lives and producing their arts, the women from elsewhere felt at home and able to give of themselves for the betterment of the Islanders. If they did not add to the improvement of their lives, they hoped to make the Sea Islanders and their culture more understood and appreciated.

The women of the Sea Islands are much like their West African and Caribbean sisters, surviving, preserving the culture, nourishing its constituents, crafting, and decorating whilst transmitting a strong feeling of coherent relationship to themselves and their environment. Broadcasting on several channels through quilting, netting, fishing, cooking, plowing, praying, singing, dancing, and showing knowledge, they send the message of who they are. Sisters and mothers in the church, devout worshippers of the powerful sun or the distant East, they maintain through good times and bad. They carry with them the African past and their realistic present.

---

[1] Ms. Janie Hunter, Johns Island, SC, Personal Communications, 1970.

[2] William Bascom, "Gullah Folk Beliefs Concerning Child Birth," paper presented at the American Folklore Society, Andover, MA, 1941.

[3] John Sale, *A Tree Named John* (Chapel Hill: University of North Carolina, 1929); Tina McElroy Ansa, *Baby of the Family* (New York: Harcourt Brace, 1989).

[4] Chinua Achebe, *Things Fall Apart* (Greenwich, CT: Fawcett, 1960).

[5] Twining, fieldwork, 1970s.

[6] Melville J. Herskovits, *Myth of the Negro Past* (New York: Harper, 1941).

[7] Herbert M. Cole and Chike C. Aniakor, *Igbo Arts* (Los Angeles: University of California Los Angeles, 1984).

[8] Ibid.

[9] Harriet Leiding, *Street Cries of an Old Southern City.* (Charleston, SC: Daggett Printing Co., 1910).

[10] Victor Uchendu, *The Igbo of Southeastern Nigeria* (New York: Holt Rinehart Winston, 1971); John Messenger, Personal Communication, 1970.

[11] Anders Boserup. *War Without Weapons* (New York: Schocken, 1975).

[12] Ibid.

[13] Marvin Harris, *Food and Evolution* (Philadelphia: Temple University Press, 1986).

[14] Anne M. Jennings, *The Nubians of West Aswan: Village Women in the Midst of Change,* Women and Change in the Developing World Series (New York: Lynne Reinner Publishers Inc., 1995).

[15] Louise Bennett, Personal Communication, 1980.

[16] Louis Lynch, *The Barbados Book* (London: A. Deutsch, 1964).

[17] Francis Bebey, *The Ashanti Doll* (Westport, CT: Lawrence Hill, 1987).

[18] Anne M. Jennings, *The Nubians of West Aswan: Village Women in the Midst of Change,* Women and Change in the Developing World Series (New York: Lynne Reinner Publishers Inc., 1995).

[19] William Saunders, Personal Communication, 1980.

[20] Julie Dash. *Daughters of the Dust,* film available at California Newsreel.

[21] Mary A. Twining, "Harvesting and Heritage," in *Afro-American Folk Art and Crafts,* ed. William Ferris (Boston: G. K. Hall, 1983).

[22] Dale Rosengarten, *Row upon Row* (Columbia: University of South Carolina Press, 1986); See installation "Man in Africa," Museum of Natural History, New York.

[23] Melville Herskovits, *Myth of the Negro Past* (New York: Harper, 1941).

[24] Candi and Guy Carawan, *Ain't You Got a Right to the Tree of Life?* (New York: Simon and Schuster, 1967).

[25] Twining, Fieldwork, 1970s.

[26] Guy Carawan, Personal Communication, 1970s.

[27] Bess Lomax Hawes, Personal Communication, 1972.

[28] A *cantefable* is a traditional narrative form, which includes songs and refrains.

[29] Bess Lomax Hawes and Bessie Jones, *Step It Down* (New York: Harper Row, 1972), 71.

[30] Bamidele Agabasegbe, "Family Life on Wadmalaw Island," in *Sea Island Roots: African Presence in the Carolinas and Georgia.* eds. Mary A. Twining and Keith E. Baird (Trenton, NJ: Africa World Press, 1991).

[31] Fanny Kemble, *Journal of a Residence on a Georgian Plantation* (New York: Harper, 1864); Charlotte Forten Grimké, *Journals of Charlotte Forten Grimké* (1854; repr., New York: Oxford University Press, 1988); Septima Poinsett Clark, *Echo in My Soul* (New York: Dutton, 1962); Harriet Beecher Stowe, *Uncle Tom's Cabin* (1852; repr., New York: Bantam, 1983).

[32] Prominent abolitionists in New England in 1800s.

[33] Willie Lee Rose, *Rehearsal for Reconstruction* (New York: Vintage, 1960).

[34] Ibid.

[35] Charlotte Forten, "Life on the Sea Islands," *Atlantic Monthly* (May 1864), republished in Sterling Brown et.al., *Negro Caravan* (New York: The Dryden Press, 1941).

[36] Charlotte Forten Grimké, *Journals of Charlotte Forten Grimké* (1854; repr., New York: Oxford University Press, 1988).

[37] William Francis Allen, Charles Pickard Ware, and Lucy McKim Garrison, *Slave Songs of the United States* (1867; repr., Freeport, NY: Books for Libraries Press, 1971).

[38] Abigail M. H. Christensen, *Afro-American Folklore Told round Cabin Fires on the Sea Islands of South Carolina* (Boston: J. G. Cupples Co., 1892); Elsie Clews Parsons, *Folklore of the Sea Islands, South Carolina,* Memoirs of the American Folklore Society, vol. 16 (Cambridge, MA: The American Folklore Society, 1923); Lydia Parrish, *Slave Songs of the Georgia Sea Islands* (New York: Farrar, Straus, 1940).

[39] Septima Poinsett Clark, *Echo in My Soul* (New York: Dutton, 1962).

[40] Lydia Parrish, *Slave Songs of the Georgia Sea Islands* (New York: Farrar, Straus, 1940). A praise house is a place where the Islanders could worship in their own cultural style of song and "shout." There are a few I know of; one on Johns Island and three on St. Helena Island, all in South Carolina.

[41] Elsie Clews Parsons, *Folklore of the Sea Islands, South Carolina,* Memoirs of the American Folklore Society, vol. 16 (Cambridge, MA: The American Folklore Society, 1923).

Ms. Janie Hunter's grandchildren about to play a ring game, 1970s.

Afterword

"But You Leave All Your Heart Behind": Issues and Insights on the Sea Islands

Studying and enjoying the culture as scholar or tourist are two approaches for information and understanding. However, social and economic issues are paramount if the people and their culture are to survive.

William Saunders, Johns Island, SC
Personal Communication

T he Sea Islands are rife with many issues, some of the most compelling of which are in the economic sphere.[1] The title "But You Leave All Your Heart Behind" refers to the outmigration from the Islands, which is necessitated by the lack of opportunities in those communities.[2] Once people have found decent jobs elsewhere, their main aim is to get back to their home stamping grounds because that is where they can truly enjoy themselves. Although the economic opportunities are few, it is also true that suitable educational chances are not forthcoming from a society whose commitment is less than complete. Education is insufficient for today's needs, and the people are not prepared properly to live in a complex society. The education system as it is presently constituted does not meet the demands of an increasingly technological society, nor does it meet the needs of a group of people whose history has been largely neglected. Suburbanization is swarming out onto even the remotest islands; developers are trampling ancient burial grounds, and governments are actively neglecting the transportation and other requirements of people living in remote areas. Jobs are not plentiful and government regulations make bringing in industry difficult. The trade agreement with Canada and Mexico bids fair to make things worse and further guarantee the destruction of the area and its people by limiting their opportunities.

The development of the onshore and offshore islands has led to serious dispute among the residents who would like to have a role in the decision making. Kiawah Island, off Johns Island, South Carolina, was purchased by some Arabs and put into the hands of a Euro-American holding company to develop into a resort. The Sephardic Jewish community in Charleston was distressed because they thought the Arabs would be prejudiced against them; the African Americans on the Islands wanted more than service jobs; the environmental advocates were upset by the implications of such development for the annual seabird nesting on that barrier island. The issues of jobs versus possible careers, pass-through traffic through populated areas, which would bring no economic benefit to the Islands, and probable disruption of living patterns disturbed the denizens who saw little future for themselves in the picture. The development and investment returns would go not only off island, but out of the country and bring small yields to the Islands. The resort was built anyway, supposedly with precautions taken for the good of the bird population and job promises proffered to the humans.

The problems are the same to a more or lesser degree on all of the Sea Islands. Where the people used to fish and hunt, live, move, and have their being, the developers are putting condominiums, timeshares, and golf courses for middle-class playgrounds and large job-bearing projects and industries seem not to be forthcoming. These developments bring with them concomitant sewage, poisonous and toxic runoff, which affect the waterways, the groundwater, and the wildlife.

The Islanders feel that there are certain strengths in their families and communities which have helped them to survive and make them a good source of labor. They feel themselves to be an untapped resource on the American scene. Among these strong points in the communities are family unity, education or socialization, religion, work ethic, and land ownership. Needless to say, these topics constitute issues also. While the developers are rampaging, making whole islands suddenly unavailable to their own residents and families, the Islanders are organizing themselves to resist being crushed by these inhumane outside forces. The strength and unity provided by church and praise house groups, family relationships, and work training have helped to provide for their families and life conditions. Well-being, however, has a spiritual dimension which is maintained as well as may be by the aforementioned linkages. The invasion of their graveyards and disruption of ancient burial patterns has been a bitter pill for them to swallow. The heartless disregard for their feelings as their parents' and ancestors' graves have been destroyed and obliterated has been shameful. The Daufuskie Islanders have taken the model of the Native Americans in similar circumstances whose feelings of outrage may be readily understood; they have sued the developers and won their case, but David is up against Goliath once more. They won the suit but the final outcome, including the enforcement of the decision (1993), is yet to be known.

The problems occur in such a wide range, from the violation of their innermost feelings to the systematic denial of chances to get ahead, that the mind comes close to boggling at the lack of prospects offered those citizens.

According to Emory Campbell, the former director of Penn Center in Frogmore, South Carolina, located on St. Helena Island, the problems created by large industry are spoiling the environment and giving little job opportunity to the Islanders.[3] The waters are being contaminated at an unprecedented rate as hundreds of thousands of gallons of refuse is being dumped, poisoning the marine life and polluting it for the humans. No systematic approach is being taken to plan for disposal or neutralization of increasing waste as the developers crowd in with their new units.

The groups that should be working together for the good of all parties are isolated from each other in their works. The school boards in each community should be cooperating with the planning and development agencies to insure that education suits the needs of the people and the industries, which are local or might relocate to that area. There is a necessity for some inclusion of African and African American studies in the education system, which would help the young people to know themselves and, in the case of the Euro-Americans, to know their neighbors. Curriculum must be adapted as it is being in many other parts of the country, to include the Africans, especially the Sea Islanders, and their accomplishments. Surely, such adaptations could stem the tide of dropout, as the young people find themselves reflected and valued in the educational system. Charlotte Forten set the example in the 1800s teaching the Islanders about Toussaint L'Ouverture and other accomplished, diasporic African people.[4] Faculty and administration need to be integrated also so that true cross-cultural exchanges could come about. When the schools were integrated, everyone thought the battle had been won. One battle had been won, but the war was still on. The fight is yet to be joined effectively to bring the African people and their great contributions to culture into the syllabi and curricula to take their place in world history.

Although the economic and environmental issues as they now stand are vital, Mr. Campbell stressed the importance of education as, in the long run, it impacts other problems. Unfortunately, public school education has been used as a political football. Questions of language learning and loyalty, social integration, and relevance of the curricula have plagued administrators and legislators not entirely equipped to handle the problems either through personal choice or educational lacks of their own. The issue of English as a second language, discussed in the Florida schools in the 1970s, has hardly been effectively addressed in the Sea Islands communities. Triumphant though the civil (or human) rights struggle was in its push for integration of the existing system, quality of education was let to slip. Quality in Southern educational public systems was not high for Euro-Americans as well as African Americans, so no one was well-served. The Euro-Americans had better facilities on the whole, but the educational standards were poor, as education was not valued very highly.

When the school desegregation decision was handed down from the Supreme Court (1954), many states, including South Carolina, made school attendance permissive rather than mandatory. Families had children who were sharing pairs of shoes so each one could go to school every other day when his/her turn with the shoes came around and no truant officer would come to assess the situation. Some families could not afford the book fees, particularly if they had a number of children. Parents who spoke Sea Islands Creole felt diffident about bringing their concerns to standard-English-speaking, Euro-American principals, PTA members, and officials. The issues that they might like to bring up would involve the relevance of their child's education to the present state of the economy and their own ethnicity. In the first instance, the young people need skills to get ahead and be tax-paying, productive citizens—a source of pride in itself. In the second example, instilling pride in themselves, their people, their history, and culture could go a long way toward cutting down substance abuse, dropout rate, and disruptive behavior. They could feel less marginalized by the neglect of the society at large and have more hope in the future for themselves.

Bill Saunders of Johns Island, a longtime champion of the people, who worked at the right hand of Esau Jenkins, has opined that the resorts are providing adequate job opportunities, as he is firmly convinced that a culture cannot survive if its practitioners cannot.[5] On the other hand, Emory Campbell takes it a step further to say that the economy and the educational system do not lend themselves to career development for the young people, therefore, they may sustain their existence with the jobs, but they cannot achieve much in the future. He indicates further that both the economy and the educational system need to diversify, maximize opportunity, and open up possibilities for a variety of people and skills.

Such opportunities have come in the past; a German firm, Chicago Bridge and Iron, and a yacht-building outfit were defeated in their efforts to relocate in the island area by the environmentalists. Clearly, the interests of the community and the ultimate impact on the environment are at loggerheads. Where does the right of people to live beyond marginal levels take precedence over the admittedly important issue of environmental protection? It would seem some more realistic rapprochement must be effected and some balance between conflicting interests must be achieved.

Land ownership is a heartbreaking issue, as many of these landowners' families have been on this land since the Civil War times. Their family plots were their only wealth in many cases. The huge amounts of money being offered by developers could tempt the strongest, and many have sold their rights for a mess of pottage which is soon gone. The outright piracy of lands and property for defaulted tax money is a shameless racket, which is causing the amount of acres owned by Sea Islanders to dwindle. Some people are land-poor; they own but can't use it or sell it, so it and the people in question are not utilized to their highest and best use.

The issue of language has been addressed. A translation of the Bible by a team of linguists and Bible scholars has been instituted on the Islands. It does answer the question of the Sea Islands Creole speakers of their culture and language being taken perfectly seriously and accepted into the world catalogue of languages. The method thus far seems to be one of translation and then presentation to the people for suggestions and corroborations. This method could be a project which would help the Islanders to learn code-switching skills such as John Gadsen had in Beaufort, South Carolina, some years ago.

The five most pressing issues, land ownership and development, the environment, education, health, and the attendant issue of housing, are also found in abundance in the Caribbean island nations. Because most of them have achieved independence, they have more control over some of the problems. One main difficulty remains, however, which is that of size and scale. Obviously, they cannot manufacture all the goods that they need as a modern society, so like the Sea Islands, they are dependent on larger nation states, which are heavily industrialized and which need markets like them. This situation, which holds them hostage to the outside world, influences their culture and society to an almost unwarranted degree. To keep their cultural heads above water they must celebrate the culture of the past, which recalls a time when they were self-sufficient in many areas. These culture facts of self-sufficiency also remind them of the struggle for social and political independence, which made them proud and free. They are not, however, free of the financial and technological off-island societies, which can inundate them with sometimes inappropriate technology. On the other hand, the more technically developed nations can also withhold certain known developments to the detriment of their client groups. When technology moves on backed by political forces, the small societal entities are virtually helpless to stem the tide. When the phosphate industry near Beaufort, South Carolina, was devastated in a great storm (1911) similar to Hugo or Andrew, the fertilizer business started up again in Charleston, thereby decimating capital invest-ments, jobs, and business climate in Beaufort and its islands. Further efforts to bring such large industries, as the bridge and yacht builders, have come to grief through obdurate attitudes of environmentalists. Hard times manufactured by the forces of politics and large-scale economics keep the Islands, both Caribbean and Lowcountry, in a predicament that makes them a fine place to retire to but a place to leave to make a living. The loyalty to the Islands is such that people go to metropolitan centers to earn good wages and return every chance they get to celebrate their own culture, hear their own language, and see friends and family.

Others in the dominant society have discovered the mild climate, beach-access timeshares, and other resort-like characteristics, and purchase condominia without realizing that they are built on the graves and sacred land of Sea Islands forebears. The search for the good life seems to sweep all before it, and we lose all values of our own and others in the stampede of progress. The establishment of some compromise could benefit everyone without standing so heavily on the shoulders of those who have contributed so much to the necessary labor to build and sustain this country and its infrastructure. The forward rush of the so-called progress brings with it jobs but no structured careers, lasting change, or hope for the young peoples' futures. Great amounts of research and surveys have been done and the results lie buried in endless reports. Concerted efforts must be made to preserve the people and their culture as all advocates like Bill Saunders and Emory Campbell strive daily to accomplish.

This foregoing may not sound much like progress, however, there are significant signs of forward movement: the State University of South Carolina at Beaufort is establishing a research unit in their facility at Beaufort, South Carolina; Penn Center and the State College of South Carolina in Columbia have teamed up to inaugurate the Gullah Studies Institute. Social, economic, and cultural questions are being addressed in the various course offerings. Credit hours are being awarded for those who need them. Many community people from the Islands and far and wide come to study in the classes and the workshops. Faculty and students come away enriched and carry the knowledge of the Sea Islands area with them. Furthermore, the Honorable James Clyburn has forwarded legislation to establish the Gullah Geechee Cultural Corridor Heritage Commission. Dr. Althea N. Sumpter is the chair of the commission and Dr. Herman Blake is the executive director of it. Now the full faith and credit of the federal government is engaged with it and two lifelong Sea Islanders are working to their best abilities to bring the management plan that has been devised by a committee of commissioners to fruition.

Their task is to research and organize situations to benefit the residents of the Islands in economic, cultural, and other areas for future management alternatives. Both of these, one a diminution of the pressure from the developers and the other an augmentation in the interest in and concern for the Islands may augur fortunately for their well-being in the future. All praise to Congressman James Clyburn for his work in this area to help the people in a neglected and marginalized region.[6]

---

[1] Some of the issues may have advanced or been resolved in ways unknown to me.

[2] The title is taken from a Sea Islands shout song collected in the late 1860s by Allen, Ware, and Garrison: "O Daniel," William Francis Allen, Charles Pickard Ware, and Lucy McKim Garrison, *Slave Songs of the Sea Islands* (1867; repr., Oak Publications, 1965), 148.

[3] I am grateful to Emory Campbell, former longtime executive director, Penn Center, Frogmore, South Carolina for a great deal of the information and understanding in this essay.

[4] Charlotte Forten, *The Journal of Charlotte Forten,* ed. Ray Allen Billington (1854; New York: Collier, 1953).

[5] William Saunders, Johns Island, South Carolina, Personal Communication, 1990.

[6] Gullah Geechee Cultural Heritage Corridor Commission: [www.gullahgeecheecorridor .org;] The National Parks Service has placed The Management Plan of the Gullah Geechee Cultural Heritage Corridor Commission in public libraries so it can be accessed by the general public.

About the Author

M ary A. Twining, PhD, has a doctorate from Indiana University (1977), co-edited and authored *Sea Island Roots* with Keith E. Baird, PhD, and published several articles on African American folklore, quilting, basketry, African American children's games, and dance. Twining's pedagogical work includes courses on Native American folklore and literature, African and African American folklore and folklife, African American science fiction/fantasy/horror writers, Southern women writers, Southern fiction and folklore, world literature, and humanities, among others. Dr. Mary A. Twining was co-chair for the 1997 Annual Writers' Conference at Clark Atlanta University on the topic of African American Science Fiction/Fantasy/Horror Writers.

About the Contributor

Keith E. Baird, PhD, born in Barbados, is a retired professor and administrator of African World studies and the humanities, most recently at Clark Atlanta University. Over the years, in addition to scholarly writing, he has published book reviews, essays, and poetry. He has occasionally done public dramatic readings. He is currently a freelance editor.

Photo by Ian Frank

Other Works by Mary A. Twining and Keith E. Baird

Sea Island Roots, edited by Mary A. Twining and Keith E. Baird, Trenton, NJ: Africa World Press, 1991.

Signs and Wonders by Keith E. Baird, Alpharetta, GA: BookLogix, 2012.

Index

Thompson, Robert F., 5, 23, 136, 209
Thornton, E. M., 172
"Throw Me Anywhere, Lord, in That Old Field," 79, 224–225
"Tom Wasn't There," 92, 98–99, *132*
"Too Great a Pride Can Lead to Disaster," 141–142
Tortoise (trickster), 136–139, 140–141
"Tortoise in the Animal Kingdom, The" (Ogundipe), 141
Towne, Laura, 55, 70
trafficking. *See* human trafficking
trickster figures, 136–140, 141–142, 142
Turnbull, Colin, 200
Turner, Clara Lee, 200
Turner, Lorenzo Dow: *Africanisms in the Gullah Dialect*, 4, 6, 39, 46, 47; field recordings by, 62; Gullah language research by, 26, 40; on shouts, 172
"turnouts," 178, 184
Twain, Mark, 58
"Twelve Gates to the City," 126
Twining, Mary A., *147, 155,* 161

U

Uchendu, Victor, 182
Umar Ibn Said, 171
Uncle Remus stories, 56–57, 58–59
Uncle Tom's Cabin (Stowe), 252

University of South Carolina, 265

V

Vance, Rupert B., 20, 24, 30
Vasquez, Lucas, 25
vendor street cries, 241
Vlach, John, *194, 195, 197, 202, 213*
voluntary beneficial associations, 184
"Voting Does Count" (Clark), 254

W

"Wade in the Water," 126
"Walk Believer, Walk Daniel," 72, 160, 220
Ware, Charles, 25, 54–55, 56, 64, 254
"Weapon of My Song, A," 107,
Weil, Peter, 198, 199
Weinreich, Uriel, 42
Welty, Eudora, 20
Wesley Methodist Church, 65, 135
West African Religion (Parrinder), 164
Westcott, Jan, 137
"We Wear the Mask" (Dunbar), 80
"What is de Hour?" (Jenkins), 12, 109–110, 111–118
When Roots Die (Jones-Jackson), 6, 63–64
whisks, 212
Whitbeck, R. H., 32
white magic, 164. *See also* magic
Whittier, John Greenleaf, 253
Wiggins, William, 85, 89
Williams, Eric, 43
winnowing baskets, 200